# ANIMALS & ETHICS

**3RD EDITION**

# ANIMALS & ETHICS

## AN OVERVIEW OF THE PHILOSOPHICAL DEBATE

### 3RD EDITION

**ANGUS TAYLOR**

**BROADVIEW** GUIDES to PHILOSOPHY

**Library and Archives Canada Cataloguing in Publication**

Taylor, Angus MacDonald, 1945-
　　Animals and ethics : an overview of the philosophical debate / Angus Taylor. — 3rd ed.

(Broadview guides to philosophy)
Originally published under title: Magpies, monkeys, and morals.
Includes bibliographical references and index.
ISBN 978-1-55111-976-2

　　1. Animal rights — Philosophy.　2. Animal welfare — Moral and ethical aspects.
I. Title.　II. Series: Broadview guides to philosophy

HV4708.T38 2009　　　　　179'.3　　　　　C2009-900881-5

Broadview Press is an independent, international publishing house, incorporated in 1985. Broadview believes in shared ownership, both with its employees and with the general public; since the year 2000 Broadview shares have traded publicly on the Toronto Venture Exchange under the symbol BDP.

We welcome comments and suggestions regarding any aspect of our publications — please feel free to contact us at the addresses below or at broadview@broadviewpress.com.

*North America*
PO Box 1243, Peterborough, Ontario, Canada K9J 7H5
2215 Kenmore Ave., Buffalo, New York, USA 14207
Tel: (705) 743-8990; Fax: (705) 743-8353
email: customerservice@broadviewpress.com

*UK, Ireland, and continental Europe*
NBN International, Estover Road, Plymouth, UK PL6 7PY
Tel: 44 (0) 1752 202300; Fax: 44 (0) 1752 202330
email: enquiries@nbninternational.com

*Australia and New Zealand*
UNIREPS, University of New South Wales
Sydney, NSW, Australia 2052
Tel: 61 2 9385 0150; Fax: 61 2 9385 0155
email: info@unireps.com.au

**www.broadviewpress.com**

Broadview Press acknowledges the financial support of the Government of Canada through the Book Publishing Industry Development Program (BPIDP) for our publishing activities.

Edited by ohn Burbidge.

Designed by Chris Rowat Design, Daiva Villa

This book is printed on paper containing 100% post-consumer fibre.

PRINTED IN CANADA

The production of the title **Animals & Ethics** on Rolland Enviro 100 Print paper instead of virgin fibres paper reduces your ecological footprint by :

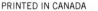

Tree(s) : 11
Solid waste : 325 kg
Water : 30 780 l

Suspended particles in the water : 2,1 kg
Air emissions : 715 kg
Natural gas : 46 m$^3$

For Zeb and Mairin

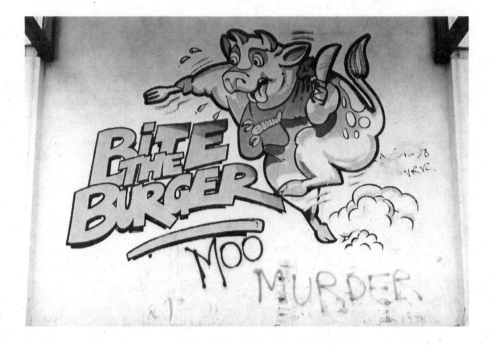

# CONTENTS

# ACKNOWLEDGEMENTS

Don LePan of Broadview Press was receptive to my initial idea for this book and has been supportive throughout the writing of it. I thank editors Alex Sager, Tara Lowes, and Piper-Lee Blackey for seeing this third edition through the production process. I am indebted to Michael Allen Fox for his careful reading of the manuscript of the first edition and for suggesting a number of improvements, and to John Burbidge for his work on subsequent editions. The good people in the Interlibrary Loan office of the University of Victoria also deserve credit; without their speedy assistance in requisitioning books from all over the continent, the bibliography, and indeed the text, would have been considerably poorer.

The quotation at the beginning of Chapter 5 from S.F. Sapontzis, "On Justifying the Exploitation of Animals in Research", *The Journal of Medicine and Philosophy* 13 (1988), pp. 177-78, is used with permission of Oxford University Press and the author.

# PREFACE

This book is intended for students and members of the general public who wish to know what philosophers have been saying about the controversial issue of animal liberation. The aim is to do justice to the arguments of philosophers involved in the debate, while presenting those arguments in a way that makes them accessible to a wide audience.

Philosophers who have written on the matter can be divided broadly into two camps. On one side are those who believe that a fundamental reassessment of our traditional view of animals is in order, and that such a reassessment leads to the conclusion that we should make radical changes in our treatment of them. On the other side are those who, while likely to find cruelty to animals abhorrent, nevertheless find the notion of "liberating" them to be without merit. However, this is not to say that there are two neatly defined positions, with all those in favour of liberation employing a common set of principles and arguments, and all those against liberation employing another common set of principles and arguments. Indeed, it would be hard to find any two philosophers who agree completely with each other on the moral status of animals. The complexity of the debate will become apparent in the course of the following chapters.

In 1632 Galileo published *Dialogue Concerning the Two Chief World Systems*, in which he set forth the respective arguments for the Ptolemaic, or earth-centred, view of the universe, and the Copernican, or sun-centred, view. Galileo's sympathies, however, were too obviously with the Copernican view, and the Church in its turn took a very dim view of Galileo, convicting him of suspected heresy. *Animals and Ethics* also concerns a debate about two radically different ways of viewing the world. However, although I have my own opinions on many of the issues raised in the following chapters, I hope to present the various arguments involved in a reasonably impartial manner, even while commenting on their strengths and weaknesses. In this way I mean to provide the reader with an understanding of the principal areas of contention in the debate, and with a good basis for evaluating competing claims about how we should treat animals.

As John Stuart Mill maintained in *On Liberty*, his famous defence of freedom of expression, familiarizing ourselves with other points of view is vital regardless of how firmly we hold that our beliefs are correct. Another view just may be correct after all, or at least it may hold part of the truth. And even if our own view is indeed the right one, it is only by understanding and evaluating the opinions of those who disagree with us that we can come to believe what we do on the basis of well-reasoned arguments, instead of holding our beliefs simply as dogma. For this purpose, Mill said, we should be exposed to opposing opinions in their strongest form, preferably in the words of those who believe them and can put the case for them most forcefully. With Mill's injunction in mind, readers of this volume are encouraged to seek out in their original form arguments that I summarize, not only those arguments they find congenial, but those that strike them as unsound or even bizarre.

In Chapter 1 animal liberation is defined and is situated with respect to the notion of the moral community. Along the way, we look at the question of whether animals can suffer. A brief overview is given of the main ethical approaches to the topic. The perspectives and implications of rights theory, utilitarianism, contractarianism, feminism, and virtue ethics are outlined and contrasted. Also introduced is an argument that plays a particularly prominent role in the ethical debate and that is encountered in subsequent chapters.

Chapter 2 provides a historical introduction to the topic of the moral status of (non-human) animals. A number of prominent pre-twentieth-century thinkers are canvassed on the subject of animals, with particular attention being paid to Descartes' view that animals are machines without minds, to Kant's view that we have no duties to animals because they are not rational, and to Darwin's claim that humans are not fundamentally different from their non-human kin.

Whether animals should be ascribed moral rights is a controversial issue even among philosophers who support animal liberation. Chapter 3 addresses this issue, focusing primarily on the work widely acknowledged to be the most comprehensive and influential pro-rights argument: *The*

*Case for Animal Rights*, by Tom Regan. Regan's argument is explicated in some detail, and is examined in terms of the criticisms (explicit or implicit) made both by supporters and by opponents of animal liberation.

Chapter 4 addresses the issues of eating and of hunting animals. How much does the suffering of animals matter and can eating them be justified by minimizing their suffering? Among the arguments considered are those of Peter Singer, author of *Animal Liberation*, and of Singer's critics. Attention is also directed to what makes killing wrong, to whether being vegetarian really makes any difference, and to the intersection of feminism and vegetarianism. The chapter also looks at the issue of hunting. Is killing for sport to be condemned out of hand, or can a case be made for it? What about the traditional subsistence hunting done by Aboriginal people?

Animals are commonly subjected to suffering and death in scientific research. Whether such research can be justified is the subject of Chapter 5. Even philosophers who favour animal liberation often agree with their anti-liberation opponents that if it comes to a conflict of basic interests, the basic interests of normal humans should prevail over those of animals. Should we conclude that scientific research involving animals is almost always justified, even in cases where it would be immoral to experiment on humans, or would a consistent application of moral principles lead us to condemn much of the animal research undertaken these days? Chapter 5 includes a look at the related topic of the genetic engineering of animals and considers whether there are valid objections to this practice.

Though at first glance it might be assumed that animal liberation is an aspect of environmentalism, a great deal of heated debate has arisen over the question whether the individualistic orientation of liberationists is compatible with the holistic orientation of environmentalists. It has been charged that liberationists must be committed to protecting wild animals from harm, and that any such policy must have ruinous consequences for the environment. In Chapter 6 the diverse arguments on both sides of the liberation/environmentalism issue are explored, together with attempts at reconciliation.

Chapter 7 concludes the book with a brief look at the wider context of animal-liberation philosophy and activism.

The ways in which animals are used by humans are numerous, and the book does not attempt to address every one of them. For example, it does not deal directly with the use of animals in circuses or in rodeos and touches only briefly on the issue of zoos and on the role of animals as companions (pets). Some works on zoos, companion animals, and circuses are included in the bibliography.

The bibliography is a feature of this book. Although there is no intention to list everything ever written on the moral status of animals, the bibliography is extensive, comprising publication data on nearly seven hundred books and articles. The bibliography forms an integral aspect of the text. During the course of the book frequent references are given to works listed in the bibliography, both to cite the source of ideas discussed and to point readers to pertinent material.

I have kept direct quotations to a minimum in the main body of text. Works mentioned in the following chapters, as well as relevant source materials, are cited in the text by author and year of publication — e.g., "Singer 2002". These citations refer the reader to the bibliography at the end of the book.

For the sake of convenience I use the word "animal" in its everyday sense, to refer to non-human animals. However, human beings are also animals, even if we are animals of a unique kind. The perceived tension between our animal nature and our uniqueness informs much of the debate about animal liberation.

The first edition of this book was published in 1999 under the title *Magpies, Monkeys, and Morals*. A second edition, titled *Animals and Ethics*, appeared in 2003. For this third edition, new material has been added to the text and some existing material rearranged. Once again, the bibliography has been significantly enlarged. For the first time the book includes a number of sidebar quotations, ones that I hope are not only pithy but also provocative.

# CHAPTER ONE

# ANIMALS AND THE MORAL COMMUNITY

*Beauvoir*: You've never liked animals.
*Sartre:* Oh, but I have, to some extent. Dogs and cats.
*Beauvoir:* Not much.
*Sartre:* Animals. As I see it they are a philosophical problem. Basically.[1]

Until recent times few philosophers wrote much about the moral status of (non-human) animals. Mention of animals, when it occurred, was usually incidental to concern with human beings. Animals were generally perceived as significantly different from, and inferior to, humans. Because animals were seen to lack some crucial quality — reason, or moral agency, or language, or self-awareness, or perhaps any consciousness at all — it was denied that they counted morally in any fundamental way. Since the 1970s, however, this consensus has broken down and fierce debate among philosophers has become the order of the day. Hundreds of books and articles have been devoted to the moral status of animals and how we humans should treat them. This explosion of interest on the part of philosophers has reflected, and to some extent influenced, a sharply increased interest in society about environmental issues, including our treatment of the other living creatures with whom we share this planet.

---

[1] Simone de Beauvoir, Adieux: *A Farewell to Sartre* (New York: Pantheon, 1984), p. 316.

## What Is Animal Liberation?

Moral philosophy is not a subject that has normally commanded public attention or exercised much immediate influence on the course of public affairs. However, the movement of recent decades to defend the interests of animals has been remarkable partly for the role played by professional philosophers. Indeed, philosophers have been called the "midwives" of the movement (Jasper and Nelkin 1992). This is not to say that animal liberation is a movement of philosophers. Rather, pro-liberation philosophers have articulated intellectual frameworks that have focused the moral sentiments of sympathizers and encouraged activism.

The term "animal liberation" was popularized by Australian philosopher Peter Singer in his book with that title, first published in 1975. In *Animal Liberation* Singer explicitly draws a parallel between the women's liberation movement and the movement to "liberate" animals. Animal liberation, he tells us, is the logical next step in the evolution of our moral sensibility. Just as we have come to realize that discrimination on the basis of race or sex is not acceptable, so we must put aside the idea that it is acceptable to discriminate on the basis of species. Human or non-human, says Singer, all animals are equal.

By this, Singer does not mean that we should treat animals in exactly the same way we treat humans (after all, it makes no sense to allow pigs to drive cars or to enrol them in ballet class), but it does mean that the interests of animals merit the same consideration as the similar interests of humans. In particular, we must not think that the suffering or the pleasure experienced by animals counts any less from a moral point of view than a like amount of suffering or pleasure experienced by humans. While giving a pig the right to vote for a political candidate makes no sense, a given amount of pain experienced by a pig is just as bad as the same amount of pain experienced by a human. After all, pain is pain, and if we think that suffering is generally something to be avoided, what difference can it make that the suffering is experienced by a creature with four legs instead of two, or by one that has a tail instead of being tailless? What difference can it make, in terms of the badness of the suffering, whether the creature can do arithmetic, or whether it can play the violin, or whether it can read a philosophy book?

Singer calls unjustifiable discrimination against non-human creatures "speciesism". The word was coined in 1970 by British psychologist and animal-liberation activist Richard Ryder as an analogue of "racism" and "sexism". Like racism and sexism, says Ryder (1983), speciesism is a form of prejudice that shows a selfish disregard for the interests and sufferings of others. Just what that implies is not clear and the term "speciesism" has been applied somewhat inconsistently (Fjellstrom 2002b). Evelyn Pluhar (2006, p. 276) defines speciesism as "The attitude or practice of giving greater weight to the interests of certain individuals than to the interests of otherwise morally relevantly similar individuals, on the grounds of species membership alone." Marjorie Spiegel (1996), for one, has no doubt that a parallel exists between racism and the way human beings treat animals. In particular, she cites many similarities between the treatment of Africans enslaved by Europeans and the ways we commonly treat animals—from the ways in which slaves and animals have been separated from their families, confined, and transported to the language used to describe them and the arguments used to justify their subordination.

Not everyone accepts that there is a legitimate parallel to be drawn between what is called animal liberation and the liberation of women, or the liberation of people oppressed on racial or other grounds. The liberation of an oppressed group of human beings generally involves recognition of its members' right to conduct their lives as they see fit, to pursue their chosen goals in life. Does it make sense to talk of liberating animals to live the lives they choose? It has been argued that Singer's concern for an end to the infliction of unnecessary suffering on animals does not, properly speaking, require either recognizing a right of animals to liberty, or liberating them from oppressive conditions that prevent them from pursuing their own goals in life (Pierce 1979). Some advocates of animal liberation maintain that animals should indeed be ascribed a right to liberty, and must be liberated from oppressive conditions in order to pursue their own goals. However, these philosophers may not share Singer's premise that the liberation of animals is fundamentally a matter of relieving their suffering. (Singer's claims and those of his critics will be addressed in more detail in Chapter 4.) Then too, animal liberation relies for its realization on outsiders—in this case, humans. By contrast, in human liberation movements members of the oppressed groups articulate their own grievances and demands, and organize themselves for struggle. To what extent, if at all, can animals do the same (Francis and Norman 1978; Lamb 1982)?

Racists violate the principle of equality by giving greater weight to the interests of members of their own race when there is a clash between their interests and the interests of those of another race. Sexists violate the principle of equality by favoring the interests of their own sex. Similarly, speciesists allow the interests of their own species to override the greater interests of members of other species. The pattern is identical in each case.
—Peter Singer, *Animal Liberation*, p. 9

We see, then, that the very expression "animal liberation" is a subject of controversy. Even some who are on the *pro* side of the debate may prefer another designation. Some philosophers or activists speak of the "animal protection" movement, the "animal defence" movement, or the "animal advocacy" movement. Despite its possible deficiencies, I shall stick to "animal liberation" because it is a widely used label for a movement whose primary concern has been to liberate/protect/defend animals from harm at the hands of human beings, and because many sympathizers believe, like Singer, that the movement has affinities with other so-called liberation movements. The expression "animal rights", while often used loosely as a synonym for animal liberation, properly has a more limited application, since not all liberationists agree that focusing on the concept of rights is particularly useful, and some even deny that animals (or humans) possess moral rights—Peter Singer (1987) being a prominent example.

Inasmuch as those who advocate animal liberation often disagree among themselves when it comes to the premises of their arguments, what, if anything, unites them philosophically? For partisans of the cause, the liberation of animals implies more than just treating them "humanely", or without obvious cruelty. Though advocates of animal liberation differ in their particular viewpoints and in the arguments they advance in support of those viewpoints, they agree that *animals must no longer be treated essentially as resources for human use*. Animals have their own lives to live and to cause them avoidable harm is morally indefensible (Clark 1977). Except perhaps in special cases, their basic interests are not to be subordinated to human interests.

This still leaves room for dispute on important issues, such as whether animals may sometimes be used for scientific research. Yet when it comes to the issue that involves a choice we make every day—whether or not to consume animals for food—liberationists generally agree that eating meat is morally wrong except in some unusual circumstances. Animal liberation is a radical idea, not a reformist one, in that it demands not better treatment of animals within the present structure of our relations to them, but rather a fundamental transformation of those relations. As such, it evokes strong responses not only among philosophers but the wider public. It has been denounced as dangerous and misanthropic (e.g., Marquardt 1993). The animal-liberation move-

In fact, I regard the present popular concern with animal rights in our culture as a reflection of moral decadence. Just as Nero fiddled while Rome burned, many in the West agonise over the fate of seal pups and cormorants while human beings elsewhere starve or are enslaved.
—Peter Carruthers, *The Animals Issue*, p. xi

ment, as a broad set of philosophical, political, and cultural activities united by a rejection of the idea that animals are essentially resources, is to be distinguished from the traditional "animal welfare" movement, which has sought to minimize the suffering of exploited animals but has not fundamentally challenged the view that animals are essentially resources (Francione 1996). What is of concern in this book is not the history or tactics of these movements; good accounts in those areas are provided by other works, such as *Blood Relations*, Charlotte Montgomery's comprehensive look at activism in Canada. (See also Beers 2006; Finsen and Finsen 1994; Garner 1993; Guither 1998; Jasper and Nelkin 1992; Phelps 2007; Ryder 1989; Shevelow 2008; Singer 1998; Tobias 1999; E. Turner 1964.) The focus of this book is the philosophical debate over the contention that animals should be liberated.

It should be noted that the term "animal" in *animal liberation* does not apply to all animals regardless of their natures. Few people advocate the liberation of insects, for example. Pro-liberation philosophers may disagree about whether crabs, say, or snails qualify as candidates for liberation. Nevertheless, there is a consensus that the concept of liberation is restricted to creatures who have interests, where having interests is taken to mean that one has feelings of well-being that can be affected by what happens to oneself. Living things that are not sentient have no such interests and thus cannot be the subject of the animal-liberation movement (Bernstein 1998; Feinberg 1974; Rollin 2006; Sapontzis 1987).

Strictly speaking, to be sentient is to have the power of perception by means of the senses. However, as employed in the debate about animals, the term typically refers to the capacity to experience pain or pleasure. Anything that is not able to experience pain or pleasure, the thinking goes, is not the sort of thing that can regard itself as being harmed or benefited by how others treat it. In particular, for the organic beings of this planet, having interests seems at a minimum to entail having a *sensory* capacity for pain or pleasure. This makes it not unreasonable to use the term "sentience" to denote the capacity to experience some events as good or bad for oneself. What is crucial, however, are the mental states of suffering (either painful sensations or emotional distress) and pleasure (or happiness), whether or not these are the direct product of sensory input. After all, we might imagine a being that has no sensory capacity for pain or pleasure, but that can experience satisfaction or frustration, joy or grief, as the result of achieving or not achieving its goals. A conscious computer might qualify, or a disembodied intelligence: such a being would still have to be aware of its surroundings, though the assimilation of information about its environment might never *in itself* be painful or pleasurable. The point to bear in mind is that unless a creature can have an experience of things going well or ill for it, it is not the sort of creature that can be liberated.

Not surprisingly, then, questions having to do with mental faculties play a large role in the debate over the moral status of animals. What faculties do different types of animals possess? What is the appropriate way of treating an animal with particular faculties? (David DeGrazia explores the meaning and applicability of pertinent concepts like sentience, consciousness, pleasure, pain, suffering, desire, and belief in *Taking Animals Seriously: Mental Life and Moral Status*. Gary Varner's *In Nature's Interests?* includes a useful account of the scientific evidence for what sorts of creatures have desires, and hence have interests that are defined by desires.)

### Can Animals Suffer?

The issue of whether we do wrong when we use animals for food, clothing, sport, or research rests on the assumption that many, or most, of those animals are conscious beings who have a subjective welfare. The arguments for animal welfare in general, and for animal liberation in particular, make little sense if what happens to animals makes no difference to them—that is, if they just don't care what happens to them. Most people believe that mammals, birds, and perhaps other kinds of animals can suffer; these animals can experience pain as the result of various physical stimuli, and perhaps can experience depression, anxiety, grief, or other emotions (Darwin 1872, 1890; M. Dawkins 1980, 1993; Masson and McCarthy 1995).

The idea that animals like dogs, pigs, and deer cannot suffer will strike most readers as simply bizarre. Yet René Descartes' seventeenth-century claim that animals cannot suffer (see Chapter 2) survives among some scientists and philosophers. For instance, as Bernard Rollin (1989, 2007) details, for most of the past century adherents of the influential behaviourist movement in psychology have followed in Descartes' footsteps. Some modern philosophers, too, take a neo-

Cartesian position on this matter. So before proceeding to examine other arguments about our treatment of animals, we must look at the sort of argument that, if correct, would dispense at one stroke with the issue of animal liberation.

The pain and joy of others cannot be directly experienced, yet few of us doubt that other human beings can feel pain and joy. In large part this is because of the resemblances between their behaviour and our own. True, many (not all) other people can tell us in words how they feel; but how much confidence would we place in the words of a computer that insisted it was happy or unhappy, and yet displayed no recognizable corresponding behaviour? That we can also infer much about the inner life of animals on the basis of behavioural resemblances between them and human beings is affirmed by many (e.g., Churchill 1989).

Peter Singer employs what has been called *the analogical argument for animal pain* (Perrett 1997). It is reasonable, says Singer (2002), to believe that animals, especially mammals and birds, can experience pain because they manifest the same sorts of physical behaviour that humans in pain manifest: writhing, facial contortions, moaning, attempts to avoid the source of pain, and so forth. These creatures also have nervous systems that respond physiologically as ours do (dilated pupils, increased pulse rate, etc.) in situations where we would experience pain. Further, the capacity for pain is an evolutionary mechanism that enhances a species' chances of survival by helping its members avoid sources of injury. It is unreasonable to suppose that nervous systems, human and non-human, that have a common ancestry and common evolutionary function operate quite differently when it comes to subjective experiences. As to just which creatures are capable of suffering, Singer has suggested drawing the line "somewhere between a shrimp and an oyster", though in the second edition of *Animal Liberation* he admits his uncertainty in this regard.

Assessing the scientific evidence for animal pain in the light of what is known about pain in humans can be a complicated matter. Indications are that mammals and birds can feel pain, and other vertebrates (fish, reptiles, and amphibians) probably can too. By contrast, evidence supporting the capacity to feel pain is much weaker in the case of invertebrates — with the exception of cephalopods like octopuses and squid. (See Allen 2004; DeGrazia 1996; DeGrazia and Rowan 1991; Varner 1998.)

Why…am I so confident that my dog, Ludwig Wittgenstein Searle, is conscious? Well, why is he so confident I am conscious? I think part of the correct answer, in the case of both Ludwig and me, is that any other possibility is out of the question. We have, for example, known each other now for quite a while so there is not really any possibility of doubt.
—John Searle, "Animal Minds", pp. 206-07

13

Peter Harrison (1989, 1991) is not convinced by the analogical argument. To begin with, he points out that even single-celled organisms withdraw when confronted with harmful stimuli and that insects struggle feebly after being crushed underfoot—yet few of us would say that these behaviours are indicative of the experience of pain. We can also imagine constructing a robot and programming it for self-preservation; it would struggle to escape from harmful situations and might cry out to summon aid. Harrison's point is that "pain" behaviour is no proof that the creature involved is experiencing pain. There is also sufficient doubt about the connection between brain states and mental states, says Harrison, to rule out the assertion that animal nervous systems that resemble ours must give rise to mental states like ours. The robot we have constructed above is a physically sophisticated system that imitates humans in the complexity of its actions, yet there is no reason to think that it has any mental states at all. Where critics of Descartes (e.g., Matthews 1978) may invoke evolutionary theory in affirming that many animals must have faculties similar to human ones, including the ability to experience pain, Harrison points out that what is crucial from an evolutionary perspective is not pain but the appropriate harm-avoidance behaviour. Whether a creature struggles, cries out, or remains silent in a harmful situation has to do with enhancing the species' chances of survival and reproduction, not with pain.

Perhaps the most interesting argument advanced by Harrison is that animals do not need the capacity for pain because they lack free will. Being free agents, humans can choose to do things that may harm them. A person may decide to run back into a burning house to save someone trapped inside—or even just to save the family photograph albums (an action that appears hard to explain on the basis of perpetuating one's genes or promoting the survival of the species). Pain is our body's voice, warning us of danger. In effect, a pain signal says, "This action may harm you. Are you sure you want to proceed?" If animals are programmed to avoid harmful situations (or, for that matter, to plunge into harm's way to rescue their offspring), they have no need of a warning voice: they have no choice in the matter.

Like Descartes and behaviourist scientists, Harrison believes that in attributing the capacity for pain to animals we invoke a superfluous hypothesis. Singer, however, turns Occam's razor (the philosophical principle that we should make the fewest possible assumptions when explaining something) back against Harrison and company. Is not the hypothesis that animals feel pain simpler than the idea that despite the physiological similarities between humans and animals, different explanations are to be invoked for their similar behaviours? Similarly, Marian Dawkins (1993), whose field of study is animal cognition, suggests that Occam's razor tells in favour of many animals' having an emotional life, including the capacity to experience pain and pleasure.

Harrison does not flatly deny that animals have minds. Rather, Harrison suggests that animals cannot experience pain because they have no sense of self. Animals are like chronic amnesiacs, who lose their identity at every moment; they are like newborn children and like those of us who cannot remember their unpleasant dreams upon waking. Without a continuity of experience, there is no "I" to own any experience of pain. Hence an animal may encounter painful stimuli and react to them, yet because it lacks any continuity of experience it does not experience pain as we do.

Colin McGinn (1999) insists that the idea of ownerless experience makes no sense; all experience must be experience *for* some subject or self, even if that self is unable to reflect on its experience. That all experience must have a subject is true regardless of how long any given subject persists and whether it is human. Rollin (1989) asserts that if it is really true that the consciousness of animals is locked into the present moment, then things are even worse for them, since when they are in pain their whole world is filled with it and they are unable to remember or anticipate its absence. Not only have scientists adduced evidence of self-consciousness in primates, but some philosophers have also argued that a distinction between oneself and the rest of the world is made by most animals. Stephen Clark (1982) notes that, unless an animal made this distinction, it would be unable to perceive a relatively stable world through which it could track its own progress; it would be unable to return to places and objects it had seen before. According to Rosemary Rodd (1990), self-consciousness could have value in any circumstances where conscious beings interact; in evolutionary terms, it might initially take a simple form. Both Clark and Rodd maintain that self-consciousness is most developed in social species.

Harrison's arguments stand or fall on their own merits. However,

15

there is another consideration that Harrison offers in support of the belief that animals cannot experience pain. The unjust suffering of animals presents a problem for those who believe in the existence of a benevolent and omnipotent deity, for how could such a god allow innocent creatures to suffer? But if animals do not suffer after all, there is no problem. Harrison believes that his arguments against animal pain assume greatest significance in the context of theodicy (the vindication of divine providence).

Peter Carruthers devotes the last chapter of his book *The Animals Issue* to arguing that animals have no conscious experiences and therefore cannot suffer. Animals do have mental states, he says, but these are not consciously experienced. Carruthers points to the example of a person driving a car along a familiar route while thinking of other things: the driver takes note of sights and sounds along the way but is not conscious of them. Animals, he maintains, live their entire lives like this and, though they "experience" pain, they are not aware of doing so. Contrary to the oft-cited claim of Thomas Nagel (1974) that there is something that it is like to *be* a bat, there is in fact nothing that it feels like to be a bat or a dog or a monkey. If consciousness is like turning on a light, suggests Carruthers, then the lives of animals are nothing but darkness.

Evelyn Pluhar (1995) takes issue with Harrison and Carruthers at some length. Among the points she makes is that Harrison's view that pain would be superfluous for animals is based on the assumption that animals are in effect machines—the very thesis he is trying to persuade us to accept. He assumes without argument that only humans can make choices, despite scientific evidence to the contrary. Pluhar charges Harrison with inconsistency when he goes on to suggest that animals encounter painful stimuli but do not experience pain the way we do. Pain that is fleeting or forgotten is still pain, says Pluhar, even for the amnesiac, the newborn child, or the forgetful dreamer; if animals are like such humans, animals still experience pain. As for Carruthers, Pluhar notes that complex habitual actions like navigating one's way by car are possible only because one has previously learned consciously to perform them. Carruthers claims that conscious experiences involve thoughts that themselves can be thought about in turn and says that animals lack the ability to do this. Pluhar points out that young children have great difficulty reflecting on their thoughts even though they can talk; are we to take it that they are not conscious? (See also Lynch 1994.)

The reader who has been convinced that animals cannot suffer may be tempted to close the book at this point and get on with other things. However, while Harrison and Carruthers present ingenious arguments to support the possibility that animals cannot suffer, they do little to show that this possibility is a likelihood. Although the adequacy of the analogical argument may be questioned — although it may be questioned whether it even provides a satisfactory explanation for our inclination to attribute feelings to animals (Cockburn 1994) — the burden of proof still rests with those who would deny the "common sense" view that many animals are sentient beings, creatures who can experience pain and pleasure. Even so, the issue of the moral status of animals remains open. An admission that they can suffer does not commit one to advocating their liberation.

## The Moral Community

Animal-liberationists, we may say, are all those who consider many non-human animals to be members of the *moral community*. But what is that? A traditional point of view would maintain that the moral community consists of those who are moral agents, that is, those who can make choices based on some commonly understood standard of right and wrong and who can thus be held accountable by others for their actions. To this group might be added some human beings, like infants, who are not moral agents but who might be looked upon, in effect, as honorary members of the moral community, either because they have the potential to become moral agents, or simply because they are human. Defining the moral community in terms of moral agency would, by most accounts, exclude all (or almost all) animals. But we would then have to find some other term to denote all those whom liberationists include within the circle of those who must never be treated essentially as resources.

Some philosophers (Clark 1982; DeGrazia 1996; L. Johnson 1983; Preece and Chamberlain 1993; Rachels 1990; Rodd 1996; Sapontzis 1987; R. Watson 1979) and scientists (Darwin 1890; de Waal 1996) have challenged the belief that the criterion of moral agency neatly distinguishes human beings from animals. But the philosophy of animal liberation does not presuppose the success of this challenge, and in any case liberationists do not claim that animals exhibit moral agency to the same degree that humans do. At least one philosopher (MacIver 1948) has argued that individuals incapable of moral agency may still exhibit good or bad traits of character, so that even a creature like a beetle may be judged to possess or to lack virtue to some slight extent. His conclusion is that non-human creatures, even insects, differ from human beings in moral status only in degree, even if the difference in degree is great. While many liberationists might hesitate to apply the notion of virtue to insects, they would agree that the general human superiority in reason and moral agency cannot be used to deny significant moral standing to members of other species.

Those who espouse animal liberation, then, disagree with those who do not over the question of *who fundamentally counts in our moral reckoning*. With this in mind, one way to describe the moral community is to say that it consists of all those to whom we as moral agents have duties. I have a duty not to assault you, and this is a duty I owe directly to you. I may have a duty not to damage your television set, but this is also a duty I owe to you; it is not owed to your television set. The television set is not a member of the moral community, but you are. You count morally in a way that your television set does not.

However, defining the moral community in terms of those to whom we have duties will not always do the trick. One problem is that we have not specified what sorts or strengths of duties are involved. If the only duty we have to some creature $X$ is to refrain from forcing $X$ to wear red mittens on Thursdays, while at the same time we have no duty not to torture or enslave $X$, then it can hardly be said that we recognize $X$ as a member of the moral community in any significant sense. More relevantly, someone may think that, other things being equal, we should not cause an animal to suffer, but that almost any human interest — in eating meat, for example, or in testing cosmetics or in fishing for sport — overrides an animal's interest in not suffering. Such a person thinks that animals count morally to some degree, that they are "morally considerable" (Goodpaster 1978), but that the moral consideration we owe them does not prevent us from subordinating their interests to ours most of the time.

Another problem with defining the moral community in terms of those to whom we have duties is that some liberationists, like Singer, are utilitarians, and utilitarians tend to avoid talking in terms of rights or, correspondingly, of duties in the sense in which duties entail rights. (Insofar as you owe a duty directly to someone, that someone has a corresponding right against you.) Utilitarians, it might seem then, do not think anyone, human or non-human, is a member of the moral community. A formulation with this implication obviously will not do if we wish to cover utilitarians.

A better way of characterizing the moral community might be to say that it consists of *all those whose interests should receive the same consideration as our similar interests.* This is not to say that all members necessarily have the same interests. For example, although everyone may have the same interest in avoiding pain, everyone may not have the same interest in continuing to live. Someone who is incurably ill with a painful disease may not have the same interest in continuing to live as someone who is healthy. Someone who is healthy but who by nature has little or no conception of having a future beyond the next few moments may not have the same interest in continuing to live as someone who can imagine having an extended future and can look forward to it. To say that a particular being counts as a member of the moral community is to say that with respect to any interest that he or she has, that being is entitled to the same consideration that we would be. Not everyone who accepts that animals share at least some interests with humans will agree that those interests should be counted equally with ours in our moral reckoning.

As is often the case in applied ethics, there is a grey area here, one that can obscure the distinction between who is a liberationist and who is not. There is disagreement about just what interests animals have, and as a result there can be disagreement about whether a given philosopher is in fact recognizing all interests. In particular, there is the question of what interest animals may have in continuing to live and whether they are significantly harmed by being painlessly killed. Complicating matters is the fact that those who ascribe rights to animals are likely to view a utilitarian approach as inherently inadequate when it comes to describing the interests of either humans or animals. Thus it is that even Peter Singer's credentials as a liberationist have been questioned (Francione 1996, 2000).

It must also be stressed that counting interests equally does not mean that there are never times when it is legitimate to favour the interests of some individuals over those of others. It is commonly, though not universally, maintained that we have special obligations to see to the welfare of members of our family and our community. Moreover, interests sometimes conflict. We may have to choose whether to devote time and resources to aiding flood victims in a neighbouring town or to aiding famine victims in another country. We may, in the extreme case, have to decide who gets a place in the lifeboat when the ship goes down. Many liberationists are prepared to say that when the basic interests of humans and animals conflict, it is generally right to give priority to basic human interests. *Why* it may be right to do so is an issue that will come up more than once in the rest of the book. Liberationists differ from their opponents in holding that when there is no such special obligation or conflict, the interests of animals must receive the same consideration as we would give to the similar interests of human beings. (For extended discussions of the notion of equal consideration of interests, see DeGrazia 1996; Francione 2000; Rowlands 2002.)

## Utilitarians Draw the Line at Sentience

The debate about the moral status of animals and whether they should be "liberated" has been conducted from several ethical perspectives. Utilitarianism, the rights view, contractarianism, and feminist theory all play prominent roles in the debate, and recently virtue ethics has arrived on the scene.

Utilitarianism is the doctrine that, in its standard form, enjoins us to choose among different possible courses of action on the basis of the net amount of happiness, for all affected, that is likely to result. If reducing pain and promoting pleasure is what morality is all about, then sentience is the dividing line between those beings that are morally considerable and those that are not. If a being is not sentient, then, morally speaking, there is nothing to take into account for its sake. There may be many good reasons for not taking an axe to that oak tree across the street, but if the tree is not sentient, then whatever wrong is done by chopping down the tree will not be a wrong done to the tree. On the other hand, if a being is sentient, we must reckon with its experience in our moral deliberations.

By underlining the moral significance of pleasure and pain, utilitarianism endorses the claim that all sentient beings count for something in the moral calculus. But whether the pleasure and pain of animals is to count as much as the pleasure and pain of humans is an issue about which utilitarians disagree. Peter Singer (2002), the most prominent utilitarian advocate of animal liberation, has championed the idea of viewing animals on equal moral terms with humans. In doing so, Singer is following in the footsteps of Jeremy Bentham (see Chapter 2), the founder of modern utilitarianism. On the other hand, R.G. Frey (1980, 1983), to take a leading example, has attacked the notion of animal liberation from a utilitarian position.

Appealing as it does to the net consequences for all those affected by our actions, the utilitarian viewpoint tends to be non-absolutist in its conclusions. What may be right in some circumstances may be wrong in other circumstances, and what is best for a particular individual may have to give way to considerations of the good of others.

### The Rights View: Respect for Individuals

A right is a claim to something (say, to be allowed to speak freely, or to possess a particular piece of property) that is recognized as legitimate on the basis of some moral or legal principles. A right may be thought of as a protective shield around an individual. The alleged good of the community is generally not sufficient reason to override this protection. In the political sphere, for example, liberal democracies combine the democratic principle of rule by the majority with the idea that the majority must not be allowed to trample underfoot certain basic individual liberties. These basic liberties are sometimes legally enshrined in a charter of rights.

In this book we are concerned much more with moral than with legal rights. Those who are interested in the relation between moral principles and laws relating to animals in the United States are referred to *Animals, Property, and the Law* by Gary Francione. Francione makes the point that in contemporary societies animals have the status of property and that their liberation would involve an end to this status. In *Unleashing Rights: Law, Meaning, and the Animal Rights Movement*, Helena Silverstein examines the ways in which the movement has sought to employ legal institutions and the language of rights in defence of animals. In *Rattling the Cage: Toward Legal Rights for Animals* (which focuses on chimpanzees) and in *Drawing the Line: Science and the Case for Animal Rights*, Steven Wise examines the mental abilities of animals in order to build the case for ascribing basic legal rights to members of some species.

Although moral rights are sometimes ascribed to individuals on the basis of a social agreement (see the following section), another tradition —what I shall designate simply *the rights view*—holds that moral rights are to be ascribed to certain sorts of beings on the basis of their natural characteristics, independently of a revocable social agreement, and independently of their utility for others. In other words, certain sorts of beings are entitled to be *respected* (in particular, never to be used as a mere resource for others) and to be treated with *justice* because they have, by nature, some significant quality. Typically, the significant quality is held to be the ability to conduct one's life through the conscious pursuit of goals, however this process may be characterized.

Historically, the concept of respecting individuals was powerfully articulated by Immanuel Kant, whose ideas about animals are discussed in Chapter 2. His moral theory is described as *deontological*, in that it speaks the language of duties and, at least implicitly, of corresponding rights. Kant stressed the capacity to reason about the morality of one's actions as the basis for membership in the moral community. However, those philosophers who attribute rights to animals, while subscribing to the idea of respecting the capacity of the individual to conduct his or her own life, reject Kant's criterion of rationality. It is not necessary, such philosophers say, to be able to reason about moral principles in order to be worthy of respect. Any being, human or non-human, that has some minimal degree of self-consciousness and the ability to act in accordance with his or her preferences deserves to be treated with respect. The case for ascribing rights to animals is most prominently associated with Tom Regan (2004a), whose views are examined in some detail in Chapter 3.

## Contractarians Say Morality Is an Agreement

If we think about either utilitarianism or the rights view, we see that both enjoin us to treat other beings on the basis of what, by nature, is in the interests of those beings. For utilitarianism, this means considering whether a being is sentient and thus has an interest in avoiding pain and experiencing pleasure. For the person who takes a rights position, it means considering whether a being possesses the requisite ability to conduct her life as she sees fit and so is entitled to be free from unnecessary interference when doing so. From either point of view, we have a responsibility to regulate our behaviour toward others on the basis of who they are, and not simply on the basis of what they can do for (or to) us.

However, there is a very different way of looking at morality, one that sees it as an agreement among rational, self-interested individuals. For the contractarian, the question is not *What obligations do I have with respect to other beings by virtue of what is in their interests?* Rather, it is *What sort of a deal must I strike with others in order to get what I want?* For those who believe that all moral obligation springs from contractual agreement, the nature of other beings imposes no restrictions on my behaviour, except insofar as it is prudent for me to consider how my interaction with them may affect me. The notion that it is intrinsically wrong to impose unnecessary suffering on others, or to intervene in others' lives against their wishes, is for the dyed-in-the-wool contractarian mere intuition, not hard fact, and therefore no sound basis for a moral theory.

The contractual view of morality sees moral rights as the product of a social agreement. In so doing, it by and large excludes animals from the moral community. (See, for example, Carruthers 1992 and Narveson 1977, 1983, 1987). Although it is possible to think of a few instances where we might describe the interactions between human and non-human as involving an unspoken contract—consider a farmer and a sheepdog or even a home-owner and a domestic cat—in general animals cannot participate fully, if at all, in the sorts of agreements to regulate behaviour that characterize human society. Animals may nevertheless be covered by a moral contract. While the framers of a contract must be rational agents, those protected by its principles need not be; one philosopher (Rowlands 1998) has even made a contractarian case for animal rights. As traditionally articulated, though, the contract view of morality has been inhospitable to the idea of animal liberation. If some animals are to be protected, this is only because we humans feel it is in our current interests to do so. I shouldn't kick your dog because that would upset you, and you are another human being, one with whom I have an understanding about how to behave.

## Should Feminists Support Animal Liberation?

In sharp contrast to contract theorists, who hold that human beings are fundamentally separate, self-interested individuals who enter into relations with each other on the basis of rational calculation, feminist philosophers maintain that relations are primary in human affairs and not just added on to our basic natures. Surely there is something important in this. However useful it may be on occasion to consider what sorts of voluntary arrangements we would like to make with others to further our personal interests, the fact is that from the moment we are born we are embedded in webs of relations with others. Many of the relations in our lives are not voluntarily chosen, and many are not between individuals equal in knowledge or power. (Consider, for example, our original family relations with our parents and siblings.)

Feminists are certainly not the first to stress the importance of understanding individuals in terms of their relations to others. In China the traditions of Daoism and Neo-Confucianism offered a holistic view of nature and of the individual in society. If European philosophers prior to the twentieth century more often than not stressed individual self-determination and took an atomistic view of nature and of society, there were prominent exceptions, such as Spinoza, Hegel, and Marx. Feminist philosophy is part of a wider trend during the past century, in social and political philosophy as well as in the sciences (from physics and biology to cybernetics and ecology), that has emphasized *wholes* and *relations*.

At the same time, feminist philosophers urge us to be sensitive to the unique qualities of individuals, and thus to the differences between oneself and the other. With this in mind, they have criticized utilitarians and rights theorists for allegedly relying on abstract, universal ethical principles to the detriment of understanding the concrete and the particular. Reliance on abstract principles is seen as linked to an overemphasis on the role played by reason in human affairs and to a neglect of the vital role of the emotions in relations among individuals (Donovan and Adams 1996; McKenna 1994; Slicer 1991).

What does this general feminist perspective as such imply for our treatment of animals? The short answer would seem to be: nothing definite. There is no consensus among feminist philosophers on the subject of our relations with animals. Feminist philosophy has many strands, and different philosophers draw different conclusions. Some of them (Donovan 1990; Gruen 1993) argue that, in order to be consistent, feminists must support animal liberation. It may be noted that most animal-liberation activists are women (Groves 1997; Guither 1998; Jasper and Nelkin 1992; Mukerjee 1997; Sperling 1988). On the other hand, it has been claimed (B.A. Dixon 1996; Pierce 1979) that there is no necessary connection between the liberation of women and the liberation of animals. Indeed, we find some feminist philosophers opposing animal liberation. For example, Nel Noddings (1984), who articulates an "ethic of caring", in which the idea of relatedness is central, sees little reason to care about animals apart from those few, like pets, for whom we deliberately assume personal responsibility. (See Chapter 3 for more on Noddings' view.) Not surprisingly, then, feminists are divided on the question of vegetarianism. It has been argued (Adams 1994, 2000) that meat-eating symbolizes and reinforces male dominance in human society. But it has also been argued (George 2000) that vegetarianism does this.

For their part, eco-feminists (ecological feminists) see an inherent link between hierarchy and domination in human society, particularly the historical domination of women by men, and attitudes and practices of human domination over the non-human world (Gruen 1993; Kheel 1985). Eco-feminism, then, in rejecting all forms of domination over others on the part of human beings, does tend to support the concept of animal liberation.

### How Would the Virtuous Person Treat Animals?

With its emphasis on caring and personal relationships, and its wariness of abstract principles, feminist ethics exhibits a kinship with a much older tradition, deriving from the moral perspective of Aristotle and the ancient Greeks, known as virtue ethics. Instead of asking what obligations we have or what rules we should follow, virtue ethics asks what traits of character we should cultivate in order to live a good life—that is, in order to flourish as human beings. Virtues are positive traits of character. They include, for example, courage, honesty, loyalty, benevolence, industriousness, compassion, and, more generally, all the traits that help us to get along with others in society and to face the hardships of life. Virtues stand in contrast to vices, such as cruelty, cowardice, and dishonesty. Until lately, virtue ethics has played only a marginal role in the debate about the moral status of animals. But now a few philosophers, like Rosalind Hursthouse (2000), seek to change that. They contend that, with regard to our treatment of animals, we ought to ask: how would the virtuous person act?

Aristotle's notion of virtue is intimately connected with his idea that humans flourish when they manifest the potential that is intrinsic to members of the human species. In his view, every living thing has its appropriate *telos*, a goal that it is striving to realize (Hauskeller 2005). An acorn, for example, will by nature grow to be a great oak tree if allowed to manifest the potential of its kind. This aspect of Aristotle's thought has influenced some philosophers recently, in particular Martha Nussbaum (2006), who has been developing what she calls the "capabilities approach". The best approach to ethics, she argues, is one that seeks to facilitate the flourishing of both humans and animals according to their intrinsic natures.

## Is Animal Liberation Compatible with Environmental Ethics?
The case for animal liberation is a case for ascribing moral standing to sentient individuals. As such, it does not seem to ascribe moral standing directly to the non-sentient elements of the natural world, whether individuals or systems, living or not. Grass, trees, rocks, rivers, forests, ecosystems—all these seem, at first glance, to be left out of the picture. As we shall see in Chapter 6, there are those who doubt that the individualistic orientation of animal liberation can be reconciled with a concern for the flourishing of the natural world. Even if we recognize the importance of natural habitat to animals, the fact that nature is "red in tooth and claw" means it is unclear that any protection of the interests of individual animals can be extended beyond domesticated creatures without having absurd implications. Not surprisingly, animal-liberation philosophers have disputed claims of irreconcilability. The issue has been one of the most hotly-contested in animal ethics.

The place that human beings and animals occupy in the natural world also brings us to an important twist in the animal-ethics debate. As will be seen, numerous philosophers have mounted a strong challenge to what has been called "human exceptionalism"—the idea that human beings possess some quality that sets all humans apart from all animals and endows all humans with a special moral worth. One response to this challenge has been to abandon the doctrine of human exceptionalism while seeking to justify continued human domination of animals. If humans are, after all, one species among many in nature, then — even if we regulate our behaviour according to moral rules within the human community — do we not have the same right as other animals to prey upon members of other species?

### The Argument from Marginal Cases

Finding our way through the debate about animals involves seeking coherence among theory, principles, and the considered judgements we make in particular cases. We cannot simply pick and choose among arguments according to the conclusions we desire, heedless of their internal consistency or their consistency with other arguments to which we subscribe.

The demand for consistency in our thinking is nicely illustrated by one argument that plays an especially prominent role in the ethical debate. This is what is called *the argument from marginal cases*. The name appears to have originated with Jan Narveson (1977), but the argument itself can be found even in the ancient world, where it was advanced by the Neoplatonist philosopher Porphyry in the third century (Dombrowski 1984, 1997).

The argument from marginal cases makes reference to the many instances of humans who fall significantly below the level of mental ability typically exhibited by adult humans. It points to the overlap in capacities (cognitive or sensitive) between humans and animals in order to make the claim that we must either include at least some animals in the moral community or else exclude some humans. If the criterion that we use as a ticket to the moral community — be it moral agency or self-consciousness or rationality or simply the ability to experience pain and pleasure — permits us to include all humans, then it will necessarily include at least some animals. And if it excludes all animals, then it will necessarily exclude at least some humans. So we have a choice: either we can bite the bullet and exclude some humans along with the animals, or we can include all humans (perhaps with the exception of those in a persistent vegetative state) and many animals too. What we cannot do, according to the argument, is draw a neat, permanent line in the sand that simultaneously includes all humans and

The argument from marginal cases provides us with a powerful argument that applies to almost any suggested morally relevant difference between humans and animals. Whatever feature is proposed, ask yourself: "Do all humans have it?" If they don't, then ask yourself: "What about those humans who don't have it?" This argument, almost single handedly, rules out most of the suggested relevant differences between humans and animals.
– Mark Rowlands,
*Animals Like Us*, p. 45

excludes all animals. For example, if we hold that only those who can reason about right and wrong are entitled to membership in the community, then many humans, including young children and those with severe mental handicaps, will not qualify. If we hold that anyone who is capable of experiencing pain or pleasure qualifies, then many animals will qualify.

Not surprisingly, most people are unwilling to disqualify any humans from the moral community (A. Taylor 2008b). According to proponents of the argument from marginal cases, logical consistency then demands recognition of many animals as members too.

The argument from marginal cases presents a powerful challenge to those who claim that no animal ought to be ascribed the same moral standing as any human. But is the argument watertight? For its part, the contract view of morality can offer a way of drawing a line between all humans and all animals, insofar as it holds that rational contractors set the rules that say who counts and who does not. If the contractors agree that all humans are members of the moral community and all animals are not, then that is the way it is. But the contract view, whatever its merits, typically ascribes no intrinsic value even to humans and puts everyone at potential risk through renegotiation of the contract.

Can a way around the argument from marginal cases be found that still guarantees permanent protection to all humans? One strategy might be to claim that there is something about just being a member of the human species that gives all human beings, regardless of their individual capacities, a unique moral standing. But it is hard to see how the simple fact of being biologically human could *in itself* carry any moral weight; if being biologically human makes a difference, there must be some relevant quality attached to being biologically human that makes the difference. Another strategy might be to claim that those of us who qualify on the basis of our capacities owe special duties of care to those humans who are deficient in those capacities. Another might be to question whether the significance of cognitive or sensitive capacities can be properly evaluated apart from species membership. Of course, any such claims require further backing if they are to be convincing.

We shall encounter the argument from marginal cases at various places in the chapters that follow. Often the argument is implicit in the discussion; in Chapter 5 it is explicitly addressed at some length. The ins and outs of the argument are explored at book length by Daniel Dombrowski in *Babies and Beasts*. Evelyn Pluhar also devotes considerable space to a discussion of marginal cases in *Beyond Prejudice*. (Some people object to the expression "marginal cases" on the grounds that it is derogatory to those humans to whom it applies. It might be noted that the expression is "marginal cases", not "marginal humans", and refers to atypical or non-paradigmatic *instances*.)

### Seeing Ourselves through Animals

It would be naïve to imagine that any of us, including philosophers, approach the issue of the moral status of animals with no preconceived beliefs or biases. In general, people do not like to change their opinions, much less their behaviour, so there is always the temptation to favour theories and arguments that reinforce the beliefs we already have. (The economist John Kenneth Galbraith is reported to have said that, faced with the choice between changing one's mind and proving there is no need to do so, almost everyone gets busy on the proof.) This is particularly true in the case of animal ethics because our relation to, and treatment of, animals is profoundly bound up with the way we conduct our everyday lives (the food we eat, the products we use, even our language) and with our sense of who we are (our place in the world, our sense of intrinsic worth, even our religious beliefs).

Animals do not just exist somewhere "out there". We eat them, hunt them, use their living bodies for labour and their dead bodies for industry, watch them on television and stare at them in zoos. They are cherished members of our families and objects for dissection in laboratories. Their symbolic images fill our languages, our myths and stories, our art and advertising (Baker 1993; Kalof 2007). Yet even our everyday language often reflects what one writer has called our "careless contempt" for animals, promoting the idea that non-humans are fundamentally different from, and inferior to, humans (Dunayer 2001). For example, unless we know an individual animal well, the animal is typically referred to as "it", rather than "she" or "he". Animals are "harvested" by hunters and "sacrificed" by scientists, rather than "killed" or "executed". A dead human body is a "corpse", while a dead animal body is a "carcass". The word "meat" renders invisible the once-living creature from which it came. When animals are not just bodies they are nobodies. In

The saddest and silliest of the superstitions to which we sacrifice animals is our belief that by killing them we ourselves somehow live more fully. We might live more fully by entering imaginatively into their lives. But shedding their blood makes us no more full-blooded.... There is no law of nature which makes *savoir vivre* incompatible with "live and let live".
– Brigid Brophy, "The Rights of Animals", p. 129

May of 2002, residents of the northeastern Quebec town of Notre-Dame-du-Lac were forced to flee their homes because of an ammonia leak from a slaughterhouse that was destroyed by fire. Canadian Press reported that "No one was injured but about 2,600 pigs were killed."

Rod Preece (1999, 2002, 2005) has argued persuasively that it would be a mistake to believe that the history of Western cultural attitudes toward animals is simply one of denigration. The true story is complex and exhibits much that is respectful of the animal realm. If Preece is right, then it is perhaps not so surprising that this other current should burst forth with special strength in propitious conditions. That we have come to a turning point in our relations with our non-human kin is a possibility but not yet a probability. For society to recognize animals as members of the moral community would be to put an end to the prevailing idea that these creatures are essentially resources. This would have far-reaching implications for agriculture and industry, for scientific research, for many occupations, for land use, and for animal populations themselves. It would signal a profound reorientation in the basic attitude of human beings to the other sentient beings who live on this planet. A world in which animals had been "liberated" would be a world dramatically changed from the one we live in at present.

## Conclusion

Although there are many aspects to the debate among philosophers about the moral status of animals, at its centre is the issue of whether it is acceptable to treat non-human creatures essentially as resources for human use. Another way to put the issue is to say that it has to do with who qualifies as a member of the moral community. The moral community can be said to consist of all those beings whose interests should receive the same consideration as our similar interests. Different philosophers have argued the issue from different ethical perspectives, and even philosophers arguing from the same general perspective may disagree with each other in their conclusions.

For anyone who is new to animal ethics and confronting all the various claims and theories, there is the danger of not being able to see the forest for the trees. The reader of this book might want to keep in mind a couple of questions raised by a deceptively simple rule of morality that most people would endorse. The rule is: If you don't have to harm someone, you shouldn't. The questions it raises are: *Who counts as someone?* and *What justifies harming someone?* The reader is also advised to bear in mind the question raised by the argument from marginal cases: *Can any rational justification be given for drawing a neat, once-and-for-all line in the sand between all humans and all animals?*

# CHAPTER TWO

# FROM ARISTOTLE TO DARWIN

...animals cannot even apprehend a [rational] principle; they obey their instincts.

*— Aristotle* [1]

A dog frames a general concept of cats or sheep, and knows the corresponding words as well as a philosopher.

*— Leslie Stephen, quoted by Charles Darwin* [2]

This chapter provides a historical introduction to the topic of the moral status of animals. A number of prominent pre-twentieth-century thinkers—including Aristotle, René Descartes, Thomas Hobbes, John Locke, David Hume, Immanuel Kant, Jeremy Bentham, John Stuart Mill, and Charles Darwin—are canvassed on the subject of animals. Particular attention is paid to Descartes' view that animals are machines without minds, to Kant's view that we have no duties to animals because they are not rational, and to Darwin's claim that humans

---

[1] Aristotle, *The Works of Aristotle* (London: Oxford University Press, 1927), "Politica", Book 1, 1254b.

[2] Charles Darwin, *The Descent of Man, and Selection in Relation to Sex*, 2nd ed. (London: John Murray, 1890), p. 89.

Chuang Tzu and Hui Tzu had strolled on to the bridge over the Hao, when the former observed, "See how the minnows are darting about! That is the pleasure of fishes."

"You not being a fish yourself," said Hui Tzu, "how can you possibly know in what consists the pleasure of fishes?"

"And you not being I," retorted Chuang Tzu, "how can you know that I do not know?"

"If I, not being you, cannot know what you know," urged Hui Tzu, "it follows that you, not being a fish, cannot know in what consists the pleasure of fishes."

"Let us go back," said Chuang Tzu, "to your original question. You asked me how I knew in what consists the pleasure of fishes. Your very question shows that you knew I knew. I knew it from my own feelings on the bridge."

– Chuang Tzu, 4th century BCE, "The Happiness of Fish" in *Chuang Tzu: Mystic, Moralist, and Social Reformer*, trans. Herbert A. Giles (London: B. Quaritch, 1926), pp. 218-19

are not fundamentally different from their non-human kin. Most of the issues raised in the course of this chapter are taken up at greater length in subsequent chapters, where the emphasis is on the debate among modern philosophers.

## Traditional Religious/Ethical Teachings

Although religion is peripheral to this book's topic except where it may impinge upon the writings of philosophers, a few words can be said here about the world's great religious/ethical traditions. These traditions have done much to shape societies' views of animals. Indeed, the complex intersection of animals and religion also has much to do with our understanding of who we are as human beings (Waldau and Patton 2006).

In the Middle Ages, Saint Augustine (354-430) and Saint Thomas Aquinas (1225-1274) articulated the Christian doctrine that animals, lacking as they do the faculty of reason, have been placed here on earth by God for human use. By contrast, for Francis of Assisi, who died just after Aquinas was born, esteeming animals was a way of honouring God (Gaffney 1986). Even the possibility that animals have immortal souls has been entertained by various Christian thinkers (Preece 2005). We shall see in Chapter 3 that a case for animal liberation has been made by a modern Christian theologian. Overall, however, it cannot be said that the major monotheistic religions—Judaism, Christianity, and Islam— incorporate the concept of animal liberation. Judaism does forbid causing pain to animals except for what are considered legitimate human needs, in particular medical needs (Bleich 1986), and a case for vegetarianism has been made on the basis of the precepts of Judaism (Schwartz 2001). Islam condones the religious sacrifice of animals, yet forbids being cruel to them. The Koran suggests that animal consciousness is not limited to instinct and intuition, and that non-human creatures worship God in their own ways (Masri 1986).

An emphasis on the continuity of the human and non-human realms is evident in Chinese Neo-Confucian philosophy, which arose during the Song dynasty (960-1279). Incorporating Daoism's concern with the *way*, or pattern, of nature, Neo-Confucianism maintains there is an underlying unity to all things. Human beings differ in degree, but not in kind, from animals. In the opinion of Zhu Xi (1130-1200), animals are not entirely without the capacity for moral reflection, though they do not possess the full capacity that humans do. According to Confucian tradition, the virtuous person has a feeling of oneness with all living things and is pained to see the suffering of others, including the suffering of animals. Still, this does not mean that animal suffering is as deplorable as human suffering; for Confucianism the prime concern of human beings should be for other human beings (R. Taylor 1986).

Traditional thought on the Indian subcontinent presents a picture relatively hospitable to animal liberation. *Ahimsa*, the doctrine of non-injury to all living beings, is a prominent part of Hinduism, Buddhism, and Jainism (Chapple 1993; Schmidt-Raghavan 1993). In Hindu thought this doctrine reflects the belief that any harm that one does to other living beings will result in future suffering for oneself. Refraining from injuring others is thus a matter of promoting one's salvation. Insofar as human life is seen as superior to animal life, and the goal of our behaviour is to seek our own salvation, we can be said to have duties *regarding* animals, but not duties *to* animals (Lal 1986). However, for that strand of Hindu thinking that renounces the concept of a hierarchy of domination in nature, the doctrine of non-injury implies recognition of the intrinsic value of every living being (Jacobsen 1994). The influence of Buddhists and Jainists in India has been instrumental in limiting the formerly widespread Hindu practice of animal sacrifice. Buddhism and Jainism both stress the interrelatedness of all forms of life. Vegetarianism is an ideal for both. All creatures, it is said, even the simplest, love life and seek protection from harm (Austin 1979). Then again, even the Buddhist tradition tends to regard humans as of greater moral worth than animals and displays features that leave it open to the charge of speciesism (Waldau 2002).

The indigenous peoples of North America, though speaking many different languages and varying greatly in culture, nevertheless have shared a view of nature as being filled with spirit. For some Aboriginal cultures animals form with humans an extended family whose members are mutually dependent and mutually supporting. For others, animals participate in voluntary economic exchanges with human beings (Callicott 1989, 1994). For all these cultures animals are intelligent beings who must be treated with respect even — especially — when they are being hunted and consumed by humans.

## Aristotle Emphasizes Human Rationality

The Western philosophical tradition can be traced to ancient Greece. Here too we find the origins of the debate over the moral status of animals. Those Greek philosophers who touched on the subject asked whether we have any kinship with animals. Is there some morally relevant similarity or difference? Aristotle (384-322 BCE), whose historical influence in philosophical matters has been enormous, argued that humans differ from animals in a crucial way.

According to Aristotle (1927), every living organism has a soul. By this, he does not mean an immortal consciousness, but rather an animating principle, the capacity to manifest its natural functions. The soul of a plant is concerned entirely with nutrition, growth, and reproduction. Animals differ from plants in having not just life but sense perception, and humans differ from animals in having not just life and sense perception but the ability to reason. Thus there is a scale, or hierarchy, in nature from simpler to more complex. Given that, according to Aristotle, each type of organism has the functions appropriate to its particular way of flourishing, it has been argued by a least one commentator (Osborne 2007) that we should not take this scale to imply a hierarchy of *value*.

Even so, Aristotle clearly believes that reason has a privileged role to play. Men, being superior in reason (so he believes), should govern women, and some people — those deficient in reason but robust in body — are fit by nature to be slaves. Those humans fit to be slaves at least can appreciate the reasoning of others, even if they cannot properly exercise the faculty themselves. By contrast, says Aristotle, animals are entirely without reason and are ruled by their instincts, and so it is only proper that they should be used for human purposes. Plants have been created for animals and animals for human beings. Indeed, it is advantageous for animals, tame or wild, to be subjected to humans, since all are thereby safer. Like slaves, animals are useful to us because of their bodily strength. Because we have nothing significant in common with a horse or an ox, says Aristotle, there can be neither friendship nor justice in our relations with them.

The influential Stoic philosophers of the Hellenistic period and the Roman Empire placed considerable importance on the idea of *belonging*. The source of justice, they said, is to be found in treating oneself and others as together forming a community. The sense of belonging-

And it is clear that the rule of the soul over the body, and of the mind and the rational element over the passionate, is natural and expedient; whereas the equality of the two or the rule of the inferior is always hurtful. The same holds good of animals in relation to men; for tame animals have a better nature than wild, and all tame animals are better off when they are ruled by man; for then they are preserved.
— Aristotle, *The Works of Aristotle*, vol. 10, p. 1254b

together that we feel with regard to our families and those close to us should be extended. Ideally, we should view all people of the world as belonging to a single community, governed by the same laws. Today, this idea of extending the circle of inclusiveness outward plays a role in the philosophies of animal liberation and environmentalism (e.g., Singer 1981). One might expect that the Stoics would have advocated including animals within the circle of belonging, particularly as they admitted that animals extend a sense of belonging to their own (animal) offspring. But they did not. Rational beings, they maintained, can extend belonging, and hence justice, only to other rational beings. However we may treat animals, then, we are not treating them unjustly. If some Stoics were vegetarian, they were so for ascetic reasons, not out of any sense of justice to animals (Sorabji 1993).

There were some Greeks who took a very different view of things. Pythagoras (late 6th century BCE), Empedocles (c.495-c.435 BCE), and even Aristotle's pupil Theophrastus (c.371-c.286 BCE) rejected the claim that we have nothing significant in common with animals and therefore cannot be said to treat them unjustly. Pythagoras and Empedocles believed that animals may be former human beings, now reincarnated in non-human form. If we kill them, we may be killing our ancestors. Pythagoras has been called the first animal-rights philosopher (Violin 1990). He advocated vegetarianism, and he and his followers rejected the use of animals in religious sacrifice. Theophrastus condemned meat-eating, saying that killing animals is unjust because it robs them of life. Animals, he said, are similar to us not only with respect to their sense perceptions and their emotions, but because they can engage in reasonings. Several centuries later, Porphyry (c.232-c.304) argued that we owe justice to animals not simply because they are rational but because they are conscious beings who can feel pain and terror (Dombrowski 1984; Sorabji 1993). This view led Porphyry (2000) to write at length against the practice of eating meat.

Despite these dissenting voices, the emphasis of Aristotle and the Stoics on rationality as the distinctive human quality, and the related claim that animals are on earth for our use because they lack reason, have been echoed by most philosophers until well into the twentieth century. An important figure is Saint Thomas Aquinas, who in the thirteenth century harmonized the philosophy of Aristotle with the teachings of the Church. Aquinas (1945) says that since humans, being rational, are masters of their own actions, they are cared for by God for their own sakes. By contrast, animals are not masters of their own actions, and therefore are by nature instruments for those who *are* self-directed.

### Descartes Insists Animals Are Only Machines

With the end of the Middle Ages in Europe, a new conception of the natural world arose, one compatible with the new science and the growth of capitalism. No longer looked upon as an organism, nature now came to be seen as a machine. And yet a key facet of the old tradition remained in place: the idea that human beings alone, on account of their unique mental faculties, are members of the moral community.

René Descartes (1596-1650), mathematician and philosopher, played a crucial role in propounding the new mechanistic vision of nature. His view is strikingly exemplified in his comments on non-human creatures. Animals, says Descartes (1985, 1991), are to be understood in purely mechanical terms. By this, he does not mean merely that animals are in some ways like machines. He means that they *are* machines, no different in principle from clocks. Animals are complex automatons constructed by nature; except for their natural origin they are what today we would call robots. Mind and matter, Descartes holds, are two quite distinct kinds of things. Despite the sophistication of their construction (ultimately attributable to God), animals are purely material objects and so devoid of consciousness.

Descartes does not deny that animals possess "sensation" (or what we might better call *sensitivity*). Animals have sensory equipment that allows them to react appropriately to their environments. By way of analogy, we might think of an automobile: it possesses equipment that allows it to "sense" the amount of fuel left in the tank and to register this on a dial, or to "sense" that a seat-belt is not fastened, or a door is not properly shut, and to announce this by means of a buzzer, or even in human language. But few of us imagine that the car is conscious of any of this. It is a cleverly constructed machine and nothing more. Scientifically minded Cartesians could therefore nail living dogs to boards and cut them open, secure in the belief that they were inflicting no pain and that the sounds emanating from the objects of their research were just the squeakings of machinery. (Sometimes it might be useful to cut the dogs' vocal chords in order to stop the irritating sounds.)

Even so, Descartes admits in the course of his argument that animals have feelings of fear, hope, joy, anger, and hunger. Yet such feelings seem to imply, contrary to his contention, that animals are not purely material. A creature that is sensitive to changes in its environment may be nothing more than a complex system of gears and levers, but a creature that is afraid or joyful is a subject of consciousness. The attribution of feelings to animals is thus apparently inconsistent with Descartes' dualist division of the world into mind and matter and his accompanying claim that animals have no minds (Cottingham 1978). On the other hand, if by fear, hunger, and so forth Descartes is simply referring to animal behaviour, and not to mental states, he need not be accused of inconsistency (P. Harrison 1992).

However we read him in this regard, the logic of his argument leads to the conclusion that animals do not possess consciousness. While people are conscious beings who *have* machine bodies, animals just *are* machine bodies. The hypothesis that animals have minds is superfluous: it adds nothing to our understanding of them. Their behaviour can be completely accounted for by mechanical principles. So we have no good reason to believe that animals think. Moreover, says Descartes, we have good reason to believe they do not think. There are, he says, two infallible tests by which we can distinguish a being possessed of consciousness from one that is purely material. Either of these tests can be used to distinguish true people from hypothetical machines of human appearance, or from animals.

The first is the language test: can the being communicate thoughts verbally or by signs? Though a machine-creature (a magpie or a parrot, for example) may be able to utter words, says Descartes, it cannot talk in the sense of being able to engage in conversation. And it should not be imagined that animals have their own languages that we cannot understand, since if they possessed any degree of reason, they would be able in one way or another to communicate their thoughts to us—which, in his opinion, they cannot do.

The second test to distinguish conscious beings from non-conscious ones has to do with the ability to perform a variety of actions. Though a machine may be able to do one or two things as well as, or better than, we can (a clock, for example, can keep time more accurately than an

…since art copies nature, and people can make various automatons which move without thought, it seems reasonable that nature should even produce its own automatons, which are much more splendid than artificial ones—namely the animals. This is especially likely since we know no reason why thought should always accompany the sort of arrangement of organs that we find in animals. It is much more wonderful that a mind should be found in every human body than that one should be lacking in every animal.
– René Descartes, *The Philosophical Writings of Descartes*, vol. 3, p. 366

unaided person can), only a thinking being can do many things well. Machines, in other words, can be *programmed* to do certain things well, but it is for all practical purposes impossible that a machine of the sort made by humans could be programmed to act in the universally adaptable way that reason permits a human being to act. Although Descartes does not place any limits on the behaviour of machines that God might in principle construct, the issue here is not whether God is able to deceive us about the nature of other beings (something Descartes believes God would not do in any case) but whether the behaviour of existing animals entails their having minds. He argues that the superiority of animals' behaviour in some areas, when combined with their gross deficiencies in other areas, is good evidence that they lack reason and are nothing but splendid pieces of clockwork (Newman 2001).

What are we to make of Descartes' tests? Is the ability to use language necessary in order to have thoughts? Theodora, a long-time friend, seemed to communicate to me quite clearly a wish to be fed, or to be let outside, or simply to sit in the same room with me, even though she did not use language to do this. Why should I not attribute thoughts to her? Making oneself understood through appropriate responses need not involve language (Midgley 1995). Furthermore, in recent years some researchers have concluded that some animals can understand and use language. Kanzi, a bonobo ("pygmy chimpanzee") at Georgia State University's Language Research Center, is reported to have responded appropriately to hundreds of spoken commands put to him in the form of English sentences he had never heard before, outperforming the two-year-old daughter of one of the researchers (Savage-Rumbaugh and Lewin 1994). Claims of some degree of linguistic competence have been made not only for Kanzi but for various chimpanzees (Fouts 1997), gorillas, parrots, and dolphins. Sceptics reply that such conclusions are unwarranted (Budiansky 1998; Frey 1980; Leahy 1991; Pinker 1994). The debate over what the facts are and what the facts imply for the moral status of animals is likely to continue for a considerable time (Allen 1996; Orlans et al. 1998; Radner and Radner 1996). Yet even if no animals can understand or use language in the sense in which that term applies to human communication, is it possible that, contrary to Descartes' contention, some can communicate thoughts by other means (Noske 1997)? It has been claimed, for example, that horses can communicate diverse ideas not only to each other but to humans by the use of "body language" (Roberts 1997). The jury, then, is still out on the question of whether, on the basis of Descartes' language test, some animals refute the claim that only human beings have minds.

Can an animal do only one or two things well? Judged by human standards, perhaps the answer is yes. But judged by the standards of an animal, how many things can a human do well? Can a human being fly like an eagle, or see objects as distinctly? Can a human smell or hear as well as a dog? And eagles and dogs, like other animals, do innumerable other things well; otherwise how could they survive and raise offspring? Modern biology and evolutionary theory have helped make us aware of the immense sophistication of nature's products. Also, of course, Descartes had no experience of computers, or inkling of their potential. Today machines made by human beings can be programmed to imitate human behaviour in ways that would have astounded anyone in past ages, and in the future machines will no doubt imitate, and go beyond, human behaviour in ways that would astound people living now. Today the prospect of constructing conscious machines is seriously debated. Conversely, the prospect of machines that can carry on conversations might be taken to imply that the ability to use language does not, after all, entail the possession of consciousness.

All this should make us reluctant to accept Descartes' conclusions. At the same time, the fact that Descartes has not made a convincing case does not prove that animals are conscious, much less that they are capable of reason. But if we are not prepared to accept that many animals are at least conscious, why should we accept that our fellow human beings are? Why not believe that they too are just robots?

Though Descartes' views were influential, they did not go unchallenged even in the seventeenth century. The claim that animals are not conscious and cannot feel pain seemed to violate common sense. The dilemma for many, however, was that to admit some degree of rationality in animals seemed to entail admitting that animals have immortal souls, while to deny them immortal souls seemed to entail denying them not only any degree of rationality but perhaps even the ability to experience pain and pleasure (Fuller 1949; MacIntosh 1996). At least Descartes' position avoided the worse of the two alternatives, for the idea that animals have immortal souls was theologically unorthodox and led to the uncomfortable conclusion that there is no fundamental difference between humans and beasts. In addition, Descartes' position neatly dispensed with a theological dilemma: how to reconcile belief in a just God with the suffering of innocent creatures, creatures who will not experience an afterlife where their suffering might be redeemed (P. Harrison 1989; Lewis 1940; R. Paterson 1984; Rachels 1990). With this issue in mind, the Cartesian philosopher Nicolas Malebranche (1638-1715) vehemently argued that, since God is both just and omnipotent, it follows that animals do not suffer, the evidence of our senses notwithstanding.

Readers who wish to learn more about Descartes' views on animals, including his language and action tests, or about the responses of his contemporaries and Malebranche, or about his legacy will find these matters addressed by Daisie and Michael Radner in *Animal Consciousness*. Today a few philosophers can still be found who doubt that animals like dogs, pigs, eagles, and elephants experience pain or perhaps even have any consciousness at all. However, this sort of view has become increasingly outmoded. The scientific community is moving in the same direction (M. Dawkins 1993; Griffin 1981, 1984, 1992; Varner 1998; Walker 1983). That a view is out of fashion does not, of course, prove it is wrong, but for the most part the philosophical debate has shifted to what *sort* of consciousness animals possess and what this implies for their moral status. Are at least some of them self-aware, and is self-awareness a requirement for inclusion in the moral community? Must a creature be not just self-aware but also able to think rationally? Or is sentience all that is required? Until lately, even those willing to grant that many animals possess consciousness were likely to find some reason to justify subordinating their basic interests to human interests, whether basic or not.

### Hobbes and the War against Animals

In the famous phrase of Thomas Hobbes (1588-1679), life prior to the establishment of the political state is "nasty, brutish, and short". Because human beings are by nature acquisitive and power-seeking, and because they are roughly equal in strength and intelligence, everyone poses a threat to everyone else, and the only right that exists is the liberty to do whatever is necessary for your own protection. However, because people recognize that this war of everyone against everyone else is to no one's benefit, they agree among themselves to institute the political state, each person giving up some freedom in exchange for security and the better life that such security makes possible.

For Hobbes, it makes no sense to talk of justice and injustice apart from the rules enforced by the state. Justice consists in abiding by these rules; injustice, in not abiding by them. Morality is what the political community, at any given time, designates as acceptable behaviour. Morality, then, amounts to an agreement among rational individuals to behave in certain ways and not in others, an agreement that is entered into for the sake of self-interest.

Animals, not being rational, cannot be contractors. Since we have not entered into any agreement with animals mutually to restrain our behaviour toward each other, we remain in an original state of war with them, according to Hobbes (1983). A beast is not bound by any principle of justice to refrain from killing a human; conversely, there is no reason why a human should not kill a beast. Our right to do as we please with animals — to press into service those that can be tamed and to destroy those we find dangerous — is not the result of any divine decree; rather, it is simply the basic natural liberty to do whatever we feel will make our lives more secure.

A similar view of animals is expressed by Baruch (Benedict) de Spinoza (1632-77). Although he rejects dualism and holds that humans, like animals, are entirely natural beings, Spinoza does not conclude that animals are sufficiently like us to qualify as members of the moral community. On the contrary, and like Hobbes, Spinoza argues that morality is a matter of self-preservation, and that human beings, by virtue of their superior powers, have no reason to treat animals as anything other than resources (Lloyd 1980).

Among those who take issue with Descartes and with Hobbes is the poet and early feminist Margaret Cavendish, Duchess of Newcastle (1623-73). Cavendish, a self-taught philosopher, holds that nature comprises rational matter and sensitive matter in addition to inanimate matter. Although animals cannot speak, she says, it does not follow that they have no intelligence. It is quite possible that, in their own manner, they know more about some things than we do — fish know more of the nature of water and the saltiness of the sea, birds know more of the nature of air or the cause of tempests. Cavendish condemns human arrogance, saying that we despise other creatures because we are ignorant of them (Grant 1957). Her poem "The Hunting of the Hare" ends with a denunciation of the notion that animals are on earth merely to be exploited by us (Cavendish 1972, pp. 112-13):

As if that God made Creatures for Mans meat,
To give them Life, and Sense, for Man to eat;
Or else for Sport, or Recreations sake,
Destroy those Lifes that God saw good to make:
Making their Stomacks, Graves, which full they fill
With Murther'd Bodies, that in sport they kill.
Yet Man doth think himselfe so gentle, mild,
When he of Creatures is most cruell wild.
And is so Proud, thinks onely he shall live,
That God a God-like Nature did him give.
And that all Creatures for his sake alone,
Was made for him, to Tyrannize upon.

## Locke and Hume Find Reasons to Exclude Animals

The great liberal philosopher John Locke (1632-1704) rejects both Hobbes' contract theory of morality and Descartes' view that animals lack minds, and yet he stops short of including animals in the moral community.

Locke (1979) maintains that animals exercise a degree of reason. The faculty of perception, he says, differentiates the animal kingdom from the "inferior" parts of nature. Plants are sensitive to their environments, but this is a purely mechanical sensitivity, involving no ideas on the part of plants. However, animals possess sensation, a term that for Locke implies perception and thus ideas. True, different animals possess sensation in different degrees, and an oyster's senses are neither so many nor so quick as those of a human being, or of various other animals. And yet, thinks Locke, even a creature like an oyster has some degree of perception. By contrast, Descartes (1991), for whom being able to think means having an immortal soul, points to the lowly oyster to argue that *no* animals think. If we were to believe that some animals think and thus have immortal souls, he says, there would be no reason not to believe this of all animals, and we would then be led to the absurd conclusion that even oysters and sponges have immortal souls. Locke, who is not convinced that mind and matter must be fundamentally distinct, finds no absurdity in the idea that even primitive animals may have perception in some form. Further, he says, many animals display the ability to store ideas in memory and recall them, as a bird does when it learns to sing a tune.

In his political philosophy Locke (1960) argues that there is a "law of nature", a fundamental moral law that arises from the nature and condition of human beings and exists independently of the laws laid down by the state. Because they have similar faculties and share in one "community of nature", human beings have no right to destroy one another or treat each other as mere resources. Everyone has the right to appropriate from nature whatever can be made use of, so long as one is not wasteful and does not worsen the condition of others. Given his contention that animals share with us the faculties of perception and memory, one might expect Locke to invoke the law of nature on their behalf and condemn our treating them as mere resources. But such is not the case. Animals, he says, show no sign of the capacity to form general ideas (for example, on the basis of the colour of milk and of snow, to arrive at the idea of whiteness) and to engage in abstract reasoning. Because they lack the rational perfection of human beings, animals are on earth for human use. In this conclusion, at least, Locke is at one with Descartes (Squadrito 1992).

Like Locke, David Hume (1711-76) rejects the Cartesian dichotomy between human and animal, declaring that animals too are endowed with thought and reason. According to Hume (1975), animals employ their imaginations to accumulate useful knowledge, inferring facts about their environments on the basis of experience. Repeated observation that a particular kind of event, *A*, is attended or followed by another particular kind of event, *B*, leads an animal to expect *B* when next it encounters *A*. Admittedly, this inferring of effects from causes is, in Hume's view, the product of habit, not reasoning. However, the sceptical Hume does not believe the case to be essentially different where human learning is concerned: all our knowledge of "matters of fact" (what is the case about the world but might logically have been otherwise) is based on the relation of cause and effect, but no chain of rea-

This faculty of laying up, and retaining the *Ideas*, that are brought into the Mind, several *other Animals* seem to have, to a great degree, as well as Man. For to pass by other Instances, Birds learning of Tunes, and the endeavours one may observe in them, to hit the Notes right, put it past doubt with me, that they have Perception, and retain *Ideas* in their Memories, and use them for Patterns. For it seems to me impossible, that they should endeavour to conform their Voices to Notes (as 'tis plain they do) of which they had no *Ideas*.
– John Locke, *An Essay Concerning Human Understanding*, pp. 154-55

soning can demonstrate the truth of our belief that nature must exhibit the same regularities in the future that it has exhibited in the past. Our faculty of making cause-and-effect inferences about nature depends on habit and is a form of instinct.

Hume maintains that the behaviour of animals is to be explained by the same principles that apply to humans (Seidler 1977). Yet despite believing that no great gulf separates human nature from animal nature, Hume excludes animals from the moral community. Justice is necessary in human communities, according to him, because human beings are social creatures and justice contributes to social cohesion. In particular, justice results in the mutual benefit to individuals that comes from respecting each other's private property. But between creatures of different kinds, where one is by nature vastly superior in power to the other and therefore has no interest in refraining from acting just how he or she will, justice has no place because it serves no useful social purpose. Animals are beyond the pale of justice because they have no power to make felt their objections to the way we treat them.

However, social utility is not the whole story. Hume believes that morality arises on the basis of the passions, or feelings, including natural sympathy for others. Consequently, one may be tempted to think that he is suggesting that the concept of justice is inappropriate in our dealings with animals *just because* sympathy for our fellow creatures should lead us to treat them as members of our family or community. After all, we should see to the welfare of members of our family independently of whatever rights they may have against us. But Hume denies this status to animals or any other beings similarly lacking in power. Indeed, he says, the fundamental inequality of power here means that humans and animals cannot be said jointly to constitute a society. Since animals are unable effectively to resist our will, the relationship we have with them is inevitably one of absolute command on the one side and servile obedience on the other: whatever we want from them they must immediately give us. The most Hume will concede is that we should give "gentle usage" to animals.

## Kant Divides the World into Persons and Things
Immanuel Kant (1724-1804) occupies a rather contradictory position in the history of thinking about animals. Kant (1997) himself excludes

animals from the moral community, claiming they are merely instruments to serve human purposes. Whatever duties we have concerning animals, he says, are really only indirect duties to human beings. However, his account of why we have duties to humans has been seized upon by some philosophers and modified to form the basis of the animal-rights view.

For Kant, there are two types of beings: persons and things. Human beings are persons because they are what Kant calls ends-in-themselves. Unlike sticks or stones or trees, a human being is not simply a tool or resource to be used for the ends of others. Human beings are ends-in-themselves because they are *autonomous* (self-governing). That is, they are able rationally to consider different courses of action and choose among them on the basis of an understanding of right and wrong. As a moral agent, a human being has intrinsic worth and deserves to have his or her autonomy respected by other moral agents. One version of Kant's categorical imperative, his basic rule of morality, is therefore as follows: *Act so that you treat humanity, whether in your own person or in that of another, always as an end and never as a means only.*

We can now see why Kant excludes animals from the moral community. Given that they are not moral agents, it follows from his argument that animals are mere things, resources available for our use. And yet Kant enjoins us not to be cruel to animals. When we are aware of the great care shown by animals for their young, he says, it will be difficult for us to be cruel in thought even to the wolf. This is somewhat surprising in terms of his own logic (Broadie and Pybus 1974). After all, if we have no duties to animals, if they are mere things available for our use, what does it matter how we treat them?

The reason Kant gives for restricting the ways we behave toward animals is that there are analogies between animal nature and human nature, and those who treat animals callously are more likely to treat their fellow human beings without respect. If a dog (a sheepdog, perhaps) has served us long and well, it would be wrong to shoot the dog once it is too old to perform its job efficiently. Why? Because someone who learned to repay the faithful service and trust of an animal by killing it would be cultivating the wrong trait of character. Being heartless to animals is likely to lead to being heartless to people. Our interactions with animals, then, function as a simulation of, and training for, our interactions with people, even though we typically are not motivated by this consideration in our dealings with animals. (For an endorsement of this sort of view by a modern philosopher, see Carruthers 1992.)

On Kant's account we do no wrong to animals themselves if we harm them, even for trivial purposes, since they cannot make moral judgements. Although we have duties *involving* animals, we have no duties *directly to* them. Kant even finds some instances of cruelty to animals acceptable. For example, the cruelty of those who experiment on living animals is justified because the aim (benefit to humanity) is praiseworthy and non-human creatures are only our instruments. Notice that, unlike Descartes, Kant does not deny that animals can suffer. His point is that their suffering does not matter because they are not rational beings. Notice also that Kant does not take the opportunity to propose, as others have done before and since, that such experimentation may desensitize those who do it.

There is something counter-intuitive about Kant's position. Most people would say that if you shoot your old sheepdog—certainly if you throw it out to starve—you are doing something wrong *to the dog itself*, and not merely cultivating the wrong character trait in yourself. But if it really is true that animals are just things, why should tossing out the sheepdog once it is no longer economically productive make us any more likely to toss out Grandma and Grandpa once they are no longer economically productive? After all, there are also some analogies between plants and human beings, but does chopping up a head of lettuce make me more likely to chop up the head of the person living next door? Of course, some people may be under the impression that animals have worth in themselves and are *not* mere things; but such people are not likely to treat animals callously. On the other hand, people who do treat animals callously are likely to believe (correctly, in Kant's view) that animals are mere things. Assuming they understand that humans are deserving of respect, these people are unlikely to transfer their treatment of animals to their treatment of humans. If some of these people nevertheless sometimes or often treat human beings without respect, this will not be the *result* of the way they treat animals.

Kant says that what enables human beings to be ends-in-themselves is their capacity for rational thought. In emphasizing rationality as the distinctive characteristic of human beings, the characteristic that separates them from other beings and gives them a special status in the world, Kant is reaffirming a long tradition in Western philosophy. (It is perhaps not surprising that many philosophers have regarded thinking rationally—and, in particular, doing philosophy—as the most exalted activity there is.) But why should being entitled to respect from others be dependent on being rational (Hoff 1983)? Is it not plausible to think that simply having a life that matters to oneself is enough to make one entitled not to be treated as a mere means by others? If this is the case, then being self-conscious in some way, or simply being conscious at all, or perhaps even just being alive, may be a sufficient qualification for being viewed as an end-in-oneself. For now, it is enough to say that Kant's idea of being an end-in-oneself rather than being a mere thing, or resource for others, has been taken over by some philosophers to provide the basis for the view that at least some animals should be treated with respect and ascribed moral rights. In Chapter 3 we shall examine in some detail the case for ascribing rights to animals, especially in its most influential form, as advanced by Tom Regan (2004a).

### The Question Is, Can They Suffer?

Jeremy Bentham (1748-1832) was the founder of modern utilitarianism. Recognizing that society's prevailing morality too often reflected the interests of those with power to the detriment of those without power, Bentham attempted to formulate an egalitarian doctrine that acknowledged the interests of human beings irrespective of social status. For Bentham, the pleasure or pain of anyone was to count no more or less than the same amount of pleasure or pain of anyone else. With this in mind, he was prepared to follow his own logic beyond the species boundary. His comment on animals was brief but significant.

> The day *may* come, when the rest of the animal creation may acquire those rights which never could have been withholden from them but by the hand of tyranny. The French have already discovered that the blackness of the skin is no reason why a human being should be abandoned without redress to the caprice of a tormentor. It may come one day to be recognized, that the number of the legs, the villosity of the skin, or the termination of the *os sacrum*, are reasons equally insufficient for abandoning a sensitive being to the same fate? What else is it that should trace the insuperable line? Is it the faculty of reason, or, perhaps, the faculty of discourse? But a full-grown horse

49

or dog, is beyond comparison a more rational, as well as a more conversible animal, than an infant of a day, or a week, or even a month, old. But suppose the case were otherwise, what would it avail? the question is not, Can they *reason*? nor, Can they *talk*? but, Can they *suffer*? (Bentham 1970, p. 283n)

These words are contained in what is a mere footnote to *An Introduction to the Principles of Morals and Legislation*, yet they have often been quoted in the debate over the moral status of animals, and with good reason. Bentham's position is really quite radical: he aims to put our understanding of our relations with animals on an entirely new moral footing. Animals have a basic interest in not suffering, and it is "tyranny" for humans to inflict suffering on them. Bentham will have none of the traditional excuse for ignoring animal suffering: that animals' lack of reason or language excludes them from the moral community. (Although Bentham is concerned with our moral obligations to animals, it should be noted that when he refers to the rights of animals, he means legal rights; he does not believe in the concept of moral rights, either for animals or humans.)

Critics of Bentham's utilitarianism said that while the doctrine may be fine for pigs, surely the proper goals of human life cannot be reduced to maximizing pleasure. John Stuart Mill (1806-73), who followed Bentham as the champion of utilitarianism, sought to counter this accusation. He defended Bentham's passage on animals, quoted above, with its implication that any act causing more pain to animals than pleasure to humans is immoral. However, in rescuing utilitarianism from the charge that it ignores what is distinctive about human life, he partially re-erected the barrier between humans and non-humans.

Mill (1957) contends that the types of pleasure that give satisfaction to pigs do not suffice for humans. It is better to be a dissatisfied human being, he tells us, than to be a satisfied pig, and the proof is that few, if any, humans would agree to exchange their lot for that of a happy pig. If the pig has a different opinion of things, it is because the pig does not appreciate what it is to be human.

Mill is maintaining that some pleasures are *qualitatively* superior to others. The difference in quality, if any, between two given pleasures can be judged by those who are competently acquainted with both. If I appreciate eating good apple pie but have never taken much interest in music, I am not in a position to judge whether the pleasure to be derived from listening to Mozart is superior, or inferior, to that to be had from eating good apple pie. If you, on the other hand, have learned to appreciate both sorts of pleasure, then you are competent to judge between them. It is Mill's firm opinion that the distinctively human pleasures are superior to the pleasures enjoyable by animals and therefore count for more in our moral calculus. Utilitarianism has traditionally had a strongly egalitarian bent to it; however, Mill seems to be saying that, when it comes to happiness, some creatures are more equal than others.

Mill assumes that we are competent to judge between the pleasure of reading Jane Austen and the pleasure of rolling around in the mud. Since a pig is not interested in nineteenth-century literature, we conclude: so much the worse for the pig. But how can we know what it is like to be a pig, or to be a bat (Nagel 1974), or any other creature, and to experience the world the way that creature does? When Mill says it is better to be a human being dissatisfied than to be a pig satisfied, how does he know (E. Johnson 1983; Sapontzis 1987)? His claim may ring true from the human perspective, but that is the only perspective we have. Each sentient creature, it could be said, has the happiness peculiar to its species and to itself as an individual, and we are foolish to try to judge these many happinesses according to our own standards (Hearne 1994). If a pig could learn to read, would she conclude that *Pride and Prejudice* is better than hunting for truffles? If a whale could learn to enjoy playing chess, would playing chess make him happier than freely roaming the length and breadth of the Pacific Ocean?

Although not a utilitarian, Arthur Schopenhauer (1788-1860) makes the capacity for suffering key to his analysis of morality. In so doing, he castigates the European tradition for denying that we have duties directly to animals. He rejects the contention that animals have no self-consciousness with the quip that "If any Cartesian were to find himself clawed by a tiger, he would become aware in the clearest possible manner of the sharp distinction such a beast draws between its ego and the non-ego" (Schopenhauer 1965, p. 176). Disagreeing with Kant, he says it is outrageous to claim that animals are to be regarded as things, or mere means for us, just because they lack the faculty of reason that characterizes our species. An admirer of Buddhist and Hindu thought, Schopenhauer insists that right conduct is based on compassion for all beings who can suffer. However, he is not prepared to carry his compassion for other sentient creatures to the length of abstaining from eating them. Intelligence, it turns out, does play a significant role in Schopenhauer's ethics; he contends that the intelligence of human beings increases their capacity for suffering and hence they have a stronger claim to our compassion than animals do. Particularly in northern lands, he says, humans would suffer more from abstaining from meat than animals suffer from a quick and unforeseen death.

### Darwin Says Humans Differ from Non-humans Only in Degree

Charles Darwin (1809-82) was not the first to argue that the plant and animal species existing in the world have evolved from earlier forms of life. However, his theory of natural selection provided a plausible explanation of how such evolution could occur. Today Darwin's theory remains controversial, and not only because creationists continue to deny evolution. Although scientists overwhelmingly agree that organic evolution is a fact of natural history, there is some dissent over whether natural selection can adequately account for the emergence of new species. Nevertheless, *On the Origin of Species by Means of Natural Selection*, published in 1859, marked a watershed in science's understanding of the history of life on earth. Over the last century and a half, Darwinian theory, supplemented by the science of genetics, has undermined the traditional view that human beings are the pinnacle of creation and that a profound gulf separates them from the other living creatures on the planet. The Darwinian view of the world proclaims that *Homo sapiens* has evolved as just one more of nature's innumerable products. Human beings *are* animals. In particular, humans are primates and, as DNA analysis has confirmed, are close cousins of the (non-human) great apes: chimpanzees, bonobos, gorillas, and orangutans (R. Dawkins 1993; J. Diamond 1993; Hawkins 2002). It was not in *The Origin of Species*, however, but in later works that Darwin addressed the issue of the relation of the human species to other animal species.

Darwin (1890) is of the firm opinion that the differences between human and non-human animals are differences not of kind but only of degree. Though modern behaviourist psychologists (e.g., Blumberg and Wasserman 1995) doubt the possibility of scientifically studying the subjective mental experiences of humans and non-humans alike, and are sceptical about attributing intentions, desires, and feelings to them, Darwin does not hesitate to do so. Influenced perhaps by his reading of David Hume (Huntley 1972), he maintains that there is no fundamental distinction to be made between the mental faculties of humans and other highly developed mammals, especially the primates.

> All have the same senses, intuitions, and sensations, — similar passions, affections, and emotions, even the more complex ones, such as jealousy, suspicion, emulation, gratitude, and magnanimity; they practise deceit and are revengeful; they are sometimes susceptible to ridicule, and even have a sense of humour; they feel wonder and curiosity; they possess the same faculties of imitation, attention, deliberation, choice, memory, imagination, the association of ideas, and reason, though in very different degrees. (Darwin 1890, p. 79)

Darwin mentions the use and making of tools by non-humans, such as their employment of sticks as levers, of branches to drive away flies, and of stones for cracking nuts or as weapons. He also believes that non-human animals can appreciate beauty, and goes so far as to suggest that dogs, in their love of, and submission to, their human masters exhibit an incipient form of religious devotion.

Against Locke and others, Darwin claims that many non-human animals possess the power of abstract thought and can form general concepts. For example, when a dog sees another dog some distance away, he perceives it as a dog in the abstract. This is evident because when he gets nearer to the other dog, his whole manner will change if he recognizes the other dog as a friend, a particular dog that he knows. Hence Darwin rejects the argument that the use of language, which involves the power of forming general concepts, constitutes an insuperable barrier between humans and non-humans. As with so many other faculties, the difference here is one of degree: humans have a much greater power of associating sounds and ideas. Animals like dogs are at the same stage of development, thinks Darwin, as infants of almost a year in age, who can understand many words and short sentences even though they cannot speak. He does not believe that non-human animals reflect on the nature of life and death; yet he believes that some may well reflect on their past pleasures and pains, and in this case could

It may be freely admitted that no animal is self-conscious, if by this term it is implied, that he reflects on such points, as whence he comes or whither he will go, or what is life and death, and so forth. But how can we feel sure that an old dog with an excellent memory and some power of imagination, as shewn by his dreams, never reflects on his past pleasures or pains in the chase? And this would be a form of self-consciousness.
– Charles Darwin,
*The Descent of Man*,
pp. 84-85

be said to be self-conscious.

Morality, Darwin asserts, arises from the social instincts, including parental and filial affection, when these are combined with advanced intellectual faculties. These instincts lead an animal to take pleasure in the company of its fellows, to feel sympathy for them, and to perform services for them. Sympathy is the key element in the development of a moral sense or conscience, though the acquisition of language plays an important role by facilitating the inculcation of rules of behaviour for the welfare of the community. (According to Darwin, it is not the general happiness as such that is the standard of morality, but the general good, in the sense of the rearing of the greatest number of individuals in full vigour and health.) Many animals—even birds—sympathize with each other's distress or danger, says Darwin, and exhibit qualities that in humans would be called moral. Dogs, he thinks, possess something like a conscience. Darwin is not claiming that the moral sense is very developed in non-human animals. However, once again he refuses to draw an absolute barrier between them and human beings.

Darwin's respect for animals is evident in his writings, though he cannot be called a liberationist. He was a man who was greatly upset by any display of cruelty to animals, and one who was also an avid shooter of birds. He said that the thought of vivisection (the painful or harmful treatment of animals for purposes of research) made him feel sick with horror; yet he refused to support the contemporary campaign against it because he believed vivisection was necessary for the progress of science.

Among those who responded positively to Darwin were Karl Marx (1818-83) and Frederick Engels (1820-95). They welcomed Darwinian theory for the scientific backing it gave to the concept of organic evolution and because it explained historical development without recourse to the idea of some pre-ordained design or purpose. As such, they believed that it lent support to their own view of human history, although they were hostile to "social Darwinist" attempts to draw lessons for social policy from the struggle for existence in nature.

Marx (1974, 1976) and Engels (1972) say that humans differ from animals in humans' unique ability to use socially accumulated knowledge to transform their environments in new ways to suit their purposes. At the same time, they reject the idea that humans have been specially created, or stand apart from the rest of nature in any fundamental way. (The tension in Marx's thought between his humanism and his naturalism is explored in Benton 1993.) Engels maintains that many animals display premeditated behaviour, and that the capacity for conscious, planned action is proportional to the development of the nervous system, being especially advanced in mammals. Association with human beings has developed in dogs and horses some ability to understand human speech, and also the capacity for feeling affection and gratitude toward people.

However, despite attaching considerable importance to a naturalistic, evolutionary view of the world, Marx and Engels show little interest in what the moral implications of all this may be for our treatment of animals. Indeed, what is striking is how little, until recently, Darwinian theory has enticed philosophers to consider the moral status of non-human creatures in the light of our biological kinship with them. (Recent investigations of the topic include James Rachels' *Created from Animals: The Moral Implications of Darwinism* and Rosemary Rodd's *Biology, Ethics, and Animals*.)

## Conclusion

Until recently, the great majority of philosophers have excluded animals from the moral community. They have done so on the grounds that animals lack the mental faculties that human beings possess. In particular, it is the alleged inability of non-human creatures to reason that time and again has been identified as the crux of the matter. Lacking rationality, animals are not moral agents. They cannot formulate or understand ethical concepts and therefore cannot participate with moral agents in a community of beings who can live according to moral rules and be held accountable to others for their actions. If we should treat animals kindly, or restrict our behaviour toward them in any way, this is not because animals have any equality of moral standing with us. An alternative to demanding moral agency as the ticket for admittance to the moral community would involve the idea that we also have obligations directly to all those who, though lacking any significant degree of moral agency, meet some other standard — for example, all those who have an interest in not suffering or who have an interest in continuing to live. Whether many beings, non-human as well as human, qualify as "moral patients" in this sense, and just what our obligations to them may be, is considered in the next chapter.

Among the philosophers of the past, Descartes and Bentham represent opposite sides of the animal issue. Most philosophers stand on Descartes' side, though few go so far as he does in declaring animals to be beyond the pale of our concern. (One might think, better to be Bentham's horse than to be Descartes' dog. But if Descartes is right about animals, it makes no difference: both the horse and the dog are simply bits of machinery, and neither has any interest in how it is treated. As Descartes says, his view is not cruel to animals but indulgent to people, since it absolves people of any suspicion of doing wrong to animals.) With Bentham and with Darwin we cross a conceptual divide. Where formerly the issue of our treatment of animals was at best a marginal one for philosophers and for society as a whole, the intellectual groundwork has now been laid for it to be taken more seriously. Ideas, however, do not take root without a social climate conducive to their flourishing. It was not until well into the twentieth century, in the context of the movements against racial and sexual discrimination and of growing concern about the natural environment, that the topic of the moral status of animals became a vigorous debate about animal liberation.

# CHAPTER THREE

# DO ANIMALS HAVE
# MORAL RIGHTS?

They have individuality, character, reason; and to have those qualities is to have the right to exercise them, in so far as surrounding circumstances permit.

—*Henry Salt*[1]

There are good and sufficient reasons ... to deter us from offensive conduct toward animals, without our resorting to talk about rights, which often opens the way to confusion and even fanaticism.

—*A.I. Melden*[2]

The animal-liberation movement is often referred to as the animal-rights movement. From a philosophical standpoint, however, the view that animals have moral rights is only one particular orientation (though an important one) within the animal-liberation movement. The rights view has articulate advocates; at the same time it has its critics not only among those who reject but among those who support liberation. This chapter begins by looking at the concept of a right and then at the traditional and the revisionist positions on whether animals can have rights. The bulk of the chapter is devoted to explicating Tom Regan's influential case for ascribing moral

---

[1] Henry S. Salt, *Animals' Rights Considered in Relation to Social Progress* (London: Centaur Press, 1980), p. 16.

[2] A.I. Melden, *Rights in Moral Lives: A Historical-Philosophical Essay* (Berkeley: University of California Press, 1988), p. 64.

rights to animals, and to the responses both of those hostile to, and of those sympathetic to, the idea of animal liberation.

## Human and Other Rights

A right can be understood as an entitlement to have, use, or do something. More specifically, in the words of Joel Feinberg (1974, pp. 43-44), "To have a right is to have a claim *to* something and *against* someone, the recognition of which is called for by legal rules or, in the case of moral rights, by the principles of an enlightened conscience." For example, you may have a claim to the use of some particular piece of land, a claim that imposes on other people the duty not to interfere with your use of that land and that is recognized as legitimate by law and/or sound moral principles.

A right, then, is a valid claim. As such, it imposes on others the duty to respect that claim. Your right to use that piece of land and the duty of other people not to interfere with your use of the land are opposite sides of the same coin. In this case, right and duty are correlative, each implying the other. However, there are cases where, it is commonly held, a duty may exist without implying any right on the part of someone else. For example, I may have a duty of charity to help those in need, but this does not mean that the canvasser who comes to my door seeking money for famine relief has a right to any of my money. Although I ought to act at some time and in some manner to fulfil my duty to help those in need, there is no particular individual who has a right against me to be helped. It makes a difference, then, whether the duties we have regarding others entail their having rights against us.

Among philosophers the idea of moral rights is a contentious one even outside the context of the debate over the moral status of animals. Especially controversial is the idea that there are some fundamental moral rights that apply unconditionally and unalterably to all human beings—so-called human rights. Insofar as these rights are attributed to individuals on the basis of their natural characteristics, they can be called natural rights. The historical doctrine of natural rights goes further, however, by asserting that recognition of such fundamental moral rights is the inescapable outcome of understanding human nature and the nature of the world. For John Locke, natural rights have their ultimate source in God. Catholic doctrine, based on the teachings of

Aquinas and Aristotle, similarly views the natural rights of human beings as grounded in divine law (Barad 1995; Reichmann 2000). On the other hand, Jeremy Bentham, the utilitarian who argued that we must include the suffering of animals in our moral reckoning, said that the idea of natural rights is "absurd" and "pernicious". In a famous phrase, he described the idea of imprescriptible (unalterable) natural rights as "nonsense upon stilts".

Nevertheless, the concept of fundamental moral rights has played an important role in the modern world. The contention that, by violating the natural rights of individuals, governments render themselves illegitimate was a key element in both the American and French revolutions of the eighteenth century. Today the idea that there are fundamental human rights that all political states must uphold is embodied in the United Nations' Universal Declaration of Human Rights. These include, among others, the right to life, liberty, and security of person, the right to freedom of movement, the right to marry and to found a family, the right to own property alone as well as in association with others, the right to freedom of thought, conscience, and religion, the right to freedom of opinion and expression, the right to work, the right to form and join trade unions, the right to rest and leisure, the right to a standard of living adequate for health and well-being, and the right to education. Although it may be said that these rights, being embodied in a legal document formulated and approved by a political body, are the result of an agreement among contracting parties, there is no doubt that many people view at least some of these rights as arising from the very nature of human beings and existing independently of any political agreements. Indeed, the Universal Declaration of Human Rights proclaims that "All human beings are born free and equal in dignity and rights", that everyone is entitled to these rights "without distinction of any kind, such as race, colour, sex, language, religion, political or other opinion, national or social origin, property, birth or other status", and that no state, group, or person has a right to engage in any activity aimed at the destruction of any of these rights.

It may be objected that such declarations of unconditional and unalterable rights make no sense since moral rights are not facts about the world that exist somewhere "out there", waiting to be discovered. A sceptic on the subject of animal rights, L. Duane Willard (1982) makes the point that rights are not properties of individuals in the way that their hair colour and their capacity to experience pain are properties. Rather, we prescribe what rights individuals are to have on the basis of our moral judgement about what ought to be permitted. So the fact that many animals can experience pain does not *in itself* give those animals any right with regard to the experience of pain. Some people will judge, on the basis of their purposes, intentions, and values regarding animals, that animals should be ascribed rights, but many other people, on the basis of *their* purposes, intentions, and values, will disagree. Therefore, concludes Willard, there is no sound basis for the claim that we can discover logically that animals "have" rights.

Willard is surely correct to hold that rights are not discoverable in the way that tectonic plates or solar flares are. We shall not hear someday that scientists have identified the gene that endows people with moral rights. Even though the possession of some particular right may entail having a certain genetic endowment (such as the ability to reason, or the ability to experience pain), rights do not exist apart from the process of valuing (Orend 2002). Still, to agree that rights are not facts about the world that exist independently of people's moral judgement is not to deny the possibility of ascribing fundamental rights to individuals on the basis of some natural characteristic or capacity of the right-holder (Povilitis 1980). After all, we can conclude that all human beings, just by virtue of their capacity to suffer, have a right not to be made to suffer unnecessarily. In so doing, we are ascribing an inalienable right on the basis of an enduring natural characteristic or capacity. Our judgement about just what characteristics or capacities underlie the various rights may change, but insofar as whatever judgement we make attributes inalienable rights to individuals on the basis of their natures, we can make sense of the notion of human rights or natural rights.

## The Traditional View: Animals Cannot Have Rights

If the subject of the moral rights of human beings is fraught with controversy, it is hardly surprising that talk of the moral rights of animals commonly meets with scepticism or outright ridicule. We have seen in the previous chapter that animals have traditionally been denied significant moral standing because they are said to lack the capacity to reason and thus to participate with human beings in a community of mutually responsible individuals. This charge forms the basis of the claim that animals are not the sort of creatures that can have moral rights.

To have rights, the thinking goes, one must be the sort of being that can claim what one is entitled to and can respect the rights of others (Cebik 1981). Indeed, argues Robert Burch (1977), the primary significance of having rights lies in the fact of being entitled to act in a certain way in one's own interest. To have a moral right is to be entitled to stand up for oneself; consequently, it makes little sense to extend rights to those who lack the ability and inclination to do so. Although animals may be able to defend themselves physically, the fact that they lack the capacity to understand moral concepts means that they cannot defend themselves morally, and thus have no moral rights.

In *Against Liberation* Michael Leahy argues that it is a mistake to anthropomorphize animals and treat them as though they were honorary, if rather simple, human beings. Animals are essentially different from humans, says Leahy; because they lack language, they cannot be self-conscious and so cannot be aware of what is in their interests. This being the case, we should reject the idea of animal rights. Leahy sides with Kant in claiming that because animals lack self-consciousness and moral agency, they cannot be ends in themselves. Although it is proper for us to take their strivings and preferences into account and to act on our instinctive impulses to avoid cruelty, this will be in terms of our purposes for them.

It is the status of human beings as moral agents that is typically held to be the key to their possession of moral rights. Unlike animals, it is argued, each human being is confronted with the question of how to live his or her life. It is because we can make moral choices that we require a sphere of personal jurisdiction within which we can exercise this capacity. Our rights define this sphere. Because animals have no capacity to make moral choices, they can have no rights (C. Cohen 1997; Machan 1991, 2004; McCloskey 1979; Reichmann 2000; Scruton 2000). This is not to say that we have no obligation to treat them humanely, but it does mean that there is nothing inherently wrong in using them for their labour or in scientific research, hunting them, or rearing them for food.

Someone who argues that moral rights are attributable only to those who can act on the basis of an understanding of the duties that moral agents have to each other may well be prepared to say that rights can in

The concept of rights emerged with the rise of human civilization precisely because it is needed by and applicable to human beings, given the specifically moral nature of human beings and their ambition to live with each other in mutual harmony and to mutual benefit. Rights have nothing to do with the lives of wolves and turtles because of what animal rights champions themselves admit, namely, the amoral nature of at least the bulk of the animal world.

– Tibor R. Machan, *Putting Humans First*, p. 12

principle be attributed to any non-human being (ape, space alien, or whatever) that displays moral agency. A. I. Melden (1988), for example, even while rejecting any general attribution of rights to animals, is prepared to say that a few animals, like dogs or whales, may exhibit some degree of moral agency and thus be candidates for rights. Richard Watson (1979) maintains that there is behavioural evidence that some chimpanzees, gorillas, dolphins, elephants, dogs, pigs, probably also some whales and orangutans, and perhaps also some cats, gibbons, and other animals are at least sometimes moral agents. If so, he says, these animals merit at least rights to life and to relief from unnecessary suffering.

The belief that some animals at least sometimes qualify as moral agents will be rejected by many, perhaps most, philosophers. But when it comes to the issue of who qualifies for having rights, the dispute is not normally about which creatures possess moral agency; rather, it is about whether moral agency is a necessary condition for having rights.

## The Revisionist View: Animals Can Have Rights

Mention of justice for animals, and even the idea of animal rights, can be found in writings as early as the seventeenth century in Britain (Ryder 1989; Thomas 1983). Nevertheless, the idea that animals have moral rights is essentially a modern one, with roots in the nineteenth century. In 1824, the same year that he helped found the Royal Society for the Prevention of Cruelty to Animals, Lewis Gompertz published *Moral Inquiries on the Situation of Man and of Brutes*. In this work, Gompertz (1997) set out systematically to defend animal interests, upholding the radical propositions that every creature, whether human or non-human, has more right to the use of its own body than others have to the use of it, and that our duty to promote the happiness of others applies equally to our treatment of all beings. In 1879 Edward Nicholson, drawing on others who maintained that the capacity to experience pleasure and pain gives rights, claimed that animals have the same abstract rights to life and liberty that humans do—though he then went on to argue that practical necessities mean that the rights of animals must be significantly limited. But, ultimately, the most influential nineteenth-century proponent of a rights position proved to be Henry Salt, whose *Animals' Rights* was published in 1892. Keith Tester (1991) maintains that the book signalled an "epistemological break" in thinking about animals: from then on the idea that animals should be liberated, an idea that is a modern invention, began to seem natural and inevitable to many people.

Salt's book was later to make a strong impression on Peter Singer, even though the utilitarian Singer is a not a believer in moral rights as such. What is important for Salt is not the issue of whether ethics should employ the language of rights. What concerns him is whether we have any justification for treating animals in a fundamentally different manner than we treat human beings. Animals, says Salt, have moral rights *if humans do*. By this he means that to ascribe rights to humans but not to animals is to be logically inconsistent. For instance, if we claim that because suffering is generally to be avoided human beings must not be made to suffer unnecessarily, we cannot then turn around and without further ado claim that it is acceptable to make non-humans suffer unnecessarily. If we claim that the capacity for self-awareness gives those human beings who have it a right to life, we cannot then turn around and say that self-aware non-humans have no right to life. We must apply our moral principles (whatever they may be) consistently if we are not to be irrational.

By reminding us of the need to apply ethical principles in a consistent manner, pro-liberation philosophers hope to hoist opponents with their own petard. To the anti-liberationist's objection, "Your claim that animals have rights is merely an opinion, one that reflects your personal moral code but has no objective basis," Salt and others (e.g., Godlovitch 1971) reply, in effect, "If we examine the principles that underlie our beliefs about how we should treat our fellow human beings, then we shall see that many of the ways we treat animals cannot be justified by our own principles. Therefore, to refuse to recognize that these ways of treating animals are wrong is to be irrational."

Joel Feinberg (1974, 1978), whose views on the nature of rights have often been cited in the debate about animals, rejects the claim that moral agency is a requirement for possessing rights. Like many others who are critical of the traditional view of animals, he points to the fact that rights are commonly ascribed to those human beings, such as infants and the severely mentally handicapped, who are not moral agents. Although such individuals may not be able to make claims for themselves, other people can act as proxies for them, speaking on their behalf. Feinberg defends what he calls *the interest principle*, which says that the sorts of beings who can have rights are those who have (or can have) interests. He arrives at this principle because, in his opinion, (1) to hold rights one must be capable of being represented, and it is impossible for something that has no interests to be represented, and (2) to hold rights one must be capable of being benefited, and it is impossible for something that has no interests to be harmed or benefited. Something that has no interests has no subjective "good" of its own. To have interests in the relevant sense, says Feinberg, a being must have desires, and having desires in turn entails having something like beliefs. Hence plants, which lack beliefs and desires, have no interests and cannot have rights. Although we may commonly speak of a plant's needing water or sunshine, such needs do not imply having interests in the sense of having an awareness of what is good for oneself. By contrast, many animals do have such interests.

To this point in his argument, Feinberg does not say that animals actually have rights. Rather, he says that animals can have rights, that it is not absurd to ascribe rights to them. What is now required in order for us to conclude that some animals do in fact have rights is the judgement that we ought to treat them in a certain way not simply for the sake of others (e.g., people who own them or have a sentimental interest in them) but for their own sake, that such treatment is something that we owe to them as their due, something it would be wrong to withhold from them. Feinberg thinks that most of us do make this judgement and hence do believe that animals have rights, whether or not we speak of their having rights.

Someone may have a particular right because it has been conferred by someone else. Your neighbour may give you a right to use his swimming pool while he is away on vacation, or may even give you that right for as long as you live. The animal-rights view is that many animals have rights not only when rights are conferred upon them but because by nature they are conscious individuals who lead lives that matter to themselves. If having interests makes a creature capable of having rights, and if many animals can act in pursuit of their interests, then it might be maintained that many animals, though not necessarily having conferred rights, have what may be more important: certain inherent rights to act in pursuit of their interests.

In *Animal Rights and Human Morality* Bernard Rollin argues that any living thing with interests is an end in itself and so must never be treated merely as a means. To have interests is to have needs that matter to oneself. Drawing on Aristotle, Rollin notes that every creature has its own *telos* (literally, goal or purpose), an intrinsic set of functions and aims that has been imprinted by evolution and that constitutes its nature (the "living spiderness" of a spider, for example). A sentient creature, whether human or non-human, may not be aware of all the functions and aims intrinsic to it; nevertheless, its feelings of pleasure, pain, frustration, anxiety, boredom, anger, and so on are indications that its needs are being met or thwarted. The essence of our moral obligations to any animal that has interests, Rollin concludes, is to treat that animal as having the right to live the kind of life that its nature dictates.

In a similar vein, Jon Lowry (1975) maintains that the concept of natural rights is applicable to animals as well as to humans. Natural rights, he says, are claims to conditions necessary for living the good life. What constitutes "the good life" from the standpoint of a human being depends on the basic nature of human beings. What distinguishes a natural right, like the right to life, from a non-natural right, like the right to collective bargaining, is that violation of the right to life would make it impossible for a person to flourish as a human being. Violation of the right to collective bargaining, by contrast, would make it more difficult to achieve some particular goal, like higher wages, but would not in itself make it impossible to live a flourishing human life. In the same way, says Lowry, it makes sense to define the natural rights of an animal as claims to those conditions necessary for an animal of that species to flourish. The particular set of natural rights possessed by an individual will depend on the kind of being that individual is, though some natural rights, such as the right to life, may be common to humans and members of many animal species.

As for so-called human rights, Paola Cavalieri (2001) reaches the conclusion that there is nothing in the basic concept that necessarily restricts it to human beings. Species membership is not in itself a morally relevant criterion, and our attribution of full moral status to almost all human beings is not affected by the widely differing psychological capacities of individuals. All that is required is that one be an agent in the sense of having goals and wanting to achieve them. The

The genetic code of a given species provides us with a clear, scientific, testable, physicalistic locus for *telos*. And it is clear that this code determines behavioral, psychological, and social aspects of a creature's nature as well as physical ones — this is the message of sociobiology. To understand the nature of an animal in a way that is relevant to ethics is not a great or profound epistemological problem; it involves only sympathetic observations of the animal's life and activities.
— Bernard E. Rollin,
*Animal Rights and Human Morality*, p. 121

theory of human rights, Cavalieri reasons, should be expanded to cover mammals, birds, and probably vertebrates in general.

Most philosophers who ascribe rights to animals make no claim about any divine source of such rights. Andrew Linzey, a Christian theologian, is a prominent exception. Rejecting Thomas Aquinas's historically influential contention that animals are instruments for human purposes, Linzey (1976, 1987, 1994, 2000) argues that animals have "theos-rights", rights deriving from their place in God's creation. Because they are loved by God and exist for God, they ought not to be seen as simply means to human ends. Indeed, says Linzey, to say that animals have rights does not encompass the full extent of our obligations to them. The proper relation of humans to animals is akin to the relation of parents to children: our position of power, far from giving us the privilege of exploiting them as we see fit, or simply requiring us to give their interests equal consideration with our own, imposes on us the moral obligation to be generous and self-sacrificing toward them, to act for their benefit. (For another recent Christian view of the moral status of animals, including an assessment of Linzey's position, see Sargent 1996.)

Linzey's position is in sharp contrast to that of Jesuit theologian James Reichmann (2000), who, in his critique of animal liberation, reaffirms Aquinas's distinction between human and animal, based on the human being's unique place in creation as a moral agent. However, in her study of Aquinas's view of animals, Judith Barad (1995) insists that Saint Thomas's position is more complex and implicitly more sympathetic than is generally believed. Aquinas holds that, despite not being rational, many animals, unlike plants and like humans, can apprehend and desire what is naturally good (for example, self-preservation and the education of their offspring); hence they have natural rights to pursue their inclinations in this respect. Given that this is his considered position, says Barad, Aquinas is being inconsistent when he consigns animals to being mere instruments for human use.

### Regan's Case for Animal Rights

Any discussion of the moral status of animals must attend to *The Case for Animal Rights* by Tom Regan. Since its publication in 1983 this work has been a benchmark for debate on the topic by critics, whether they are friends or foes of the rights view. Regan's book is four hundred pages in length, ranging from the issues of animal awareness and animal welfare to a close examination of ethical theory and thence to the rights view and its implications. In the short space available here it is impossible to give more than the core of its argument.

The key concept in Regan's philosophy is *inherent value*. Inherent value is a quality that Regan attributes to every creature that (to put it briefly for the moment) has a life that matters to it. To say that a being has inherent value is to say that it has a value that is independent of any use that it may have for others. Inherent value, then, is to be contrasted with instrumental value. To have inherent value, in Regan's view, is to have the fundamental right never to be treated merely as an instrument, or means, for others.

The inherent value that may be attributed to someone is to be distinguished from whatever intrinsic value that individual's *experiences* may be said to have. A hedonistic utilitarian, for instance, will want to say that what is intrinsically valuable is the pleasure that someone derives from a particular event, and what is intrinsically bad is the suffering that is experienced. From this perspective, says Regan, individuals are not thought of as valuable in themselves, but are looked upon as mere receptacles for what is of positive or negative value: namely, their experiences. A person is like a cup that can hold liquids of various sweetness: the sweeter the liquid, the better; the more bitter the liquid, the worse — but the cup itself has no value. The concept of inherent value, by contrast, implies that (to continue with Regan's image) the cup has value, apart from the value of whatever it contains.

Regan's rights view, then, in affirming the fundamental moral significance of individuals apart from the quality of their experiences, rejects the utilitarian idea that the interests of the individual must be subsumed under the aggregate of everyone's interests. Utilitarianism, says Regan, has historically played a progressive role insofar as it has affirmed the equality of individuals (everyone's pain or pleasure counts equally with the like pain or pleasure of everyone else), but it must be rejected because the aggregative nature of its moral calculus can lead to treating individuals in ways that deny their inherent value. In other words, when we consider the pain and the pleasure that would result from each possible course of action, we may well find that what is best for the group at large in terms of net happiness involves treating some individuals in ways that most of us would find repugnant. A group of sadists might derive enormous pleasure from having someone physically or emotionally abused. A cure for some widespread and debilitating disease might be hastened by subjecting a small number of people to painful medical experiments against their will. Making slaves of some minority group might result in an overall increase in a society's happiness. In each of these cases some individuals would be treated as mere means to the ends of others.

Recall Kant's injunction that all human beings are to be treated with respect because they have inherent worth, being ends-in-themselves and not merely instruments for the use of others. Regan's view owes much to Kant, but there is a crucial difference, one that has profound consequences for our treatment of animals. According to Kant, human beings merit respect because they are autonomous. To be autonomous is, for Kant, to be rational and hence able to govern one's life on the basis of an understanding of right and wrong. In other words, what makes human beings worthy of respect, and what is distinctive about them, is that they are moral agents. For Regan, too, autonomy demands respect, but Regan allows a notion of autonomy that is considerably broader than Kant's.

The kind of autonomy that Regan says many animals possess is *preference autonomy*. To have preference autonomy, as he defines it, is to have preferences and the ability to initiate action with a view to satisfying them. In Regan's view, preference autonomy is the key to having a life that matters to oneself, to being what he calls the *subject-of-a-life*. Those who are subjects-of-a-life are those who "have beliefs and desires; perception, memory, and a sense of the future, including their own future; an emotional life together with feelings of pleasure and pain; preference- and welfare-interests; the ability to initiate action in pursuit of their desires and goals; a psychophysical identity over time; and an individual welfare in the sense that their experiential life fares well or ill for them, logically independently of their utility for others and logically independently of their being the object of anyone else's interests" (Regan 2004a, p. 243). Regan believes that normal mammalian animals of at least a year in age meet this criterion and thus have inherent value and hence moral rights. Birds are probably subjects-of-a-life, and some other creatures may be too (Regan 2003).

The subject-of-a-life criterion, while endowing many animals with strong protection in the form of rights, does not entail rights for every sentient creature. Arguably, some animals are sentient but are not subjects-of-a-life. However, as Regan sees things, the subject-of-a-life criterion advances a sufficient, but not a necessary, condition for ascribing inherent value and hence moral rights. That is, every individual who is the subject-of-a-life has moral rights, but it remains an open question whether moral rights may be ascribed to individuals on other grounds as well.

Is there good reason for us to accept the subject-of-a-life criterion, or is the concept *ad hoc*, something that Regan has adopted specifically to bolster his claim that animals have rights? It is to be noted that Regan does not derive the concept that some individuals have inherent value from the observed fact that these individuals are subjects-of-a-life. He does not proceed by saying, "Any creature that is the subject-of-a-life must have inherent value. That rabbit, for example, is the subject-of-a-life. Therefore that rabbit must have inherent value. And therefore that rabbit has rights." In other words, he does not make the subject-of-a-life criterion a *premise* of his argument. Rather, he arrives at the subject-of-a-life criterion during the course of it. He begins his argument by asking us to consider what it is about people that typically makes us ascribe moral rights to them.

Although traditional moral theory points to moral agency as the quality that endows people with moral rights, Regan, like other revisionists, finds this notion unconvincing. We commonly attribute rights to people, such as young children and the severely mentally handicapped, who are not moral agents in any normal sense. Although such persons have little understanding of what it is to act according to moral principles and hence are often not held morally responsible for their behaviour, this fact does not relieve the rest of us of having duties to them. We have duties to behave in certain ways and not in others toward a young child, even if the child does not yet have the mental faculties to recognize reciprocal duties on his or her part. A young child may not be a moral agent, then, but is still what Regan calls a "moral patient". The child is not to be treated in many of the ways we feel we are entitled to treat a stone or a plant.

Whether persons are moral agents or not, we typically treat them as having a special value, a value that is independent of whatever use they may have for others. Further, in Regan's opinion, this inherent value that we ascribe to persons depends neither on the quality of their experiences nor on whether they are saints or sinners. All who have inherent value have it equally, he says, and it does not matter whether someone is Mother Teresa or an unscrupulous used-car salesperson.

This claim that inherent value is possessed equally by all who have it is a contentious aspect of Regan's philosophy, and we shall return to the matter when we come to some of his critics. Still, the claim has some plausibility if we understand that Regan is pointing to a quality of individuals that acts as a prohibition against their being treated disrespectfully. Analogously, we might note that everyone who has a right not to be robbed has that right equally; in principle your right not to be robbed is the same as everyone else's and does not vary according to whether you are clever or stupid, short or tall, rich or poor.

Now, asks Regan, what is it that accounts for our ascription of inherent value to someone, regardless of whether that individual is a genius or a moron, regardless of whether that individual is a morally responsible agent? What relevant similarity can we point to among individuals who have inherent value? Regan answers that what plausibly accounts for our ascription of inherent value to them is the fact that the individuals in question have lives that matter to them, that fare well or ill for them, independently of their usefulness for others—in other words, that each individual is the subject-of-a-life. It is because a typical human being is the subject-of-a-life that we treat him or her as having inherent value and hence moral rights. Logical consistency then demands that we recognize any being who is the subject-of-a-life as having inherent value and hence as having moral rights. Since many animals are, in Regan's opinion, subjects-of-a-life, they too must be ascribed rights.

If many animals have rights, what rights do they have? Whether they are moral agents or moral patients, says Regan, all those who have inherent value have the basic right to be treated respectfully. That is to say, it is unacceptable to use them as mere means for the goals of others, even when the goal is to increase the aggregate welfare of a group of individuals. The right to be treated with respect is basic because it is not dependent for its existence on anyone's voluntary acts or on the posi-

It is not an act of kindness to treat animals respectfully. It is an act of justice. It is not "the sentimental interests" of moral agents that grounds our duties of justice to children, the retarded, the senile, or other moral patients, including animals. It is respect for their inherent value. The myth of the privileged moral status of moral agents has no clothes.
— Tom Regan, *The Case for Animal Rights*, p. 280

tion occupied by the possessor in some institutional arrangement. In other words, it is an *unacquired* right, as distinct from a right that you might acquire because of some institutional position you occupy (like your right as a police officer to stop cars on the highway) or because of someone's voluntary act (like your right to a skiing vacation because of a promise made to you). Further, as a basic right it is possessed equally by all relevantly similar individuals.

To be entitled to respectful treatment is to have a basic right not to be harmed, says Regan. The right not to be harmed is a *prima facie* (i.e., at first sight) right. In other words, it is not an absolute right, but one that may legitimately be overridden in certain cases where the rights of individuals conflict. Sometimes we have situations where someone's right not to be harmed can only be upheld at the expense of someone else's right not to be harmed. For cases like this, Regan proposes two guiding rules that he holds are consistent with the concept of equal inherent value: what he calls *the miniride principle* and *the worse-off principle*.

The miniride (or minimize overriding) principle says: "Special considerations aside, when we must choose between overriding the rights of many who are innocent or the rights of few who are innocent, and when each affected individual will be harmed in a *prima facie* comparable way, then we ought to choose to override the rights of the few in preference to overriding the rights of the many" (Regan 2004a, p. 305). The worse-off principle says: "Special considerations aside, when we must decide to override the rights of the many or the rights of the few who are innocent, and when the harm faced by the few would make them worse-off than any of the many would be if any other option were chosen, then we ought to override the rights of the many" (Regan 2004a, p. 308).

As an illustration of this, let us imagine the following situation. Suppose that a disaster at a coal mine has left twenty miners trapped in one shaft and one miner trapped in a second shaft. The twenty miners in shaft number one can be rescued unharmed, but only at the cost of sealing up the second shaft and having the miner there die — or, alternatively, the one miner can be brought out unharmed, but only at the cost of sealing up the first shaft and having the twenty miners die. What is the right thing to do? (We assume here that death is a comparable harm for all involved.) According to the miniride principle, we should rescue the twenty miners in shaft number one, since this will result in overriding only one person's right not to be harmed rather than in overriding the right of twenty people not to be harmed.

Now let us imagine that the alternative to having the one miner die is not death for the other twenty miners but a broken arm or leg for each of them by the time they are brought out. Here, the worse-off principle tells us to save the life of the one miner even though a price will be paid by each of the twenty. In this case the cost to each of the twenty (a broken limb) is less than the cost to the one miner (loss of life) of the alternative course of action.

In what may come as a surprise to the reader (but philosophy is full of surprises, and a philosopher's position is seldom as cut and dried as it may appear at first glance), Regan says that an animal is harmed less by death than a normal human being is. This is because an animal's death forecloses fewer opportunities for satisfaction than a normal human's death. What this means is that when it comes to an unavoidable choice between having an animal die and having a human being die, then normally we ought to choose to have the animal die. Regan gives the example of five survivors—four normal adult human beings and a dog—in a lifeboat that cannot support all of them. One must be thrown overboard or all will perish. The dog should go because its death, though a harm, would not be as great a harm as the death of any of the humans. Even in a case where we must choose between four humans and a *million* dogs, the million dogs should be sacrificed because death would be less of a harm for any of them than it would be for any of the humans.

Every individual who has inherent value has the *prima facie* right to pursue his or her own welfare. To say otherwise would be to hold that the treatment each is due is contingent on how others will be affected— something that the rights view denies. I have the duty to treat others with respect but, in turn, I have the right not to be treated as just a means for the purposes of others. With this in mind, Regan (2004a, p. 331) advocates what he calls *the liberty principle*, which says: "Provided that all those involved are treated with respect, and assuming that no special considerations obtain, any innocent individual has the right to act to avoid being made worse-off even if doing so harms other innocents."

Regan's two override principles and his liberty principle are not the heart of his rights philosophy; rather, they are introduced to resolve cases where rights conflict, whether or not animals are involved. Still, as we shall see in following chapters, these principles arguably can be invoked to qualify the strict protection for animals that the rights view seems to entail. Be that as it may, Regan's rights view has revolutionary implications for our treatment of animals. Recognition by society that many animals have a basic right to be treated with respect would mean, except in special circumstances, an end to allowing them to be harmed for purposes of providing humans with food or clothing or recreation or for purposes of scientific research.

For Regan, our basic, unacquired duties to animals entail that we ought to refrain from interfering with their conduct of their own lives. That is to say, we must not intervene in their affairs against their will (except in some instances when our own rights or the rights of others are at stake). Duties of non-interference are sometimes called "negative" duties, and generally we can fulfil them just by "minding our own business". However, Regan emphasizes that when someone's right not to be interfered with is being violated by others, we cannot simply fold our arms and ignore the matter; we have a *prima facie* duty to assist the individual in question, one that we ought to carry out unless there are more pressing moral demands on us.

## Utilitarian Responses

As mentioned previously, Regan's case for animal rights has drawn critical attention from many quarters. Let us begin a survey by looking at responses from a couple of utilitarians, Peter Singer and R.G. Frey. Although they share a general philosophical approach, Singer and Frey are on different sides of the liberation debate.

Given that Regan repeatedly emphasizes the opposition between his rights view and utilitarianism, it is perhaps surprising that Singer (1987) accepts Regan's contention that subjects-of-a-life have inherent value and that it is wrong to treat them as mere things. A utilitarian, says Singer, recognizes that the welfare of animals matters and that their interests must not be discounted. He rejects Regan's contention that utilitarianism regards individuals as mere receptacles of experience and so denies inherent value to them. This analogy is misleading, says Singer. A sentient creature (a pig, for instance) is not separable from its experiences, the way a bottle is separable from the wine in it. In fact, in proposing his subject-of-a-life criterion for inherent value Regan is saying that having inherent value cannot be separated from the capacity to have certain sorts of experiences — and surely this renders problematic any distinction between assigning inherent value to individuals and assigning inherent value to their experiences. Further, says Singer, it does not follow that, in advocating the best aggregate consequences, the utilitarian denies inherent value either to those benefited or to those who may be harmed in achieving this result. Someone who is harmed here is not treated merely as a means for others; on the contrary, his or her interests are given as much consideration as the interests of anyone else. Singer concludes that, in assessing our proper moral stance toward animals, nothing is gained by attributing rights to them.

Like Singer, R.G. Frey (1980, 1983) does not believe that the language of rights adds anything useful to the discussion of moral issues. In any event, he says, it makes no sense to attribute rights to animals. In *Interests and Rights: The Case against Animals* Frey claims that, even if we accept Feinberg's interest principle (that the sorts of beings who can have rights are those who have, or can have, interests), animals do not qualify for rights because they cannot have interests. This assertion rests on the bold argument that animals cannot have interests because they cannot have desires, that they cannot have desires because they cannot have beliefs, and that in turn they cannot have beliefs because they do not have language.

Frey is quite prepared to say that animals have interests in the sense that they have a good or well-being that can be harmed or benefited. For example, it is not good for a dog to be deprived of a nutritious diet or of a certain amount of exercise. But in this sense even a tractor can have interests: it can be in its interests to be well-oiled and otherwise taken care of. The relevant sense of having interests with respect to Feinberg's interest principle, however, entails having desires. A dog, like a tractor, needs water in order to function properly, but does the dog desire to have water? Frey doubts that it does. Having a desire for something — let us say, your having a desire to own an original Gutenberg Bible — can be traced to certain beliefs, such as that you do not currently own one of these books and that your book collection is thus deficient. According to Frey, this involves your believing that the sentence "My collection lacks a Gutenberg Bible" is true. In order for a dog to desire to have water it would have to have certain beliefs, such as that water would quench its thirst, and this in turn would require that the dog believe in the truth of a declarative sentence such as "Water will quench my thirst." Since it is unreasonable to believe that a dog has the linguistic ability to believe in the truth or falsity of declarative sentences, it is unreasonable to believe that a dog can desire water, or have an interest (in the sense relevant to having a right) in having water.

Regan (2004a) finds Frey's argument unpersuasive, in part because it would seem to rule out the possibility of young children being taught to use a language. If in order to believe anything one must believe that certain sentences are true, then young children cannot believe anything before they can understand sentences. And if they lack beliefs, says Regan, then they cannot be taught to use a language. Consider a baby being taught the word "ball" by our repeatedly holding or pointing to a ball and saying the word. Unless the baby comes to believe that we are referring to a particular object when we say "ball", she will never learn the meaning of the word. That is, she must have *preverbal* beliefs in order to begin her linguistic education. (For other critiques of Frey's language argument, see Clark 1982; Miller 1983; Sapontzis 1987.)

Frey (1987) disputes both Regan's claim that human and animal lives are of equal inherent value and the idea that preference autonomy can confer value on a life. Frey holds that the value of a life depends on its quality, which depends on its richness, which depends in turn on its potential for enrichment. He is prepared to bite the bullet and say that, since not all human lives are equal in this respect, some human lives are more valuable than others. If human lives are not equal in value, we cannot claim that animal lives have the same value as normal human lives. Indeed, Frey doubts that the lives of some severely handicapped humans are worth living and thus have much value at all. As for preference autonomy, Frey says that even people with severe Alzheimer's disease have desires and initiate action on the strength of them, but this can hardly be said to support the idea that their lives have the same value as the lives of normal people. Something more is required in order for a life to have significant value: the ability to assess and control our desires in the service of some conception of the good life. Frey sees no reason to think that either animals or severely mentally-handicapped human beings have such an ability.

We shall return to the arguments of Singer and Frey in the next chapter.

For me, the value of life is a function of its quality, its quality a function of its richness, and its richness a function of its scope or potentiality for enrichment; and the fact is that many humans lead lives of a very much lower quality than ordinary normal lives, lives which lack enrichment and where the potentialities for enrichment are severely truncated or absent.... If not all human life has the same value, then Regan's claim of the equal inherent worth of animals collapses; for we do judge some human lives of less value than others.
– R.G. Frey, "Autonomy and the Value of Animal Life", pp. 57-58

## Contractarian Responses

One of Regan's most severe critics has been Jan Narveson, a philosopher who sees morality as an agreement among rational, self-interested individuals. To have rights, on his view, one must have one's interests protected by such an agreement. In the tradition of Thomas Hobbes, who claims that in a state of nature no principles of justice exist to restrain the behaviour of individuals toward one another, Narveson (1977, 1983, 1987, 1999) argues that, because animals cannot be party to an agreement with us, whatever protection they are afforded will depend entirely on our interests.

Two things, says Narveson, are necessary for a moral agreement to be reached among individuals. First, all concerned must be able to understand the nature of an agreement and be able to carry out its terms. Second, all concerned must have something to gain by being party to the agreement. Now, an animal cannot understand the terms of an agreement. Perhaps there are some instances (such as a sheepdog and a farmer) where we might speak of an implicit agreement between animal and human. In general, however, the ability of animals to enter into agreements of the kind we typically make with each other is quite limited or non-existent. And while it would certainly be in the interest of animals to have restrictions placed on human behaviour, we humans have little incentive to restrict the ways we behave toward animals. (Morality involves recognizing restrictions on the way we may legitimately treat others.) Unlike our fellow human beings, animals have little power to make life difficult for us if we treat them in ways they don't like. If necessary, we can always shoot them or cage them. What all this amounts to is that animals simply do not count, morally speaking.

What then of those humans who are not rational agents and so cannot be moral contractors? Is it all right to shoot them, cage them, or perform painful medical experiments on them? Narveson points out that almost all non-rational humans, young or old, are the objects of some contractors' affections. We want to protect our children and our mentally incapacitated relatives and acquaintances from harm, and so it makes sense to agree with other contractors to protect these human non-contractors. We also have a personal interest in making sure that the senile elderly are well treated because we may end up in that condition ourselves one day. We have an interest in seeing that all children are well cared for; otherwise they are more likely to grow into nasty adults who may harm us. By contrast, there is little reason to extend such consideration to most animals.

Note that Narveson is not saying that we ought to violate animal interests. To prescribe how we ought to treat animals (or humans) would be to violate the tenets of his contractarianism. There is nothing about Narveson's position that says you must not be sympathetic to the interests of animals. If you are sympathetic, then there is no reason why you should not personally refrain from causing them suffering, or why you should not help animals in distress, or why you should not try to persuade other people to act similarly. If you do not like the idea of animals being killed by hunters, then you can get together with like-minded people and buy some land where animals will be protected from human predators. As a political libertarian Narveson thinks you should not impose your beliefs on other people through government regulations. If you point out that people impose their beliefs on animals all the time, he will say this objection is irrelevant because animals do not count. Whether Narveson's contractarian view that animals do not count is consistent with a liberal/libertarian emphasis on the right of individuals to conduct their own lives as they see fit is an interesting question (A. Taylor 1996b).

As things stand, we have agreed among ourselves to place some restrictions on the treatment of animals. There are laws against "cruelty" and we have different rules for pets than for animals raised for food or experimentation. But on Narveson's view animals have no rightful claim on us to have any of their interests protected. If some interests of some animals are protected, it is because we humans have decided, for the time being at least, to grant such protection, and not because we are under any pre-contractual obligation to do so. If some animal interests are protected, it is because we feel that it is in our interests to protect them.

Contractarian Peter Carruthers (1992) declares that the present popular concern with animal rights, in a world where there is so much human suffering, is a reflection of moral decadence. He maintains that, though animals are not to be accorded rights, they have indirect moral significance because the way we treat them will often express something of our character. Like Kant, then, Carruthers evaluates our treatment of animals in terms of what he sees as really important, namely, our

One person will befriend a cow, and that's fine; but the next will milk the beast, and eat her later on. People differ. The question, then, is this: why should those of us who want to eat cows have to submit to the self-ascribed "moral" ministrations of those who want to make them charter members of the moral republic?
– Jan Narveson, *Moral Matters*, p. 132

attitudes toward human (rational) beings. Both Carruthers and Narveson charge Regan with failing to provide us with an adequate account of the source of moral ideas and with relying instead on intuition. They also say that his conclusions about our proper treatment of animals are too inconsistent with the considered beliefs of most people to be plausible. Louis Pojman (1995) goes further, claiming that once we accept the radical egalitarianism of Regan or Singer we are on the road to moral nihilism, to saying that because there are no relevant moral distinctions among beings we have no moral duties at all. Instead Pojman argues for a contractarian ethic based on sociobiology's insight that cooperative self-interest is an evolutionary strategy for survival.

That an account of morality like Narveson's offers no once-and-for-all rules for the treatment of others—so that, for example, we cannot say that slavery is always wrong or that there is something intrinsically objectionable about performing painful medical experiments on the mentally handicapped—may be taken by some as a defect (Jamieson 1981). On the other hand, sympathizers will see advantages: a rejection of the quixotic hope of making people conform to rules that may not be in their perceived interests, and a straightforward explanation for the fact that socially acceptable behaviour varies over time and from one society to another.

Of the major ethical theories, contractarianism has been least hospitable to the notion of animal liberation. Recently, however, Mark Rowlands (1998, 2002) has made a contractarian case for animal rights. In contrast to what might be called the Hobbesian contractarianism of Narveson, Rowlands draws on the work of political philosopher John Rawls (1971), who maintains that since neither our initial place in society nor our natural characteristics (our race and sex, our intrinsic mental and physical abilities) are a matter of choice, no one is morally entitled to benefit from them at the expense of others. In propounding his idea of "justice as fairness", Rawls therefore asks us to consider what basic political, economic, and other social arrangements would be agreed to by self-interested contractors behind a "veil of ignorance", that is, in an imagined position of equality, where they did not know what their socio-economic status in society would be to begin with, or what particular natural characteristics they would have. Behind the veil of ignorance, says Rawls, they would choose principles of justice that maximize individual liberty and are such that inequalities in starting positions and natural capacities tend to advance the interests of even the least fortunate members of society.

In Rawls' opinion the capacity of animals to experience pleasure and pain imposes duties of "compassion and humanity" on us, but he says that this fact lies outside the scope of his contractarian theory of justice. Michael Pritchard and Wade Robison (1981) argue that this represents a major inconsistency in Rawls' thinking, since the principles adopted by self-interested human contractors are likely to conflict with any duties to treat animals as other than simply resources. Rowlands takes a different tack. Expanding on what he sees as the implications of Rawls' thesis, Rowlands points out that rationality and species membership are unchosen characteristics, and thus are ones that no one is morally entitled to benefit from at the expense of others. Although contractors must be assumed to be rational agents when formulating the contract, they ought not to know who, once the veil of ignorance is lifted, will be a human and who will be a sentient non-human, one who might be abused or killed by humans if not protected (a point made previously by VanDeVeer 1979b). In this modified original position, says Rowlands, contractors will choose to attribute rights to sentient animals.

Rawls himself gives short shrift to the idea of justice for animals. But rather than trying to show how his theory could be made compatible with animal rights, Ruth Abbey (2007) takes his brief comments on our duties of compassion and humanity as support for the idea that not all moral obligations can be "shoehorned" into the language of justice and rights.

## Feminism and the Ethics of Care

In the opinion of Mary Midgley (1983a, 1983b), the term "right" is too closely tied to a legal and political context, and in particular to the notion of contract, to be employed usefully in the context of whatever moral duties we may have to animals and the rest of the natural world. The notion of rights has developed within a liberal tradition that emphasizes the pursuit of self-interest. By contrast, Midgley insists that we are always embedded in networks of relations. According to Carol Adams (1994), a value of thinking relationally is that we are led to acknowledge that humans are not radically different from non-humans and that we may have significant relationships with animals. Having a relational epistemology encourages us to reject the Cartesian mind-body dualism that sees animals as merely bodies to be used.

Like David Hume and Charles Darwin, many feminists ground morality in a natural human feeling of sympathy for our fellows. (In Darwin's opinion, remember, natural sympathy is to be found among non-humans too.) Josephine Donovan (1990) points to the importance of making a sense of emotional bonding with animals a basis for liberation theory. Despite Regan's disagreement with Kant, Donovan sees Regan's subject-of-a-life criterion as still wedded to the idea that rationality (albeit in a less demanding form) and individuality are the keys to moral standing—a charge that is echoed by Lynda Birke (1994). In a similar vein, Brian Luke (2007) criticizes Regan and Singer for working exclusively within a "justice" framework that presents animal liberation as a matter of logical consistency and fair treatment. This approach, says Luke, ignores the fact that, typically, people's moral condemnations of the ways animals are treated arise directly from sympathy and not from considerations of fairness.

The feminist critique here is motivated less by any disagreement with Regan's or Singer's conclusions about how we should treat animals than by the aim of establishing a different starting point, one that emphasizes the role of emotion and sympathy in morality—what has been called the "care" perspective (McKenna 1994; Slicer 1991). Feminists like Adams and Donovan do not totally reject the rights and utilitarian versions of animal-liberation theory but rather find them inadequate, limited by their association with dominant philosophical traditions. Adams says that her position is "informed" by animal-rights theory, while Donovan approves of the central role played in Singer's argument by the capacity for feeling. Donovan describes both Regan's and Singer's contributions as impressive and useful arguments for the ethical treatment of animals but insists that it is necessary to ground such an ethic in what she calls "an emotional and spiritual conversation with nonhuman life-forms" (Donovan 1990, p. 375).

It might be objected that, without some further account of the connection between feeling and ethics, we have no clear guide for the application of feminist theory. Feelings are likely to differ from person to person. Human history is all too full of harms perpetrated on the basis of feelings about how different groups of people ought to be treated.

Moral theories that stress the rights of individuals or the overall happiness of the group have aimed to avoid the danger of prejudice by evaluating our behaviour in terms of rationally defensible principles that apply equally to all. Feminist philosophers, it might be said, do a valuable service by reminding us of the legitimate role of feeling in morality and the harm that comes from suppressing feeling, but we cannot ignore the need to articulate principles that can justify or condemn the particular ways in which we treat others, principles based on respect for such qualities as life, sentience, and moral agency (Lekan 2004; Regan 2001; Warren 1997).

One prominent feminist writer who has articulated the principles underlying an ethic of care, Nel Noddings (1984), has also devoted some thought to its implications for our treatment of animals — and her conclusions are not sympathetic to animal liberation. For Noddings, the ethical ideal is rooted in the natural longing of human beings to relate to others through caring and being cared for. The true relation of caring is necessarily a reciprocal one, in which the caring individual finds satisfaction or joy through the resulting behaviour of the one cared for. Such behaviour may take the form of a direct response to the one caring, or it may take the form of delight on the part of the one cared for, or it may take the form of that individual's personal growth. What establishes a moral obligation to care for someone else is the existence of, or potential for, a relation between oneself and the other, or else the potential for growth in one's relation with the other.

According to Noddings, it is natural for human beings to be able to care for other human beings. But the capacity to care, or feel affection, for animals varies greatly from person to person. As a result, we cannot demand that everyone conform to the same standard of behaviour with regard to the treatment of animals. Even though animals may be conscious, claims Noddings, they are not perceived by us as *subjects* in the way that normal humans are perceived as subjects. We are, however, aware that animals can experience pain, and we can be aware of the relief they feel when their pain is removed. This awareness on our part does impose an obligation not to inflict unnecessary pain on animals, and to relieve their pain when possible. Yet in our relations with animals the possibility of reciprocity is strictly limited, in part because there is no intellectual or spiritual growth for us to nurture.

What all this means is that whereas caring for other human beings (those with whom we have some more or less direct connection in our lives) is an obligation that imposes itself on us, we have no inescapable obligation to animals apart from refraining from subjecting them to unnecessary suffering. Any other obligation that we may have to an animal is one that we voluntarily assume, as, for instance, when we take a dog or cat into our home as a pet and thereby take on the responsibility of feeding it and seeing to its health and general welfare. Because in general we have no inescapable obligation to care for animals, eating them is permissible so long as they are killed painlessly.

Now, the injunction not to inflict unnecessary pain on animals and to relieve their pain when possible could open a large hole in Noddings' argument. It could be taken to mean that the basic interest of animals in not suffering is to be considered equally with our own interest in not suffering, and that not only must we normally refrain from causing animals suffering but we must intervene in nature when we can to rescue them from suffering. This would mean that we have strong obligations with regard to all animals, both domesticated and wild, and not simply with regard to our household companions.

This cannot be Noddings' intention. She believes that animal pain does not pain us as much as human pain and that inflicting pain on animals is therefore justified if this is necessary to prevent human suffering. How much suffering are we talking about? Is no amount of animal suffering too great if it will prevent some human suffering? Noddings does not make herself clear on this point but she clearly rejects the idea that animals have, even roughly, the same level of moral claim upon us that human beings do.

Noddings' perspective appears to offer a neat response to the dilemma posed by the argument from marginal cases: namely, how can it be acceptable to treat animals in ways that we would never allow human beings of similar mental capacity to be treated? If our moral obligations arise mainly on the basis of our feelings and the kind of response we evoke from others, and if animals have little capacity for the appropriate response, then animals may indeed have little or no claim to have their interests considered. Even an ethic-of-care viewpoint that judges the killing of domesticated animals for food to be morally problematic (a possible violation of our duty to care for those we have made dependent on us) can still give preference to human beings, regardless of their cognitive faculties (Engster 2006).

### Hursthouse and Virtue Ethics

Rather than asking what rights or duties we have, virtue ethics asks us to consider how the virtuous person would act in a given situation. How would someone who is courageous, loyal, benevolent, and so forth act in these circumstances? Virtue ethics is open to the charge that, by eschewing straightforward rules, it is too vague to be workable. Rosalind Hursthouse (2000) prefers to say that virtue ethics is "subtle" rather than "vague". Its flexibility is a strength, not a weakness, since it recognizes that the motives and emotions that accompany acts properly enter into our assessment of their moral worth. As an example, she asks us to imagine someone who carefully preserves the coppices in which foxes live. Such behaviour would be virtuous if done from concern for the foxes' well-being. But if, instead, the person in question takes a sadistic pleasure in killing foxes and the motive for preserving their coppices is simply to ensure a ready supply of foxes for organized hunts, the act of preservation appears in a very different light: as the expression of a vicious nature and therefore wrong.

Hursthouse recognizes that rational argument plays a limited role in virtue ethics, so that sincere people may come to different conclusions about particular issues. (For example, is fox-hunting a manifestation of courage or of cruelty and self-indulgence?) But, she contends, this limitation to the role of rational argument is an inescapable feature of moral life and is no reason to abandon virtue ethics.

### Rights Again

Mary Anne Warren (1983, 1987, 1997) maintains that sentience is both a necessary and a sufficient condition for having at least some sort of moral rights. Her criterion for rights, then, sets the bar lower than Regan's subject-of-a-life criterion. However, against Regan, she argues that being the subject-of-a-life is plausibly regarded as a matter of degree: some creatures have a greater sense of self and ability to anticipate the future than do others. If so, then we should reject the thesis that all subjects-of-a-life have equal moral status. She asks us to consider the moral status of a spider. If Regan's view is right, she says, then "We are forced to say that either a spider has the same right to life as you and I do, or it has no right to life whatever—and that only the gods know which of these alternatives is true" (Warren 1987, p. 166). This is not an exceptional case, in her opinion: Regan's subject-of-a-life criterion provides us with no clear moral guidance for our dealings with most animals.

Warren instead advocates what she calls the "weak animal rights" position. She maintains that, while all sentient animals have rights (including the right not, without compelling reason, to be killed or made to suffer), their rights are not as strong as the rights of human beings and hence can more easily be overridden in light of social or ecological considerations. She favours a "sliding scale of moral status", according to which we have stronger obligations to those creatures that display higher degrees of sensitivity and mental sophistication. Hence our obligations to scorpions and tadpoles are relatively weak; by contrast, it should almost never be permissible to treat dolphins, apes, or elephants in ways that would violate their rights if they were humans. Warren's position seems intuitively plausible, but it raises questions. Rights have been described as being like trumps in a card game: they override other considerations. What value are these weaker rights to animals in practice? And just how are we to specify the different strengths of different creatures' rights?

Taking issue with Regan from another angle, Lori Gruen (1991) doubts our ability to judge impartially that a human being thrown overboard from a lifeboat is harmed more by the thwarting of her desire to get home and write that play she's always wanted to write than a dog thrown overboard is harmed by the thwarting of his desire for one more run by the river. If we think the human is harmed more, isn't that because we see things from a human perspective? This is like the objection that can be raised against John Stuart Mill: are we not biased in believing human pleasures to be qualitatively superior to the pleasures enjoyed by pigs? Indeed, Lewis Petrinovich (1999) thinks that Regan's favouring of humans in lifeboat cases is based on an unacknowledged assumption by Regan that humans have greater inherent value than non-humans. Petrinovich contends that bias for one's own species has a biological basis. Our legitimate pro-human bias is an aspect of evolved human nature: the emotional bonds that we have with other members of the human community support the social contract that underlies morality.

Gary Francione (2000) derives the basic right of animals not to be treated as property or mere resources directly from the principle of equal consideration, which he says is a logical requirement of *any* sound moral theory. The principle says that we must treat like cases alike. If John is allowed to run for public office, then Jennifer must also be allowed to run for public office if the circumstances are relevantly similar. That Jennifer is female is not a good (i.e., morally relevant) reason for denying her the opportunity to run; that she is insane or a child may be a good reason. There are many ways in which animals differ from humans. But if we judge that animals have morally significant interests — in particular, if we judge that animals, like humans, have a morally significant interest in not suffering — then, logically, we must ascribe to animals the same right that humans have not to be treated as mere things. While we cannot protect either humans or animals from all suffering, giving meaningful content to our belief that the infliction of unnecessary suffering is wrong cannot be squared with animals' current status as property, any more than it can be squared with the practice of human slavery.

Francione's position, then, ascribes the basic right not to be treated as property to all sentient individuals, not just to those who meet Regan's definition of "subject-of-a-life". While his theory differs in some respects from Regan's, Francione makes the point that the concept of equal inherent value is an alternative way of expressing the basic right of all those who have an experiential life not to be treated merely as means to the ends of others, and that neither the concept of this basic right nor the concept of equal inherent value relies on any questionable metaphysical doctrine.

## Nussbaum's Capabilities Approach

Both Regan's modified-Kantian approach and Singer's utilitarianism, despite their significant breaks with traditional views of the moral status of animals, have been criticized for being too anthropocentric — too wedded to the idea that many animals have moral standing because they are like humans in important ways. These liberation philosophies are sometimes labelled "extensionist", in that they extend traditional moral theories to include various animals as morally considerable on the basis of characteristics shared with humans. Feminist ethic-of-care philosophers and others (e.g., Fellenz 2007; Steiner 2005, 2008; Wolfe 2003a) argue that respect for difference, not just similarity, is important if animals are to be appreciated for who they are and not viewed simply as deficient versions of humans.

Desiring to give due recognition to the great variety of forms and capacities to be found among sentient creatures, Martha Nussbaum (2004, 2006, 2007) has constructed what might be described as a neo-Aristotelian argument for animal rights. She calls it "the capabilities approach". Unlike Kant, she does not consider the rationality of humans to be opposed to their animality, but sees rationality as just one aspect of the human animal. Drawing on both Aristotle and Marx, she views humans as social creatures whose essential needs and abilities arise from their nature as a specific kind of animal. If they are to live flourishing lives, humans must be capable of manifesting their innate powers in effective ways. The central capabilities, those that we ought to promote, are those evaluated as being necessary for human flourishing. Among others, they include life, bodily health, emotions, practical reason, affiliation with others, and control over one's environment.

Nussbaum goes on to apply the capabilities approach to members of non-human species. With Aristotle, she views with wonder the endless forms of life on this planet, believes they all deserve to be studied and appreciated, and considers it a waste when an organism is not able to develop and exercise its natural powers. But Nussbaum does not limit the moral community to rational beings or understand the exercise of reason to be the highest good. There is no natural ranking of forms of life, she says; rather, every form of life has its appropriate way of functioning. Animals are of many types and pursue a variety of activities and goals. When it comes to sentient beings, each is to be respected as a subject and agent; each is entitled, as a matter of justice, to positive opportunities to flourish.

That is to say, not just every human, but every sentient animal, has the right to what Nussbaum calls a dignified existence. This is not simply a matter of avoiding pain or fulfilling conscious preferences. For example, a dog that has always been confined in a small space may not be in pain, and if her condition has rendered her unable to imagine roaming freely, she may not feel frustration at her deprivation. Yet such confinement is wrong because her power to flourish is being stunted. What counts as harm to a creature depends on the species nature of that creature, but among the typical requirements of a dignified existence

Each form of life is worthy of respect, and it is a problem of justice when a creature does not have the opportunity to unfold its (valuable) power, to flourish in its own way, and to lead a life with dignity. The fact that so many animals never get to move around, enjoy the air, exchange affection with other members of their kind — all that is a waste and a tragedy, and it is not a life in keeping with the dignity of such creatures.
— Martha Nussbaum, "The Moral Status of Animals", p. 33

for an animal, Nussbaum says, are physical activity, sensory stimulation, freedom from non-beneficial pain, opportunities for emotional expression and attachment, opportunities for rewarding interaction with members of the animal's own species and of other species, and the territorial integrity of the animal's habitat. Each sentient creature is entitled to continue its life, so long as that life is worth living.

Nussbaum's capabilities approach is a significant contribution to the animal debate. Her approach is still in the process of development, and various details and implications remain to be discussed and clarified.

## Continental Philosophy

The modern debate over the moral status of animals has been conducted primarily in the English-speaking world, with some contributions, often in English, from philosophers in other countries. Indeed, recently there has appeared a book (Jeangène Vilmer 2008) billing itself as the first introduction of the animal-ethics debate to a French-speaking audience. Notably absent from this debate has been any substantial representation of philosophers in the so-called continental tradition of Europe.

It is perhaps not surprising that the existentialism of Jean-Paul Sartre and Simone de Beauvoir, with its emphasis on the radical distinction between (human) consciousness and the natural world, has little to say about animals. In their view, the realm of consciousness is the realm of autonomy and perpetual self-creation, while the rest of the world is what is in essence given, inert, uncreative and what is thus alien to humanity. For Beauvoir, the emancipation of women is the struggle to free themselves from the historical constraints of nature (particularly the limitations imposed by reproduction) and the cultural manifestations of these constraints, and to join men as equals in the realm of freedom. Sentient non-humans are an ill fit with this dualistic schema of human (being-for-itself) and other (being-in-itself) — as suggested by Sartre's brief remark quoted at the beginning of Chapter 1.

The absence in the work of almost all continental philosophers of any sustained exploration of the status of animals is remarkable, given the concern of many of them with moving beyond the humanist tradition that places the rational, autonomous subject at the centre of knowledge, action, and value. Friedrich Nietzsche (1844-1900), a precursor of postmodernism, who undertakes a radical critique of dominant philosophical assumptions and calls for a "revaluation of all values" with a view to achieving a new understanding of what it means to be human, employs a wealth of animal imagery in his writings. Even so, he does not attempt to understand animals for their own sake and fails to question the traditional hierarchical ranking of humans over animals (Langer 1999). Michel Foucault, Nietzsche's prominent twentieth-century heir, who is concerned with the connections between knowledge and power in human society, has next to nothing to say about our understanding of animals and our exploitation of them. At least for Nietzsche, the "will to power" is part of humanity's animal — or, more generally, biological — heritage. But in Foucault even this connection with the non-human is missing. Ultimately, says Paola Cavalieri (2008), Foucault fails to overcome a humanist bias.

Jacques Derrida (2002), the one major continental philosopher to consider the animal question at some length, notes that the term "animal" tends to obscure the multiplicity and variety of non-human life. He asserts that the concept of the human is constructed in opposition to this generalized notion of "the animal", and that this opposition facilitates the abuse of non-humans. Noting that recent times have seen unprecedented, systematized violence directed against animals, Derrida goes so far as to suggest an analogy between the industrial uses of animals and genocide — the difference being that animals are deliberately bred so that the death camps can be perpetuated. He points approvingly to Jeremy Bentham's conceptual revolution of framing the animal question in terms of suffering rather than rationality. We share the capacity for suffering with animals, and their suffering can evoke our compassion. Nevertheless, Derrida refuses to ascribe equal standing to all who can suffer. He rejects the idea of a continuity between humans and animals, and speaks of an "abyssal rupture" separating them. He warns against a biological reductionism that would treat humans like animals (Lawlor 2007). And despite calling our attention to the horrors of modern animal industries, Derrida (1991) shies away from endorsing vegetarianism, or indeed from taking any firm ethical stance.

While various continental philosophers have attempted to challenge traditional notions of what it means to be human, they have thrown little light on the moral status of animals and offered little by way of prescription for our treatment of animals (Aaltola 2002). Still, there are those who see unrealized potential in their work (Acampora 2006; Calarco 2008; Calarco and Atterton 2004; Palmer 2001; Steeves 1999). Take, for example, the philosophy of Emmanuel Levinas. According to Levinas, when we encounter another human, we recognize in that person's face a vulnerable being with his or her own view of the world. This fact about the other, which is most apparent when the person speaks, obligates us to respond ethically. By contrast, says Levinas, animals do not have a "face" that evokes an ethical response from us when we encounter them. Animals, it would seem, are not the sorts of beings we can engage with in a meaningful way. But Barbara Jane Davy (2007) perceives in Levinas a contradictory subtext — that the expressivity of the other need not be manifest in language — and she uses this idea to reconstruct his thought in a way that does not limit ethics to encounters between humans.

## Conclusion

One important way of understanding the notion of rights, whether legal or moral, is to interpret them as valid claims. The issue of moral rights, not without controversy when applied to humans, is especially controversial when applied to non-humans. Nevertheless, a growing number of philosophers have been prepared to consider that there may be a case for ascribing moral rights to animals. Opposition to the idea of animal rights comes, in the first place, from philosophers who are opposed to animal liberation and who argue that the concept of rights is normally not applicable to beings that cannot reason about moral principles, make claims for themselves, and be held accountable to others for their actions. Opposition, or at least criticism, also comes from many who are sympathetic to animal liberation but who prefer other ethical approaches, such as utilitarianism or feminist theory.

Despite the nuances of philosophical debate, in the public arena both advocates and opponents of animal liberation commonly refer to the "animal rights" movement. The language of rights resonates powerfully in the public mind, as is evident whenever the idea of human rights is invoked to condemn abuses of people's fundamental interests. The assertion that animals have rights puts in strong and uncompromising form the demand that many of our traditional practices involving non-humans must be radically altered. It is to the consideration of those practices that we now turn.

CHAPTER FOUR

# IS IT WRONG TO EAT OR HUNT ANIMALS?

But for the sake of some little mouthful of flesh, we deprive a soul of the sun and light, and of that portion of life and time it had been born into the world to enjoy.

*Plutarch (46-c.122)*[1]

[Samuel Johnson:] There is much talk of the misery which we cause to the brute creation; but they are recompensed by existence. If they were not useful to man, and therefore protected by him, they would not be nearly so numerous.

[James Boswell:] But the question is, whether the animals who endure such sufferings of various kinds, for the service and entertainment of man, would accept of existence upon the terms on which they have it.[2]

Each year human beings kill thousands of millions of animals. In the United States alone thousands of millions of birds (most of them chickens) are slaughtered annually for food, along with tens of millions each of pigs, sheep, and cattle, while hunters kill one or two

---

[1] Plutarch, "Of Eating of Flesh", in Tom Regan and Peter Singer, eds., *Animal Rights and Human Obligations* (Englewood Cliffs: Prentice-Hall, 1976), p. 113.

[2] James Boswell, *The Life of Samuel Johnson*, vol. 2 (London: Charles Dilly, 1791), p. 71.

hundred million wild animals (Nicoll and Russell 1990; Singer 2002). Opposition to the raising and killing of animals for human consumption has been a prime focus of the animal-liberation movement and of liberationist philosophers. In this chapter we consider the arguments for and against using animals for food (and, implicitly, for other purposes such as clothing, for which their dead bodies provide material). We then go on to examine a related but separate matter: the issue of hunting, first where hunting for sport is concerned and then in the matter of subsistence hunting, with reference to the Inuit of Arctic Canada.

## Vegetarianism

Generally speaking, vegetarians are those who deliberately abstain from eating meat. Vegans try to avoid any food or other product that involves animal exploitation. (Many vegans do not refer to themselves as vegetarians because they see consuming eggs and dairy products as no better, ethically, than eating meat.)

Vegetarianism has a long history (C. Spencer 1993; Walters and Portmess 1999). In India, where Buddhism, Hinduism, and Jainism preach reverence for all life, it has been common for more than two thousand years (Chapple 1993; Perrett 1993). In ancient Greece vegetarianism was associated with the mathematician and philosopher Pythagoras and his followers. Indeed, until the middle of the nineteenth century in Europe, vegetarianism was often referred to as the Pythagorean diet. Prominent vegetarians of the past include Leonardo da Vinci, George Bernard Shaw, and Mohandas Gandhi. (Gandhi's ethical commitment to vegetarianism was solidified when, as a student in London, he read a book on the subject by animal-rights philosopher Henry Salt.) The ancient-Greek philosopher and biographer Plutarch rejected the idea that humans are meat-eaters by nature and denounced the callousness of those who consume flesh when they have no need to. The poet Percy Bysshe Shelley argued that a vegetable diet is conducive to spiritual as well as physical well-being (Morton 1994). Leo Tolstoy, who converted to vegetarianism in 1885, wrote vividly of his visit to a slaughterhouse, where he was particularly horrified by the indifference to suffering displayed by the workers. Isaac Newton is reported to have found meat-eating repugnant. Albert Einstein praised vegetarianism and became vegetarian himself near the end of his life. Voltaire denounced the consumption of animal flesh; so did Henry David Thoreau, who stuck primarily to a vegetarian diet. Benjamin Franklin, who was vegetarian for some years, reverted to meat-eating after seeing one fish inside the body of another. His reasoning was: if animals eat each other, why shouldn't he eat them?

Adolf Hitler, of all people, is often said to have been a vegetarian, influenced by the dietary views of his hero, the composer Richard Wagner. This claim may originally have been designed to portray the German dictator as an ascetic who was totally devoted to serving his nation. Hitler did restrict his consumption of meat for health reasons, though some reports have it that he remained fond of liver dumplings and Bavarian sausages; not only did he eat meat now and then, but once in power he banned vegetarian organizations (Berry 2004; Schwartz 2001). Whatever the truth about the Nazi leader's personal habits, there are those who are haunted by a spectre from that time. Isaac Bashevis Singer, vegetarian and Nobel-laureate Yiddish writer, has the protagonist of one of his stories ("The Letter Writer") reflect that "for the animals it is an eternal Treblinka," thus likening our mass killing of sentient beings to the Holocaust. This controversial comparison has been raised by others too (Almeida and Bernstein 2000; Coetzee 1999; Derrida 2002; C. Patterson 2002; Sztybel 2006b).

In recent decades various reasons have been adduced in support of vegetarianism (Goodall 2005; M.A. Fox 1999; Hill 1996; Robbins 1987; Stephens 1994). These include good health (since diets high in animal fat and low in vegetables and fruit are correlated with heart disease and cancer), alleviation of world hunger (since each pound of protein produced in the form of meat requires the consumption by animals of many pounds of vegetable protein that might have been consumed by humans), and protection of the environment (since use of land for grazing and for cultivating feed significantly reduces wildlife habitats, requires enormous energy consumption, and results in much pollution, and since tropical rainforests, which play a major role in the health of the biosphere, are being devastated to clear more land for livestock production). While these reasons involve ethical considerations, the reasons in support of vegetarianism to be considered here have to do with the suffering and death of animals.

The issue of suffering and the issue of death are not to be conflated. In the same passage in which he maintains that we are wrong to torment

In his thoughts, Herman spoke a eulogy for the mouse who had shared a portion of her life with him and who, because of him, had left this earth. "What do they know—all those scholars, all those philosophers, all the leaders of the world—about such as you? They have convinced themselves that man, the worst transgressor of all the species, is the crown of creation. All other creatures were created merely to provide him with food, pelts, to be tormented, exterminated. In relation to them, all people are Nazis; for the animals it is an eternal Treblinka. …"
– Isaac Bashevis Singer, "The Letter Writer", in *The Séance and Other Stories* (New York: Farrar, Straus and Giroux, 1968), p. 270

animals, Jeremy Bentham (1970, p. 282n) argues that "If the being eaten were all, there is very good reason why we should be suffered to eat such of them as we like to eat: we are the better for it, and they are never the worse. They have none of those long-protracted anticipations of future misery which we have. The death they suffer in our hands commonly is, and always may be, a speedier, and by that means a less painful one, than that which would await them in the inevitable course of nature." Bentham's distinction between suffering and being killed is a potentially important one when we consider the issue of eating meat.

## Meat and Suffering

In *Animal Liberation* Peter Singer advocates vegetarianism not on the grounds that killing is wrong but on grounds of the suffering inflicted on most animals raised for consumption, who are not allowed to exist in conditions where they might exercise their natural faculties and lead satisfying lives. (See also R. Harrison 1964; Mason and Singer 1980.) Sweden has passed a law requiring, among other things, that cattle be allowed to graze and that pigs and chickens not be confined in a manner that prevents them from moving naturally (Rollin 1995). Sweden, however, is an exception to the rule. On the basis of a pleasure/pain calculus, a strong case can be made for refraining from eating the flesh of intensively reared (or "factory farmed") animals. At the same time, this path suggests the moral acceptability of eating meat from "free range" (non-intensively reared) animals, provided that these animals are killed with little or no pain —a goal that is frequently violated in the meat industry (Eisnitz 1997).

Indeed, Roger Crisp (1997) goes so far as to argue that, while we should abstain from eating the flesh of intensively-reared animals, we have an obligation to eat the flesh of non-intensively reared animals, since doing so will maximize the number of animals leading pleasant lives. The claim that it is actually wrong to abstain from meat will seem odd to most people, including meat eaters, depending as it does on the notion that we ought to bring into existence beings (human or non-human) just for the sake of maximizing utility in the world. It may be doubted that enough animals could be reared non-intensively to provide everyone with meat, but it could be argued that we should eat meat whenever we can obtain it from non-intensively reared animals. (See also Matheny and Chan 2005; Schedler 2005.)

The kind of position sketched above relies on *the replaceability argument*. This argument says that if an animal lives a life that involves more pleasure than pain, and if it would not have existed unless it had been deliberately brought into existence by humans, then it is acceptable to kill the animal and replace it with another animal that will lead a similar life. Thus, for example, it might be said that, if we kill a pig painlessly and replace it with another pig leading a similarly pleasant life, we do nothing wrong. A number of objections can be raised against the replaceability argument; for instance, although the argument is normally advanced to justify killing that is done for the purpose of bringing some alleged benefit to oneself or others, its logic appears to license the infliction of pain on an animal for no good result, provided that, on the whole, the animal's life is still worth living (Cave 1982b).

Would we be willing to apply the replaceability argument to human beings? What about painlessly killing a happy person — say, a child we have brought into existence — and then bringing into existence another happy person to replace her? If that is not acceptable, why not? Singer (1979, 1993a, 1993b) rejects the replaceability argument in cases of beings who are self-conscious. Self-conscious beings, unlike merely conscious beings, can have the desire to live, a desire that would be thwarted by their being killed. This means that the death of a self-conscious being is not balanced by the creation of another, similar, being.

In taking this position, Singer rejects hedonistic utilitarianism in favour of preference utilitarianism. This version of utilitarianism measures utility not in terms of pleasure and pain but in terms of the satisfaction and frustration of preferences. It makes an important difference, on this view, which animals are self-conscious and which are not. Those that are not self-conscious, unlike those that are, may rightly be raised and killed for food, provided that they live pleasant lives and that their deaths result in the coming into existence of other animals that lead similarly pleasant lives. Just which animals are self-conscious is not clear, but Singer suggests that chickens, for example, are not. The conclusion that some meat-eating is justified is not speciesist, says Singer, since it results not from a prejudice in favour of our own species but from a consideration of the fact that not all beings have the capacity to desire to go on living. (The replacement option will thus also apply to human infants insofar as they have not yet attained self-consciousness, even though few parents will want to kill and replace their babies — and fewer still will want to do this in order to eat them.)

In light of the above, we can envisage that liberationists who subscribe to Singer's principles might sometimes eat meat without logical inconsistency. In addition, many liberationists who oppose even painless killing of free-range animals will see no violation of principle in eating animals that have died from old age, illness, or accident (Sapontzis 1987). However, because liberationists are likely to have a gut (!) revulsion against the idea of consuming any animal flesh, eating meat is probably rare among those who are philosophically committed to ending the idea that animals are essentially resources. Singer's intent, of course, is not to justify meat-eating — quite the contrary. He emphasizes that the suffering of factory-farmed animals rules out most meat consumption. And though he holds that eating some free-range animals may be justified in principle, he thinks that in practice eating any meat is bound to lead to the callous attitude that animals are mere means to our ends.

In *Rights, Killing, and Suffering* R.G. Frey contends that the ethical arguments advanced by Singer in support of vegetarianism fail. Frey doubts that any of the animals commonly raised for food are self-conscious; if Frey is correct, then they are all candidates for being killed and replaced according to Singer's criterion. Singer says replacement is not an option where animals lead unpleasant lives; Frey thinks it is possible to improve the lives of intensively-farmed animals to a level where killing and replacing them becomes acceptable. Like Michael Leahy (1991), Frey believes that a concerned individual can without inconsistency continue to eat meat while advocating improvements to the factory-farming system on behalf of animals.

While most philosophers agree that the suffering that most animals experience while being raised for meat is of direct moral import, one strand of thinking dissents from this opinion. For most contractarians the suffering of animals is of only indirect moral import. That is, animal suffering is something to be avoided only insofar as it negatively affects human beings. Thus Peter Carruthers (1992), who, as we have seen in Chapter 1, is prepared to argue that animals do not suffer, holds that even if they do, their suffering is of no account unless it bothers people. His solution: practices that may cause pain to animals, like unusual sexual practices, should not be flaunted in public because of the likelihood of giving offence to some people. Carruthers does believe that inflicting pain on animals for trivial reasons is to be avoided but, as previously noted, his idea here is that such behaviour may develop the wrong character traits in us in that we may be led to treat human beings badly. He thinks that factory farming does not inflict pain for trivial reasons, since many people earn their livelihoods in this industry.

Carruthers also suggests that people who are upset by animal suffering should just not think about it. Modern society facilitates this to some extent by hiding the workings of slaughterhouses from public view and typically selling meat in small chunks wrapped in paper or cellophane. A twist is to take the sting out of the issue by joking about it: bizarrely, much advertising for meat products and for restaurants shows images of happy animals begging to be eaten. One Internet blogger calls this "suicide food" and maintains a site devoted to reproducing pictures of pigs, chickens, cows, and fish wielding knives and forks, gleefully serving up the bodies of their fellows, or barbecuing themselves, or boiling themselves in cauldrons. The ubiquity of such images suggests they have much to say about the psychological attitude of people in industrial society to the animals they consume.

Nick Fiddes (1991) insists that meat-eating is more than just an act of consumption: killing, cooking, and eating the flesh of animals provides human beings with authentication of their superiority over the rest of nature. Indeed, Fiddes claims that meat is esteemed by society not *in spite* of the consequences for the animals involved but precisely *because* of those consequences and what they symbolize: our mastery of the non-human world. He notes that meat assumed a new importance in the diets of most European peoples from the seventeenth century onwards, when science was emphasizing the need to dominate nature and when mechanistic philosophers were portraying animals as machines. Fiddes suggests that today's rejection of meat-eating by many people is part and parcel of a rejection of the ideology of domination, domination that is manifest both in relations among human beings and in relations between human beings and the natural environment.

> The symbolism of meat-eating is never neutral. To himself, the meat-eater seems to be eating life. To the vegetarian, he seems to be eating death. There is a kind of gestalt-shift between the two positions which makes it hard to change, and hard to raise questions on the matter at all without becoming embattled.
> —Mary Midgley, *Animals and Why They Matter*, p. 27

## What Makes Killing Wrong?

Whether Singer's moral distinction between self-conscious and merely conscious creatures can be sustained has occasioned some debate

(Jamieson 1983; E. Johnson 1983; Lockwood 1979). For Ruth Cigman (1981) the ability or inability of animals to imagine a future for themselves makes all the difference insofar as the morality of killing them is concerned. She believes that almost all animals lack the capacity to have what she calls categorical desires, that is, desires that entail that one wishes to remain alive in order to do something with one's life. (An example would be the desire to become an opera singer, or to raise a family.) To a subject possessing categorical desires, death must appear as a misfortune insofar as it prevents the accomplishment of one's long-term projects. However, death cannot be a misfortune for beings that lack the capacity to have categorical desires. And for beings for whom death cannot be a misfortune it makes no sense to talk about their having a right to life. Cigman does not rule out the possibility that a very few animals, like chimpanzees and dolphins, may be candidates for having a right to life, though she is sceptical even there. Her conclusion is that although the sufferings of animals may rightly be of moral concern to us, their quick and painless deaths should not be. Eating meat is therefore probably justified if the animals' deaths are quick and painless, but not if they suffer as they are prepared for death.

Steve Sapontzis responds at length to Cigman in his book *Morals, Reason, and Animals*. He says that Cigman's argument turns on the idea that, although animals may *have* an interest in life, they cannot *take* an interest in life, since they cannot understand the full significance of death (that it puts an end to one's experiences in this world). Sapontzis denies that this fact about (most or all) animals disqualifies them from having a right to life. Taking an interest in or valuing $X$ is not a necessary condition for having a moral right to $X$. After all, if we believe in the existence of human rights we shall ascribe them to people who may never have heard of a charter like the Universal Declaration of Human Rights and who may even have been brought up to believe that there are no such things as human rights. We shall also ascribe rights to young children who cannot understand or value them. Just as death is a misfortune for human beings whose enjoyment of life is cut short by death (even by an unexpected and instantaneous death, so that they never have knowledge of their loss), so death is a misfortune for animals who would have enjoyed life had they not been killed. Sapontzis concludes that it makes sense to extend to animals a right to life in order to protect them from this misfortune. Except for those extraordinary cases where people have no other way to survive, killing sentient animals for food cannot be justified.

Similarly, Rosemary Rodd (1990) suggests that a creature's possession of simple consciousness is sufficient to make killing it wrong, since killing a conscious creature deprives it of future enjoyments whether or not it can anticipate those enjoyments. She also says that the capacity to anticipate future events (a rat's anticipation of feeding time, a dog's anticipation of a walk) does not require a sophisticated level of self-consciousness and is enough to bring into play a utilitarian injunction against killing based on frustration of desires and preferences.

The question of what makes killing wrong (when it is wrong) is complex, and one that arises also in the debates over abortion and euthanasia. As suggested above by several philosophers, a plausible position has it that the wrongness of killing is inseparably involved with the harm that is done to the victim by depriving that individual of the value of future experiences. But this in turn raises difficult issues of identity, having to do with the continuity (or lack of continuity) between the present psychological states of an organism and that organism's past and future psychological states. Jeff McMahan (2002, 2008) maintains that killing animals is not as wrong as killing human persons because animals normally lose less by dying than humans do: not only are the psychological goods of an animal's future normally of lesser quality and quantity than those of a person's future, but, among other reasons, the psychological unity of the individual over time is considerably less in the animal's case, making the animal's interest in continuing to live doubly weak. Still, says McMahan, the wrongness of killing animals based on loss of future goods is great enough to support the argument for vegetarianism. Further, though the psychological goods available to a person significantly exceed those available to an animal, an animal's capacity to experience bodily pain means that the suffering of an animal can approach that of a human. Hence we have no excuse for ignoring or discounting the enormous harm inflicted on animals by factory farming.

By contrast, Meredith Williams (1980) stresses the moral relevance of the unique interests and cultural life that rationality makes possible in human beings. While the fact that animals suffer is reason for some concern, the lesser value of their lives (something Singer admits in his discussion of what makes killing wrong) undermines Singer's case for equal consideration and hence his argument for vegetarianism. Leslie Francis and Richard Norman (1978) maintain that, though there should be changes in the factory-farming of animals to minimize suffering, animals have no right to life; they lack the communication abilities and sorts of social relations (economic, political, and familial) that would entitle them to the same moral consideration as human beings. The argument of Francis and Norman is somewhat similar to that of Nel Noddings: animals are necessarily excluded from the same considera-tion that we accord humans because we cannot enter into the same rela-tions of caring and response with them.

The rights view appears to provide a stronger case for vegetarianism than does a utilitarian approach. While both Peter Singer and Tom Regan believe that we are morally obligated to be vegetarian, the ways they reach that conclusion are quite different. The case advanced by Singer (1980) rests on the alleged long-term benefits to humans and animals of our switching to a meatless diet. But, counters Regan (2004a), in view of the enormous economic interests involved in the meat indus-try, it is not *obvious* that better aggregated consequences will follow from everyone's becoming vegetarian than from continuation of the present state of affairs. Frey (1983) and Leahy (1991) both invoke the spectre of potentially disastrous economic consequences to bolster the case against obligatory vegetarianism. Singer eschews any absolutist position on the issue of vegetarianism; on a utilitarian view the matter is largely an empirical one of discovering what the best overall conse-quences will be. Regan's rights view, by contrast, enjoins us to become vegetarian as a matter of justice. Animals who are subjects-of-a-life have the right to be treated with respect, including the right not to be harmed. To raise farm animals for slaughter, to treat them as renewable resources (whether or not they are treated "humanely"), is to violate their basic rights. We cannot justify continuing to consume animals by an appeal to the economic consequences of ending the practice any more than we would be able to justify the continuation of human slavery by an appeal to the harmful economic consequences of ending that practice. No one, says Regan, has the right to be protected from harm by the continuation of an unjust practice, one that violates the rights of others.

Is the rights case for vegetarianism watertight? Given that many wild animals—mice, rabbits, birds, and others—are killed in crop production by farm machinery, pesticides, and habitat destruction, Steven Davis (2003) has suggested that a diet that includes meat from grass-fed (not grain-fed) animals actually kills fewer animals than a strictly vegetarian diet. But his calculations have been disputed (Lamey 2007; Matheny 2003). Given the much smaller amount of land required to produce an equivalent amount of food in vegetable form, even a diet involving meat from pasture-raised animals arguably results in more deaths and more harm to animals.

Hugh Lehman (1988) maintains that a rights view may sometimes condone killing animals for food. He claims that with regard to world population and present food resources we are in effect in a lifeboat situation: not all creatures, human and non-human, can survive. Any overnight prohibition against eating meat would result in there being insufficient food to support all human beings; many people would die, while others would become ill from malnutrition. Hence Regan's worse-off principle implies that, given that death is a greater harm to humans than to animals, it is right to sacrifice animal lives to save human lives. What this means is that meat-eating should continue unless and until food-production systems can be modified to support the world's human population on a vegetarian diet. The details and practicality of a widespread conversion to vegetarianism have not been adequately studied, says Lehman.

Lehman's incremental approach finds a surprising ally in Martha Nussbaum (2004, 2006), who says that the effects on human health and the environment of a total switch to vegetarianism are not yet known, and that therefore we should begin by improving the conditions of animals raised for food. But is Nussbaum's position here consistent with the fundamentals of her capabilities approach? On the one hand, she says that every sentient creature is entitled, as a matter of justice, to continue its life and never to be used merely as a means to the ends of others. On the other hand, she is not convinced that it is wrong, on balance, painlessly to kill and then eat an animal that has been leading a good life. How does the absence of pain excuse killing someone with a right to life, asks Anders Schinkel (2008), especially when Nussbaum's approach holds that an individual need not be conscious of a deprivation in order to be wronged? The array of capabilities to which Nussbaum says animals are entitled, in order to be able to flourish as individuals, surely means little if they have no secure right to life. Nussbaum suggests that killing for food may involve a tragic conflict between the well-being of humans and the well-being of animals. But, says Schinkel, that idea only makes sense if killing animals for food does indeed involve serious wrongdoing and if at the same time eating meat is necessary for human well-being.

### Does Being Vegetarian Make Any Difference?

Resort to utilitarian or rights arguments will not persuade those who do not accept the underlying ethical principles. Perhaps a simple but compelling case for vegetarianism can be made on the basis of premises that nearly everyone is likely to accept, such as the idea that it is wrong to cause unnecessary suffering, or that it is wrong to kill animals when using plants will serve our purposes just as well (Curnutt 1997; Engel 2000; Tardiff 1996). In any event, one may be tempted to assume that, if raising animals for meat is a bad thing (because, for example, it inflicts a great deal of unnecessary suffering and death), then it must be morally incumbent upon everyone (at least, upon everyone who can thrive without eating meat) to become vegetarian. But does this follow? If I abstain from eating meat, will any animals really be saved from suffering and death? It may be that the market for factory-farmed animal bodies is not sensitive enough to register the difference in demand made by a single consumer. If that is the case, why should I bother to abstain from eating meat, even if I agree that the meat industry is evil, since my abstention will apparently have no effect? (The same question can be asked with regard to abstaining from milk, cheese, and eggs, production of which almost inevitably results in exploitation and death for the female animals used and the male animals discarded.)

One response might be that, even if it takes a fairly large increase in demand to affect the number of, say, chickens that are raised for slaughter, there must be some threshold at which the purchase of one more chicken will tip the balance and result in many more chickens being raised for slaughter. If I purchase that particular chicken, I bring about serious harm. Even if the probability of my purchasing the chicken that tips the balance is small, by purchasing *any* chicken I do something the expected outcome of which (a serious harm multiplied by the probability of bringing about that harm) is not negligible (Almeida and

Bernstein 2000; Matheny 2002). But the issue is complicated; the numerous market factors that affect the relation between individual purchases and meat production may call the threshold argument into question (Chartier 2006).

Another response might be that, if I belong to a group of people (even a loosely structured group of consumers) who *could* act collectively to reduce the evils of factory farming but fail to do so, I bear partial moral responsibility for those evils. I cannot excuse myself from blame by saying that on my own I cannot make a difference, particularly if I have done nothing to try to persuade other members of the group to act (Hudson 1993).

There is yet another way to look at the matter, and that involves the idea of virtue. Few of us would maintain, for example, that it would be acceptable to join a gang of racist bullies even if the gang's activities (throwing rocks through windows at night, taunting children on their way to school) would provide us with excitement and we were convinced that our participation or abstention would not affect the number or severity of the incidents. Similarly, whether or not I believe that my eating meat will have any direct effect on the treatment of animals, I ought not to do it, because eating meat displays a disregard for their suffering and death and so is not the sort of thing that a virtuous person would do (Nobis 2002; Shafer-Landau 1994). Further, virtuous behaviour (in this case, being vegetarian) may well influence others to give up meat, people whose example will in turn influence others and thus in the long run have some real effect on animal welfare.

But is the notion of virtuous behaviour misplaced in this regard? Why should we extend it beyond human society? After all, it is often said, nature is "red in tooth and claw", an arena where "the law of the jungle" prevails. When we kill and eat animals we are only doing what they themselves do. Why should we extend to animals treatment that they do not extend to others? One problem with this line of reasoning is that not all animals hunt, kill, and eat other animals. Many are herbivores. In fact, most of the animals we hunt, eat, and experiment on do not kill and eat other animals. If we were to apply a rule that says our treatment of animals should depend on how they themselves act, then it would sometimes be acceptable for us to kill dogs, cats, lions, or eagles, but it would hardly ever be all right to kill cattle, rabbits, deer, or baboons.

We often speak of "animals", as if they were all members of a single species, thus ignoring the innumerable differences in behaviour among non-human creatures. When someone is behaving in a particularly anti-social manner, we speak of the person acting "like an animal" or being "brutish" or "beastly". Yet human beings outdo all other creatures in terms of cruelty and unnecessary aggression against members of their own and other species. Can it be that in attributing "beastly" behaviour to non-human animals we are projecting the dark side of our own natures onto convenient scapegoats (Mason 1993; Midgley 1973)?

## Feminism and Vegetarianism

Vegetarianism has become a bone of contention among feminists. We have seen in the previous chapter that the ethic of care articulated by Nel Noddings excludes animals from the moral community. Noddings (1984, 1991) justifies meat-eating on the grounds that we have no obligation of caring toward animals in general except to see that we inflict as little pain as possible on them, in particular when we raise them and kill them for food. In addition she believes that, if we all became vegetarian, there would not be enough resources to support the whole human and animal population, contrary to the pro-vegetarian claim that there would be more food resources for humans and more habitat for wild animals. Noddings' position has drawn fire from feminists like Josephine Donovan (1990, 1991), who accuses her of speciesism.

The most sustained attack on meat-eating, however, has come from eco-feminist philosopher Carol Adams, author of *The Sexual Politics of Meat* and *Neither Man nor Beast*. Adams insists that the very word "meat" attests to the ideological hegemony of an animal-consuming culture. It is a term that, like "water", denotes a mass of something; meat remains meat regardless of the amount. It has no individuality and obscures the fact that what is consumed was once a unique living creature. Behind every meal of meat, says Adams, is an absence: the death of the animal that has now been transformed from some*one* into some-*thing* (e.g., the idea of a living pig has been banished, to be replaced by a consumable object called "pork"). The function of what she calls the "absent referent" is to disconnect the act of eating meat from awareness of the animal and its suffering.

As an eco-feminist, Adams stresses the way in which, historically, the

Behind every meal is an absence: the death of the animal whose place the meat takes.... The function of the absent referent is to keep our "meat" separated from any idea that she or he was once an animal, to keep the "moo" or "cluck" or "baa" away from the meat, to keep some*thing* from being seen as having been some*one*. Once the existence of meat is disconnected from the existence of an animal who was killed to become that "meat", meat becomes unanchored by its original referent (the animal), becoming instead a free-floating image, used often to reflect women's status as well as animals'.
— Carol J. Adams, *The Sexual Politics of Meat*, p. 14

essence of being human has been identified with white Euro-American maleness and opposed to what is seen as *other*: other races, other species, the other sex, all of which have tended to be identified with the world of nature, not culture. Although modern feminists have sought to demonstrate that women are, equally with men, representatives of culture, in general they have not challenged the pernicious equation of animals with otherness, says Adams, so that for most feminists (but not eco-feminists) animals continue to be viewed as objects to be exploited.

Adams details the ways in which meat-eating has been identified with masculinity, not only in Western cultures but around the world. Vegetables and other non-meat items, on the other hand, have typically been seen as women's food. Adams notes how in the feminist movement of the nineteenth century and early twentieth century there was often an explicit link made between vegetarianism and the liberation of women. She devotes a chapter in *The Sexual Politics of Meat* to the significance of the fact that Frankenstein's monster in Mary Shelley's 1818 novel is vegetarian. By including animals within the scope of its moral concern, the creature's rejection of meat challenges the barrier of *us* and *them* that separates humans and animals and simultaneously symbolizes the creature's own desire to be admitted into human society.

As well as meat's being seen to be men's food, animals are often presented culturally in sexualized (female) ways and women's bodies are often presented as a form of meat. This linkage is evident today in many images confronting us in everyday life—in advertising, in cartoons, in posters, on menus (Adams 2004). Hunting magazines commonly link the hunt with sex, and animals with women (Kalof, Fitzgerald, and Baralt 2004).

The idea that feminists should advocate vegetarianism has been challenged by Kathryn Paxton George (2000). George maintains that arguments for universal vegetarianism, particularly in its vegan form (that is, a meatless diet without eggs or dairy products), tacitly assume male physiology to be the human norm. She claims that requiring girls and women to be strict vegetarians would typically mean imposing an inadequate diet on them, given the specific nutritional requirements of human females. There are also many males for whom a strict vegetarian diet is unsuitable, says George. Strict vegetarianism is a viable ideal only for well-off adult males (and for healthy, well-off, younger adult females who do not bear children) living in technologically advanced societies. It is normally only this minority who have the physiological capacity, the education, and the access to the necessary food sources (including vitamin and mineral supplements) to lead healthy lives on a strict vegetarian diet.

George is prepared to say, for the sake of argument, that animals have *prima facie* rights but argues that, even so, the eating of meat by those who need it for their health is condoned by Regan's liberty principle (which says that, provided all those involved are treated with respect and assuming that no special considerations obtain, any innocent individual has the right to act to avoid being made worse off, even if doing so harms other innocents). Indeed, Regan and other pro-vegetarian philosophers do excuse from the requirement to be vegetarian those who must consume meat to stay healthy. George, however, says that *excusing* such people (the majority of people, in her opinion) from an ethical ideal is unsatisfactory because it suggests that these people are a moral underclass, physiologically incapable of doing what is right. Rather, she says, we must reject the notion that one type of diet can embody the ethical standard for all individuals.

George's position has been vigorously disputed by Evelyn Pluhar (1992, 1993), who denies the assertion that most people's health would suffer on a vegetarian diet. Much of the disagreement between George and Pluhar has to do with the scientific evidence about human nutrition; readers who are interested in the details should consult their writings. Pluhar also disputes George's contention that Regan's rights view will frequently condone the eating of meat. If the liberty principle is to be interpreted in a manner that is consistent with the idea that all subjects-of-a-life have equal inherent value, says Pluhar, then we cannot prevent ourselves being made worse off by killing and consuming our fellow subjects-of-a-life. Unless we assume that subjects-of-a-life have the right to their own bodies, one person would have the right to kill another person for his or her heart if it were needed for the first person's survival. That our fellow subjects-of-a-life, having the same inherent value that we do, have the same right to their own bodies that we have to ours is a "special consideration" that prevents our invoking the liberty principle to justify killing them. Pluhar notes that Regan's view does not preclude us from consuming eggs and dairy products so long as this involves no animals (female or male) being treated without respect—a condition that is not easily met these days.

Cora Diamond (1978) thinks that the sorts of arguments advanced by Singer and Regan are fundamentally misconceived—not because we should not be vegetarian but because a case that rests on the capacities and interests of animals is not compelling. It is not mainly on the basis of the biological capacities and attendant interests of other human beings that we are inclined to refrain from eating them; it is in the first place because they are individuals with whom we share a common life. It is in the context of our lived relations with other people that we evaluate our proper responses to their joys and sufferings. Similarly, suggests Diamond, when we think of animals as fellow creatures, as companions on life's journey, we shall be more likely to respond to them with pity (i.e., compassion) and less likely to treat them as consumable objects.

## Sport Hunting

For much of human existence, people hunted wild animals in order to provide themselves with food and with materials with which to clothe and shelter themselves. Today the materials required for food, clothing, and shelter are for the overwhelming part obtained from other sources, either from non-animal sources or from animals raised on farms. Nevertheless, a significant minority of the population in industrialized nations continues to hunt. It has been estimated that the animals killed by hunters in the United States every year include 50 million doves, 25 million rabbits and squirrels, 25 million quail, 20 million pheasant, 10 million ducks, 4 million deer, 2 million geese, 150,000 elk, and more than 20,000 black bears (Swan 1995).

As hunting's role in the economy and culture of society has diminished, it has became more controversial (Dizard 1994; McLeod 2007). Despite the fact that most people are happy to eat meat from farmed animals, many of these same people—not just advocates of animal liberation—disapprove of the killing of wild animals. Hunters typically come from small-town or rural backgrounds and often view opponents of hunting as effete city dwellers who are out of touch with nature. In his treatise on the history of hunting, Matt Cartmill (1993) notes an interesting fact in this regard: that hunters generally consider Walt Disney's *Bambi* to be the most powerful piece of anti-hunting propaganda ever produced, a film that, in their opinion, has presented generations of children with a false and sentimentalized view of wild animals.

Those who hunt do so from a variety of motives. In particular, two sorts of hunting stand out as special candidates for philosophical debate: subsistence hunting and "sport" hunting that is done from an avowed love of nature. Subsistence hunting involves killing wild animals not to supplement the food bought at the supermarket but as a central element in one's survival and way of life; in the modern world subsistence hunting is normally part and parcel of maintaining a traditional Aboriginal culture. Subsistence hunting by the Inuit (Eskimos) will be discussed shortly. Sport hunting is done not in order that the hunter may survive but either for recreation or, according to some of its proponents, to provide the hunter with an intimate and even spiritual connection with the natural world.

As with the issue of using animals for food, it makes a difference whether a liberationist adopts a rights or a utilitarian perspective on sport hunting (Wade 1990). The rights position on sport hunting is clear. While everyone has the right of self-defence (you need not let yourself be mauled to death by a grizzly), hunting an animal for sport is a violation of the animal's basic right not to be harmed by moral agents.

On the other hand, those who defend hunting often do so on utilitarian grounds of aggregate benefit to humans and animals. Hunting, it is said, not only brings pleasure to hunters but spares animals the drawn-out and painful deaths they would otherwise likely suffer from hunger, disease, or natural predation; and where natural predators are scarce, hunters function to maintain ecologically healthy population levels among animal species. A problem with the claim that hunting is good for ecosystems is that hunters typically aim to kill healthy adult members of, say, a deer population, while animal predators usually take the least fit members. However, it has been asserted that to the extent that hunters do enhance ecological values, they do what is right (List 1997). Robert Loftin (1984) says that the sport hunter has a stake in the preservation of wildlife habitats and that lobbying by the hunting community toward this end benefits not only those species that are hunted but many more that are not hunted. Sport hunting can be justified on utilitarian grounds, he says, because, among other things, it results in one animal being replaced with another.

Ann Causey (1989) rejects utilitarian assessments as missing the heart of the matter. Hunting, she claims, is a deep-seated human instinct that harks back to our palaeolithic ancestors. As such, the desire of hunters to kill is morally neutral. However, because violent death is an intrinsic part of nature, the hunter's desire to participate in this aspect of the world can be valuable. Senseless killing or hunting done merely to obtain trophies is morally offensive; on the other hand, those hunters whose primary motive is the spiritual enrichment that comes from immersing themselves in natural processes are engaged in a morally legitimate activity.

In making her argument, Causey is following in the footsteps of Spanish philosopher José Ortega y Gasset (1883-1955), whose *Meditations on Hunting* is the classic defence of hunting as a spiritual activity. According to Ortega, the primary goal of the true sport hunter is not to kill an animal for consumption or sale. The primary goal of the sport hunter lies in the activity of hunting itself. Hence the sport hunter is not interested in the death as such of the animal hunted; yet, paradoxically, killing is an essential aim of this hunt. This is because the whole activity of hunting is predicated on striving to take the animal's life; it is a battle of cunning and physical skill between hunter and hunted, with the life of the hunted at stake. Alternatives, such as pursuing animals with a camera in order to bring home photographs, miss the point. Without the striving to kill, hunting is a charade, devoid of its true significance. This is what Ortega (1972, pp. 110-11) means when he says, "To sum up, one does not hunt in order to kill; on the contrary, one kills in order to have hunted."

But why hunt? For Ortega, the answer to this question has to do with our very roots as human beings. Through the activity of hunting, modern man (the great majority of hunters are men) escapes from the routines and burdens of civilization and becomes temporarily like his palaeolithic ancestors, immersed in the natural world. The sport hunter becomes again like an animal himself. He hunts his prey through achieving an understanding of its way of thinking and being, and in this there is ideally a mystical union with the animal hunted. Hunting is a kind of religious rite in which the hunter is submerged in the mysteries of nature, of life and death. Despite this re-emergence of the hunter's animal nature, however, the hunter remains superior to the prey. There is, Ortega maintains, a hierarchy of species in nature; life is marked by conflict and every kind of creature is in a relationship of superiority or

To the sportsman the death of the game is not what interests him; that is not his purpose. What interests him is everything that he had to do to achieve that death — that is, the hunt.... To sum up, one does not hunt in order to kill; on the contrary, one kills in order to have hunted.
—José Ortega y Gasset, *Meditations on Hunting*, pp. 110-11

inferiority with regard to every other kind. Hunting in its essence involves a member of a superior species taking possession of a member of an inferior species.

Ortega's defence of hunting as an activity that can give the hunter a profound and intimate sense of connection with the natural world is echoed by many pro-hunting writers, including environmental philosopher Holmes Rolston III (1988). Similarly, Theodore Vitali (1990) defends sport hunting as an exercise in predatory skills that brings pleasure to the hunter and generally enhances ecosystems, which function efficiently through the competitive taking of life. (More will be said on the subject of animals and ecosystems in Chapter 6.) According to Vitali, the pleasure that the good hunter seeks is not pleasure in the death as such of the animal, which would be morally "troublesome", but pleasure in the exercise of predatory skills. At the same time, like Ortega, he stresses that the act of killing is essential to the activity of hunting. Predation involves killing and only by killing can a person test his or her skills as a predator. Hunting with a camera or with paint pellets is not really hunting, since in neither case does one achieve the "definitiveness" and "radical completeness" that killing brings to predatory activity.

While not engaging directly in the debates of philosophers, James Swan (1995) emphasizes that for those he calls "nature hunters" hunting is a quasi-religious experience. Urban civilization divorces us from nature and from our hunting instinct. By contrast, the nature hunter feels a deep reverence for the natural environment; he feels respect and even love for the animals he kills, says Swan. The act of killing can be a "peak" experience, involving intense emotional excitement and a confrontation with the most profound issues of life and death. Adopting a virtue-ethics perspective, some have argued that, insofar as hunters unflinchingly confront the inevitability of death and take responsibility for their part in the cycle of nature, hunting promotes *eudaimonia*, or human flourishing (Jensen 2001; Tantillo 2001).

Those who know their political philosophy may perceive a disturbing likeness between the picture of the world painted by Ortega and his sympathizers and the picture painted by fascist ideologues. Nature, according to fascism, is an arena of eternal conflict where one must vanquish others or be vanquished; only by recognizing that we are beasts of prey and by immersing ourselves in the struggle for survival can we overcome the alienating and debilitating effects of modern civilization, with its misguided notions of equality and individual rights, and achieve a mystical union with the forces of nature.

The claim that human beings are natural predators who have a hunting instinct is questionable (Cartmill 1993; Cohn 1999; Mason 1993; Moriarty and Woods 1997; Preece 1999). If, for the sake of argument, we accept the claim, we might want to say that it is surely better to manifest our predatory instincts by means of aggression against animals rather than by means of aggression against people. Hunting, then, might be seen as an invaluable outlet for urges that are arguably necessary for psychological health but would prove mutually destructive if expressed in conflict among humans. Yet Cartmill finds the equation of reverence or love with killing—what he calls the "murderous amorousness" of some hunters—not just disturbing but pathological. He finds in the imagery of sport hunting and in some of the feelings expressed by hunters—including a false and contemptuous affection for the victim and a refusal to think of the victim as an individual—a symbolic attack on women, in which hunting is akin to rape. This conclusion is also drawn by eco-feminist Marti Kheel (1995).

Ortega and others admit to feeling ambivalent about the rightness of killing the animals they hunt. For his part, Ortega attributes this ambivalence to the fact that we humans see ourselves as emerging from animality (at once transcending that state and yet connected with it) and to a general confusion about the norms that ought to govern our relations to other beings, including those in our environment, particularly when it comes to the matter of death.

Most hunters are not so philosophical in reflecting on their activities. Opponents of hunting are sceptical about the claims that killing is necessary in order to exercise the skills involved in hunting and that hunters take little joy in the actual killing of animals (Pluhar 1991; J. Williams 1995). In defence of sport hunters it can be said that many of the more thoughtful among them at least sound sincere in their professions of respect and admiration for animals and of feeling guilt at inflicting suffering and death. Then again, such guilt could be expunged, the hunting experience intensified, and the confrontation with death made all the more meaningful if hunters were to restrict themselves voluntarily to *hunting each other*. As it is, many adhere to a code of ethics

It is not that "romance" connotes only sex when applied to heterosexual relations and connotes only power when applied to hunting. Rather, hunting and predatory heterosexuality are instances of romance because each is simultaneously sexual and an expression of power.
—Brian Luke, *Brutal*, p. 84

that enjoins them, among other things, to kill their prey as quickly and painlessly as possible and to take no more animals than they intend to use. Brian Luke (1997) argues that this "Sportsman's Code" implies both a recognition of the intrinsic value of individual animals and a personal responsibility to minimize one's imposition of suffering on them. But the paradox, he says, is that these non-anthropocentric values can best be realized by not hunting animals at all.

Sport fishing, or angling, can be said to be a form of hunting but it has received comparatively little attention from philosophers. This is probably because there is considerable doubt that fish qualify as sub-jects-of-a-life under a Regan-type rights view and because their capac-ity for suffering is not obvious to most people. The analogical argument is somewhat harder to apply to a fish than to a mammal, a bird, or a rep-tile. In particular, fish do not emit shrieks or moans when hooked or when hauled out of water. Still, at least one writer (de Leeuw 1996) argues that there is reason to believe that angling imposes significant and needless suffering on fish, suffering that, because it is intrinsic to the pleasure taken by anglers in hooking fish, playing with them, and landing them, probably cannot be justified even according to the ethical code of hunters.

## Subsistence Hunting: The Case of the Inuit

Most of those liberationist philosophers and activists who oppose sport hunting will say that a stronger argument can be made in favour of sub-sistence hunting. The Inuit of Canada's eastern Arctic provide a case study in the issue of subsistence hunting and the impact thereon of modern technology and economy.

The hunting that the Inuit do is not recreational. It is no weekend outing. During the long, dark Arctic winter, when the sun is rarely to be seen and the temperature may hover around -35° Celsius, hunters spend hours travelling by snowmobile to areas of offshore ice to look for breathing holes used by seals. Then they stand nearly motionless above active holes, often for hours and often without success, waiting for the appearance of their prey. Ortega's maxim that "one does not hunt in order to kill; on the contrary, one kills in order to have hunted" has little relevance here. Traditionally the Inuit hunt to kill and thereby to survive.

Hunting animals has always been not simply the means by which the

Inuit have provided themselves with food, but a central aspect of their culture. The hunt has been the core around which the Inuit have organized their lives. In recent decades, however, the technology and the economy of the industrialized world have significantly intruded into these lives. Modern houses, electricity, radio, snowmobiles, motorboats, rifles, and many other modern tools and artifacts are evident, along with the capitalist market. Some critics of the hunt say that these changes have effectively destroyed the traditional subsistence economy and with it the moral legitimacy of hunting as a necessary activity. Today's Inuit hunt for profit and are part of the fur industry, they say.

In his study of modern Inuit hunting and the controversy surrounding it, George Wenzel (1991) charges that such critics have been misled by their focus on technological artifacts like snowmobiles (which have replaced dog teams) and rifles (which have largely replaced harpoons). They have failed to look at the social context of the use of these tools. Because of resettlement of Inuit by the Canadian government in the 1950s, hunters today must traverse great distances and snowmobiles are a necessity; in turn, the sale of some sealskins is necessary in order to bring in the money required to buy and maintain the snowmobiles and other tools. While the Inuit have adopted modern technology, what remains largely intact, says Wenzel, is the web of Inuit social and cultural relations, organized around the hunt. Without the hunt, the traditional way of life would disappear. He concludes that the campaign to stop seal hunting is myopic and morally flawed.

Wenzel makes a good case for regarding modern Inuit hunting as a continuation of a traditional way of life using other means, a case that should give pause to thoughtful anti-hunt activists. In fact, many activists who oppose sealing by non-Natives (in particular, the Newfoundland seal hunt) are prepared to recognize the legitimacy of subsistence hunting by Native people. In one important sense, however, Wenzel's argument may be said to beg the question. Although he notes the high moral status accorded animals in traditional Inuit culture, Wenzel fails to consider seriously the idea that the moral worth of individual animals may make present-day hunting of them wrong even in the light of other considerations. As a result he assumes what requires to be demonstrated: that the moral legitimacy of "harvesting" seals and caribou rests solely on the questions of cultural tradition and ecological sustainability. Wenzel is not alone in focusing exclusively on these criteria. Controversy has also arisen over the hunting of bowhead whales by Baffin Island Inuit. The public debate has centred not on the moral status of the whale but on the sustainability of this endangered species and on the Inuit's claim that hunting the whale is a matter of cultural sovereignty.

Wenzel notes that in traditional Inuit culture animals are viewed as forming a single moral community with human beings, all members having reciprocal rights and obligations. Animals are believed to be sentient and even intelligent beings who are aware of the thoughts and intentions of hunters. Hunted animals willingly sacrifice themselves to those human beings who have the right attitude. If they are to be successful, hunters must approach animals with an attitude of respect, that is, with appreciation for an animal's generosity in allowing itself to be used, and with the intent of using the animal's body as fully as possible for food and of sharing it with other members of the hunter's community.

This attitude of respect for animals is common in Aboriginal cultures. It differs in its implications from the kind of respect inherent in the animal-rights position in that it allows and even encourages the killing and consumption of wild animals. Nonetheless, these two versions of the concept of respect share something fundamental: each admonishes us to treat animals as ends in themselves, never simply as means. If animals really do give their consent to being killed and consumed, then it is possible for humans to kill and consume them without treating them simply as means.

Human beings do not normally give consent to being killed and consumed by other people. It is unlikely that Wenzel would defend any present-day hunting and killing of humans, even if some instance of this could be shown to support the continuation of a traditional cannibal culture and not to deplete the long-term supply of harvestable humans. Given that present-day members of a traditional cannibal culture could make their living by other means, few observers would claim they ought to be allowed to perpetuate their age-old subsistence culture.

Taking issue with Wenzel's implicit double standard, Wendy Donner (1997) argues that if we are going to say that individual human beings matter, and not just the human species as a whole, then consistency demands we say that individual animals matter, and that it is wrong to kill any animal except for important purposes: to satisfy basic needs for

Inuit do not segregate the qualities enjoyed by human beings from those enjoyed by animals. Animals share with humans a common state of being that includes kinship and family relations, sentience, and intelligence. The rights and obligations that pertain among people extend to other members of the natural world. People, seals, polar bear, birds, and caribou are joined in a single community in which animals give men food and receive acknowledgement and revival.
— George Wenzel, *Animal Rights, Human Rights*, pp. 60-61

food, clothing, and shelter. Donner is willing to go along with Wenzel's contention that the Inuit must sell some furs in order to acquire the money necessary to buy and maintain hunting equipment. But she insists that we cannot uncritically accept that every new element incorporated into the Inuit's way of life is consistent with maintenance of their traditions. To the extent that the Inuit do in fact depart from their traditional way of life, says Donner, they lose the moral advantage in the hunting debate.

Now, few would hold that satisfying basic needs always justifies inflicting suffering or death on others. Our imaginary modern cannibals can satisfy their basic needs by hunting and killing other people, yet few of us would say they would be justified in continuing their traditional method of making a living. The reason is that, although their basic needs can be satisfied by hunting other people, modern cannibals have no need to hunt people. One way or another they can feed, clothe, and shelter themselves by alternative methods and, morally speaking, this would seem to make all the difference.

Do the Inuit need to hunt in order to survive? The answer to this question is not obvious, since it is not obvious what is entailed by "survival". Even if abandonment of the hunt meant that their traditional culture would not survive, on an individual level modern Inuit can, at least in principle, survive by filling any of the roles for people in industrial society. Especially now that the eastern Canadian Arctic has become the political territory of Nunavut ("our land" in the Inuktitut language), more Inuit are directly participating in the economic and organizational processes of the modern world. And where a wage-paying job in the work force is not available, there is, as for other Canadian citizens in similar straits, government welfare. Indeed, many of Nunavut's residents today are on welfare, while rates for suicide, teen-age pregnancy, and the abuse of alcohol, drugs, and other substances are far above national averages.

Can Regan's worse-off principle be invoked to justify continuance of the hunt? Supporters of the hunt argue that anti-fur campaigns have had devastating effects on Aboriginal communities (Barber 1997). Is the harm that befalls individual Inuit with the ending of the hunt and the hunting way of life greater than the harm to individual seals of losing their lives? And do we take into account those Inuit not yet born who will have lost their ancestors' culture? If the hunt ends, new generations of

Inuit will grow up for whom the old ways will be just stories in history books and museums. They will become astrophysicists and social workers and check-out clerks, watch basketball and soap operas on television while eating prepackaged dinners from the suburbs of Toronto, and look forward to winter vacations in Trinidad or Morocco or on the far side of the moon. Will they be better off or worse off than if they had been seal hunters — and by how much?

### Hunters and Supermarket Vegetarians

It should also be noted that Regan's miniride principle has been invoked by one hunter and writer in defence of his own hunting of elk for food. Ted Kerasote (1993) points to the many wild animals killed in crop production in order to supply food to what he calls "supermarket vegetarians". He reasons that because supplying himself with food by hunting results in fewer animal deaths, such hunting is preferable to adopting a vegetarian diet.

Kerasote's argument is certainly food for thought. At least two issues arise from it. First, there is the matter of intentional infliction of harm versus harm that is the unintentional but foreseeable side effect of one's actions. A utilitarian is likely to see no moral difference between the two, since utilitarianism holds that it is consequences that count and not intentions. Hence a utilitarian must give Kerasote's less-harm argument serious consideration. On the other hand, a deontologist, who focuses on rights and duties, may well hold that the intentional infliction of harm (in this case, the intentional killing of elk or other animals for food) is worse than the unintentional deaths that result from an action (growing and harvesting plants) that in itself is benign.

A second issue that arises from Kerasote's argument is whether hunting for one's food is practicable on a large scale. There are now six-and-counting billion human beings on the planet. It is unlikely that all or most of these people could feed themselves largely by hunting, and the attempt to do so might well result in the extermination of many animal species. On the large scale, then, the choice would seem to be between supermarket vegetarianism and supermarket meat-eating, that is, between a diet that depends on commercial agriculture but not on meat and a diet that depends on commercial agriculture including the farming of animals.

## Conclusion

It may appear that philosophers are deeply divided on the issue of vegetarianism, and so they are—up to a point. With the important exception of most contractarians, there is something of a consensus that little
of the suffering inflicted on animals raised for meat can be justified. In
particular (contractarians aside again), few are prepared to defend the
factory-farming of animals. The implication is that, at a minimum,
most of the meat industry ought to be drastically reformed or outright
abolished. Nevertheless, even pro-liberation philosophers typically concede that meat-eating is acceptable in some circumstances. A rights
view, in principle, places stricter limitations on meat-eating than does a
utilitarian view, though just what the practical implications of these two
views are is a matter of debate.

Although feminist philosophers in general have not made the issue
of vegetarianism central to their concerns, a few have. Yet those who
have are divided in their opinions. Against vegetarianism, it has been
maintained that an ethic of care implies only that we ought not to inflict
unnecessary suffering on animals when raising them for food; it has
also been claimed that not everyone can maintain good health on a vegetarian diet and that, as an ethical ideal, vegetarianism is generally not
suitable for girls and women—a conclusion that has been disputed by
some other feminists. Many eco-feminists equate meat-eating with the
ideology of male dominance in society and see vegetarianism as an integral part of the struggle for women's liberation.

Defenders of sport hunting often point to its alleged environmental
benefits: in the modern world hunters act as substitutes for natural
predators, limiting the growth of prey populations; hunters also lobby
for the maintenance and enhancement of wilderness areas, which would
otherwise likely be destroyed by the spread of urban areas and industrial activity. More than this, however, many defenders of sport hunting
see it as an important means by which people are able to rediscover
themselves as natural beings, confronting the mysteries of life and death
in what may be felt as a profound, even religious, experience. Critics
attack sport hunting from various angles: it violates the rights of animals; it is a pathological expression of aggression, often with anti-
female overtones; its beneficial aspects can be achieved by other means,
such as wildlife photography; the intrinsic value of animals, implicitly

recognized by the hunter's code of ethics, can only really be respected by refraining from hunting.

Subsistence hunting has generally seemed morally less problematic than sport hunting, and philosophers have devoted less attention to it. A prime issue here has been whether the technology and economy of the modern world has intruded into traditional cultures to such an extent as to undermine the moral legitimacy of hunting by members of these communities. While critics claim that even Aboriginal people now hunt largely for commercial reasons, a case can be made that people like the Inuit have adopted modern methods in order to maintain their traditional social relations. Even so, the question remains: if animals have intrinsic value and should be treated with respect (as Aboriginal people believe), is hunting them acceptable when one could adopt a different way of life and not hunt?

# CHAPTER FIVE

# IS IT WRONG TO USE ANIMALS FOR SCIENTIFIC RESEARCH?

Norman led Jennie into the laboratory and had her sit on a metal table near the windows. She sat there quietly while Norman and Peter fitted her with a helmet containing electrical monitors and couplings for attaching the helmet to other devices. She was watching the people walking across the lawn outside the windows. When they had finished, she had to lie down while the helmet was secured to a large machine and her arms and legs were secured to the table. All she could see now was the ceiling. Peter and Norman hooked up the monitoring devices in the helmet to a large console, checked out their equipment, and then turned it on. Jennie's head was given a tremendous blow by a piston that crashed into her helmet. She was knocked unconscious and stayed that way while Peter pried off her helmet. When she regained consciousness, she went into convulsions for five minutes. When the convulsions stopped, Peter and Norman ran some tests on her. She was blind now and could not control her arms sufficiently to grasp and carry to her mouth some food placed in her hands. Finally, she was wheeled into another room, where she was given an injection. Jennie died in less than a minute, and Norman and Peter began the work of decapitating her, describing the condition of her brain, and preparing slices of her brain tissue for microscopic analysis.

*S.F. Sapontzis*[1]

---

[1] S.F. Sapontzis, "On Justifying the Exploitation of Animals in Research", *The Journal of Medicine and Philosophy* 13 (1988), pp. 177-78.

Of course, says Steve Sapontzis, Jennie was not human; she was a squirrel monkey. To do such a test on a human being would be immoral. The question then is, what justifies using a monkey? In this chapter we turn our attention to the use of animals for scientific research. The arguments for and against the use of animals in scientific research to a considerable extent overlap those we have encountered in the debate about the use of animals for food, clothing, and sport, since much of what is at issue is the justifiability of subjecting animals to suffering or death for human purposes. What gives the issue of animal experimentation its distinct edge is, first, that the infliction of pain and injury is frequently a *desired* aspect of the activity and, second, that such treatment of animals is said to be a *necessary* condition for the relief of human suffering. This chapter also addresses another, recent, aspect of the use of animals in scientific research: genetic engineering. Here the issue is not just the infliction of suffering or death; rather, it has to do with re-creating the very nature of animals, the better to exploit them for human purposes.

Globally, about 115 million animals were used for research in 2005, according to a joint report by the Dr. Hadwen Trust and the British Union for the Abolition of Vivisection. Most of those used in research are rodents, but pigs, fish, dogs, cats, monkeys, chimpanzees, and others are also objects of experimentation. Animals are used for basic biomedical research, where the purpose is to gain original knowledge that does not necessarily have immediate application to the treatment of diseases. Animals are also used for the development and testing of drugs and for the testing of consumer goods (cosmetics, food additives, herbicides, pesticides, etc.). In addition, they are used for educational purposes, including dissection, surgery practice, and high-school science projects (Orlans 1993; Rollin 2006; Singer 2002).

Two types of experiments that have drawn particular public attention are the Draize test, in which cosmetics and other potentially hazardous products are tested on rabbits' eyes, and the LD50 (lethal dose 50 per cent) test, in which toxicity is measured by administering a substance to a group of animals and determining how much it takes to kill half of the group within fourteen days. Protest campaigns by activists have succeeded in reducing the frequency of these tests and the numbers of animals used (Singer 1998). Experiments that harm primates tend to arouse particularly strong emotions, as in the case of videotapes taken from a laboratory at the University of Pennsylvania in 1984 that showed lab personnel making fun of paralyzed baboons whose heads had been smashed by a hydraulic piston during experiments on head trauma — an incident that eventually sparked a major sit-in by protesters at offices of the National Institutes of Health and led to a minor fine being imposed on the university for violations of the Animal Welfare Act (Orlans et al. 1998).

"Vivisection", strictly speaking, refers to the dissection, or cutting up, of living animals for scientific research, though in a broader sense the term includes any painful or harmful treatment of living animals for scientific research. Much, but not all, animal experimentation falls under the heading of vivisection in the broader sense. The issue of vivisection has long provoked strong emotions on both sides (Rudacille 2000). Experimenters have often been portrayed as immoral monsters. The Victorian and Edwardian eras witnessed a notable anti-vivisection movement, one in which women played the major part (French 1975; Lansbury 1985; Rupke 1987; Ryder 1989; J. Turner 1980; Vyvyan 1969). Among them was British feminist Frances Cobbe, co-founder of what became the National Anti-Vivisection Society.

As noted in Chapter 2, Charles Darwin, while sickened by the thought of vivisection, refused to lend his support to the movement because he believed that experimentation on animals was necessary for the progress of science. Alfred Russel Wallace, who independently originated the theory of natural selection at about the same time Darwin did, decided that vivisection should be totally abolished. He reached this conclusion despite believing that no animals have the same highly developed capacity to experience pain that humans have. According to Wallace (1911), pain is not as prevalent in nature as we are likely to imagine, since the capacity to experience pain only develops in species to the degree that it is useful for the preservation of life. Nevertheless he insisted that vivisection was not to be condoned. This was because, in addition to whatever suffering it caused, vivisection produced callousness in the experimenters and more often than not was carried out for trivial reasons.

Most scientists, however, have not displayed Darwin's ambivalent attitude, much less Wallace's antipathy. Even today some scientists deny that animal experimentation raises any moral issues at all. Some still hold a neo-Cartesian view and refuse to use the word "suffering" because it implies that animals are conscious beings. In general, though, the scientific community has come to subscribe to what are called the "three Rs", three goals for the researcher concerned about animal welfare. These are (1) *replacement* of animals altogether by the use of alternative methods, (2) *reduction* in the numbers of animals used, by means of statistical techniques, and (3) *refinement* of experiments so as to cause less animal suffering (Mukerjee 1997; Rollin 2006). Even so, many scientists (e.g., Botting and Morrison 1997) insist that significant use of animals remains essential to scientific progress and that it is wishful thinking to imagine that animal experimentation now or in the foreseeable future can be completely replaced by in vitro ("test-tube") methods, by computer simulations, or by any of the other alternatives that are becoming available.

While there is evidence that many scientists are becoming more aware of the moral dimension of their research, there remains much resistance in the scientific community to engaging in dialogue with supporters of animal liberation (Bowd and Shapiro 1993; Orlans 1993). Liberationists are often dismissed as sentimental and irrational and are portrayed as being interested in hypothetical animal rights to the detriment of human rights (Baldwin 1993; Lansdell 1988; Pardes, West, and Pincus 1991). Thomas Gennarelli, who directed the experiments on baboons at the University of Pennsylvania's Head Trauma Research Center, refused to discuss the studies publicly because of the likelihood of stirring up what he called "all sorts of unnecessary fuss" (Orlans et al. 1998, p. 74). Two scientists at the University of California, Berkeley, have characterized an anti-vivisection rally on their campus as being attended by "a motley crew" of "frenzied fanatics"—whom journalists are said to have described as ranging from "purple-haired punks to violent vegetarians" (Nicoll and Russell 1990, p. 985).

The Berkeley scientists, co-founders of a pro-vivisection group called Coalition for Animals and Animal Research, conducted their own survey of some of the best-known books of pro-liberation philosophy. They found that the space devoted in this literature to the use of animals in research and teaching is out of all proportion to the number of animals "consumed" by humans in this way. In other words, while only a small percentage of the animals killed by humans are killed for purposes of research and teaching, the animal-liberation movement directs a great deal of its criticism at the use of animals in science. The two scientists' conclusion: the movement is fundamentally anti-science, anti-intellectual, and misanthropic. They describe its members as "latter-day Luddites", a reference to the craft workers in early nineteenth-century England who destroyed the new machinery that was threatening their traditional livelihoods — the scientists' implication being that those who are opposed to vivisection are opposed to science-based progress.

Surveys of public attitudes toward animal experimentation do not support a simple Luddite thesis. A combination of rational and emotional factors determines the attitudes of people on both sides of the issue. Although those who are anti-vivisection and pro-liberation tend to be more sceptical about the benefits of science than the general population, they also tend to be younger and better educated than their opponents; a high percentage of activists are employed in professional occupations. They are also more likely to be female than male (Galvin and Herzog 1992; Groves 1997; Guither 1998; Herzog 1993a, 1993b; Jasper and Nelkin 1992; Jerolmack 2003; Mukerjee 1997; Sperling 1988).

## Cohen's Case for Animal Experimentation

We begin our look at the philosophical literature with an oft-cited essay by Carl Cohen, "The Case for the Use of Animals in Biomedical Research". Cohen adamantly endorses the use of animals in biomedical research, and indeed urges that the use of animals be increased. He considers and rejects the idea that biomedical research involving animals is wrong either because it violates the rights of animals or because it causes them suffering. Invoking Kant, he maintains that animals cannot have rights because they are not moral agents. From this his principal conclusion follows: we cannot violate the rights of animals for the simple reason that they have no rights to violate. Like others (e.g., McCloskey 1987) who subscribe to the traditional view that only moral agents qualify for moral rights, Cohen maintains that our duty to respect human persons justifies, and even requires, our experimental use of animals. However, he adds, we do have an obligation to treat sentient animals "humanely".

Turning to utilitarian arguments, Cohen begins by saying that he finds Peter Singer's equation of speciesism with racism and sexism not only unsound but atrocious. Racism and sexism have no rational foundation; because human beings are moral agents, they have rights we must respect. By contrast, animals are not moral agents and therefore do not have the same moral standing. Cohen finds it offensive that anyone should claim that we owe the same moral regard to animals as to humans. He then makes a second point: even if, for the sake of argument, we were to grant Singer's claim that the interests of animals ought to be accorded equal consideration with the like interests of human beings, the use of animals for biomedical research would still be justified on utilitarian grounds, since the sum of benefits that result from this research is so very great.

Like others who defend the use of animals for experiments that involve pain or death, Cohen must confront the argument from marginal cases. How can we justify doing to an animal something that we would find morally repugnant if done to any human being possessing similar mental faculties? Singer (2002) asks researchers to consider whether they would be prepared to conduct their experiments on orphaned human infants or brain-damaged humans. David Sztybel (2006a) proposes that, in the name of ethical consistency, researchers might consider signing living wills, making themselves available as experimental subjects should they ever suffer mental debilitation.

The issue is one of kind. Humans are of such a kind that they may be the subject of experiments only with their voluntary consent. The choices they make freely must be respected. Animals are of such a kind that it is impossible for them, in principle, to give or withhold voluntary consent or to make a moral choice. What humans retain when disabled, animals have never had.
—Carl Cohen, "The Case for the Use of Animals in Biomedical Research", p. 866

Cohen rejects this sort of argument on the grounds that what counts in assessing the moral standing of any individual are not the capacities of that individual but the *kind* of being he or she is. Moral agency, he asserts, is natural or essential to the human kind. The free choices of moral agents ought to be respected; hence they may be subjected to experiments only with their consent. Those human beings who are not full moral agents are still to be considered members of the moral community precisely because they are members of humankind. Further, says Cohen, the fact that many animals may be said to exhibit desires and preferences, to care passionately for their young, to communicate or even to reason misses the crucial point, which is that animals cannot conduct themselves on the basis of moral judgements — they cannot discern and apply moral rules.

Against Cohen, James Rachels (1990) advocates "moral individualism", the idea that the proper treatment of an individual depends on his or her own characteristics and not on the group to which he or she belongs. Rachels offers the following thought experiment. Suppose there is an unusually intelligent chimpanzee, one who can read and speak English, who can converse about science, literature, and morals. Suppose this chimpanzee wishes to attend university. Would it make sense to refuse him admission to university on the grounds that normal chimpanzees cannot read? Rachels thinks that doing this—judging him not on the basis of his own qualities but on the basis of the qualities of others—would be not only unfair but irrational.

We might also ask whether we could justify subjecting an unusually intelligent animal—let's say a rat who could use a computer to write a philosophy textbook—to painful biomedical experiments and death by pointing out that normal members of her species are often subjected to such treatment with few qualms. Of course, it is hard to imagine that there could ever really be such an intelligent rat (though the prospects for genetic engineering may make us think twice on that score). The issue before us, however, is not the potential intelligence of rats but whether an individual's moral status depends on species membership.

## Is Species Membership Morally Relevant?

The very concept of species is untidy and controversial (Graft 1997; Waldau 2002). Since Darwin, biologists have generally abandoned the idea that every species has an immutable essence that distinguishes it from every other species. It cannot even be held without exception that a species is a group of individuals that can breed among themselves but cannot breed with members of other species to produce viable hybrids. There are cases where members of one species can breed with members of another species (for example, lions with tigers); there are other cases where recognized species contain subgroups that cannot interbreed. In Britain the herring gull and the lesser black-backed gull are two non-interbreeding species; yet they form the two ends of a chain of inter-breeding populations of gulls that circles the globe. Similarly, says Richard Dawkins (1993), living human beings and living chimpanzees form the two ends of a chain of individuals that extends back through time to common ancestors who lived sometime between five and seven million years ago. The idea of species, it might seem, is a shaky founda-tion on which to erect a defence of human interests.

One problem with the strategy of basing the treatment of individuals

If Darwin is correct, there are no absolute differ-ences between humans and the members of all other species.... Therefore, the fundamen-tal reality is best repre-sented by saying that the earth is populated by individuals who resemble one another, and who dif-fer from one another, in myriad ways, rather than by saying that the earth is populated by different *kinds* of beings. Moral individualism is a view that looks to individual similarities and differ-ences for moral justifica-tion, whereas human dignity emphasized the now-discredited idea that humans are of a special kind.

—James Rachels, *Created from Animals*, pp. 174-75

on the attributes of some or most other members of the class(es) to which they belong is that it opens the door to all sorts of absurdities (Nobis 2004). Should students who have failed their exams be given passing grades because most of their classmates have passed? Should human beings be treated like plants because most organisms are not sentient? Then there is the error of attributing to a class what can only belong to some of its individual members. A species is not an experiencing subject. It cannot feel, think, or be held morally accountable. If a species has value, that value derives not from possessing moral agency but from, say, its place in the web of life, or perhaps from the fact that its continued existence supports the existence of individuals who are moral agents. A human lacking moral agency cannot derive intrinsic value of the sort conferred by having moral agency simply from membership in the human species (McMahan 2005). The attempt to refute the argument from marginal cases by appealing to moral agency as a typical human capacity — what David Graham, with regard to Tibor Machan (2004), has dubbed "the argument from species normality" — is questionable, at best.

This is not to say that species membership is wholly irrelevant. Elizabeth Anderson (2004) has argued that species membership matters in that it bears on the question of just *which* set of rights an individual is entitled to. For example, the fact that chimpanzees or parrots may have the same facility for language acquisition as a mentally handicapped human does not mean they should be accorded the same right to be taught a language, since they do not have the same intrinsic interest in participating in human society, being normally able to flourish without such participation. The argument from marginal cases, says Anderson, is undermined by the illegitimacy of deducing that individuals who have the same capacities have the same rights.

Anderson's reasoning is not the same as Cohen's. She is not attributing elevated moral status to disabled humans on the basis of morally relevant capacities not possessed by them but possessed by other members of their species. She is not saying we should treat them as if they had those absent capacities. Instead, she is saying that the argument from marginal cases fails to capture the complexity of human and animal lives. Our treatment of disabled humans must take into account not just their intrinsic (non-relational) capacities but also what is required for them to live as members of a human community. In general, the ascription of rights to individuals, human or non-human, depends in part on their natural and social relations to moral agents (Gunnarsson 2008).

Daniel Dombrowski (2006) responds that the argument from marginal cases is perfectly consistent with recognition of the fact that the interests of an individual depend in part on species membership. What the argument inveighs against is the *unfair* treatment of individuals. It is not only the social relationships peculiar to humans that can entitle one to rights. Animals, like humans, have intrinsic capacities (like the ability to feel pain) that vindicate rights, something not negated by humans' having additional rights as participants in human society.

As Evelyn Pluhar (1995) sees it, we have an unacquired duty not to interfere with the freedom or well-being of others, including animals, unless they pose a threat to us. In addition, she says, we have acquired duties to those beings (human or non-human) whose existence or living conditions have resulted from our choices. Whatever acquired duties we have to various human beings are independent of genetic kinship. (If you have acquired duties to members of your family, this is because your lives are entwined and not because you are genetically related.) Having acquired duties to humans does not allow us to disregard the basic interests of non-humans. Similarly, in his examination of our obligations to companion animals, Keith Burgess-Jackson (1998) makes the point that our obligations to see to the welfare of those animals that we choose to bring into our lives are in addition to obligations that result from their intrinsic natures.

## Steinbock on the Significance of Human Suffering

If those who condone harming animals in scientific research are to avoid the charge of being speciesist, they must either present a convincing utilitarian case based on the consequences of such research, or show (not merely assert) that there are morally relevant differences between humans and animals that justify subordinating animal interests to human interests. Bonnie Steinbock (1978) believes that there are such morally relevant differences and that because of these differences the suffering of humans ought to count more than the suffering of animals.

While agreeing with Peter Singer that there is no justification for not taking into consideration the suffering of animals, Steinbock disagrees with his assertion that the suffering of any being ought to count equally with the like suffering of any other being. Mere sentience, she says, should not be sufficient for equal consideration of interests. Humans have certain capacities that animals lack, including the capacity for moral autonomy, the capacity to act from altruistic motivations, and the desire for self-respect. Humans cannot exercise these uniquely valuable capacities if they are severely afflicted by pain or disease. To live a fully human life, a human being must be free from significant suffering. Hence, concludes Steinbock, we are justified in making animals suffer if that is the only way to free humans from pain and disease. In short, then, human suffering is more deplorable than comparable animal suffering. Steinbock provides the rationale that is missing or merely hinted at in Cohen's essay: namely, that freedom from pain and disease is a necessary condition for the exercise of those unique capacities that make possible a fully human life.

Of course, pain and disease impede a rat or a monkey from exercising those physical and mental capacities that make possible a full rat life or a full monkey life. If that is so, why sacrifice a rat or monkey for the benefit of a human? Steinbock's argument rests on her judgement that the distinctive capacities of human beings make human lives more valuable than animal lives. What then of those disabled human beings who lack the distinctive human capacities—are they, like animals, suitable material for experiments designed to benefit normal humans? Steinbock attempts to meet the challenge of the argument from marginal cases by responding as follows. First, she says, animals can manage their lives very well without special care from us, whereas severely disabled humans cannot, and it seems worse to experiment on those who are dependent on us than on those who are not. Second, we identify more closely with the disabled human than with a monkey; we can imagine having been born mentally handicapped, whereas we cannot imagine having been born a monkey. Steinbock claims that even if this sense of identification points to no morally relevant difference between the human being and the animal, it is not wrong to extend special care to members of our own species, just as it is not racist to provide special care to members of our own race—provided we do not fail to carry out our basic obligations to all people regardless of race.

Is Steinbock's claim about dependent human beings consistent with her main thesis? Animals are commonly denied equal consideration with

I am willing to admit that my horror at the thought of experiments being performed on severely mentally incapacitated human beings in cases in which I would find it justifiable and preferable to perform the same experiments on non-human animals (capable of similar suffering) may not be a moral emotion. But it is certainly not wrong of us to extend special care to members of our own species, motivated by feelings of sympathy, protectiveness, etc.
– Bonnie Steinbock, "Speciesism and the Idea of Equality", p. 256

humans because animals typically have a lesser capacity for autonomous behaviour. Indeed, this is a key element of Steinbock's thesis about the moral weight we should attach to suffering. However, in those instances where animals exhibit a greater capacity for autonomous behaviour than some human beings, then on Steinbock's view their greater capacity also counts against their suffering being considered equally with similar human suffering. Either way, it seems, animals can't win.

What about her claim that it is acceptable to provide special care to members of our own species? The idea is that, so long as we do not fail to meet our basic moral obligations to anyone, human or non-human, then, when it comes to those instances where we must choose between individuals of similar faculties, we do no wrong if we favour humans. We might liken this to someone of Ukrainian background contributing to a medical fund for victims of the Chernobyl nuclear accident. Surely there is nothing wrong here with giving special consideration to others of one's own kind. As long as there are no morally relevant differences between individuals, and some of them can be spared pain, surely we may choose to spare whichever ones we like. However, now imagine a biomedical researcher who dislikes other humans but is fond of dogs. If a potentially valuable experiment requires cutting up either an unwilling dog or an unwilling human being of similar mental capacities, is the researcher doing anything wrong if she chooses to experiment on the human being? (See Cushing 2003.)

## Fox's Case for Animal Experimentation

In *The Case for Animal Experimentation*, Michael Allen Fox defines the moral community in a traditional way, arguing that its members must be autonomous beings who can function as rational moral agents. Because animals do not have the capacity to examine their own lives reflectively and to assess the quality of those lives, their lives have no intrinsic value. We are therefore under no obligation to refrain from using animals for our purposes. Such value as animals possess is instrumental only; in other words, all of their value derives from their use to us. As for the utilitarian defence of animals mounted by Peter Singer, this fails because it confines itself to consideration of the capacity for pleasure and pain and ignores those other attributes possessed by humans that give their lives a special value. Fox points out that Singer actually admits that human lives have a special value (recall Singer's views on the wrongness of killing self-aware beings); Fox doubts that this admission on Singer's part can be squared with utilitarianism.

Fox does not deny that animals have interests, but these interests, he says, are simple ones that do not have the moral significance of the interests possessed by moral agents. Hence we have no duty, in the strict sense of the term, to prevent animal suffering. Nevertheless, as independently developing creatures with characteristics that resemble to a greater or lesser degree those human characteristics we associate with having full moral status, animals are still proper objects of our moral concern. Hence we should refrain from treating them cruelly, we should provide for the natural needs of those in our care, and when we kill them we should do so as quickly and painlessly as possible.

What about marginal cases? According to Fox, our relations with infants should be guided by the fact that most of them are potentially fully autonomous beings. As for those humans who were autonomous but are now senile or otherwise incapacitated, and those who never have been and never will be autonomous, our actions should be guided by charity. Just as we can be said to have special obligations to members of our own families, so we can be said to have an obligation to extend preferential treatment to members of the human family.

Because Fox denies intrinsic value to animals and assesses their worth in terms of their use to us, his injunction to treat them humanely has little force whenever it can be shown that experimentation provides benefits to humans. An example of this is his judgement on the notorious "maternal deprivation" experiments of Harry Harlow. For many years Harlow, a psychologist at the University of Wisconsin, and his colleagues conducted experiments in which monkeys were separated from their mothers at birth and reared in total isolation, without even human contact (M.A. Fox 1986; Orlans et al. 1998; Singer 2002). Some monkeys were isolated for as long as twelve months before being introduced to the company of other monkeys. The experimental animals exhibited severe psychological problems, including fear of others, an inability to form affectionate bonds with others, and extreme passivity. Some baby monkeys in isolation were provided with a surrogate mother made of cloth or metal that would rock violently, or emit a jet of compressed air, or suddenly eject sharp brass spikes from its surface. Researchers also employed an alternative to these abusive surrogates: some female monkeys raised in isolation were impregnated so that they became mothers themselves; these mothers tended either to ignore their offspring or else to abuse or even kill them. Researchers invented various other experimental devices to produce psychopathology in their subjects, including what they called a "well of despair" and a "tunnel of terror". Despite describing Harlow's experiments as "nightmarish and regrettable", Fox says that in retrospect they can be morally justified by the usefulness of the information obtained.

## Fox's Case against Animal Experimentation

There is a surprising postscript to add to Fox's book. Not long after the publication of *The Case for Animal Experimentation*, its author publicly repudiated the main views expressed in it, now calling those views arrogant, complacent, and arbitrary. Fox (1987) attributes his former willingness to embrace a strongly anthropocentric position to a combination of factors. These include social conditioning and a philosophical training that emphasizes the application of abstract principles and argument for argument's sake, thus ignoring the important role that feeling and emotion should play in morality. In addition, there is the praise and approval that he received from members of the scientific community in the wake of the book's publication.

In particular, the new Fox draws our attention to the harm-avoidance principle, or "principle of non-maleficence", which says that we have an obligation to avoid harming the innocent. He now rejects the idea that experimentation that harms animals is justified if the benefits to humans (and/or other animals) "outweigh" the harm done to the animals experimented upon. Those scientists and others who accept this cost/benefit approach, he says, ignore the deeper question of whether it is morally acceptable to benefit from the harms we cause to other beings. In other words, to show that we would be worse off if we stopped animal experimentation is not to resolve the moral issue. Fox goes on to say that if we are not prepared to forgo the benefits we derive from animal experimentation, despite the moral argument against it, we ought at every opportunity to seek alternatives to such experimentation and perform only those sorts of experiments that *might* be morally justified. These include, in the first place, experiments that cause no harm, experiments that benefit the individual experimental animals, and experiments in which the animals are willing participants (such as language learning by apes or the training of dolphins).

Fox's new emphasis on the moral imperative of doing no harm to the innocent individual is in line with an animal-rights view but is likely to be challenged by utilitarians, even those sympathetic to animal liberation. For example, Peter Singer (2002), who is highly sceptical about the alleged benefits of vivisection and calls for an end to most of it, is not prepared to issue a blanket condemnation. After all, utilitarians may ask, what is so wrong about the cost/benefit approach? If much suffering, whether human or animal, can really be averted by subjecting some animals to a lesser amount of suffering, can it be right to opt for allowing the greater amount of suffering to occur?

## Scepticism about the Benefits of Animal Experimentation

It appears to be regarded as a truism by most supporters of animal experimentation that such research has had, and continues to have, far greater benefits than costs. In particular, thanks to animal experimentation there is much less suffering in the world than there would have been otherwise. The belief that a simple utilitarian calculation of this kind can be used to justify animal experimentation is challenged at length by Hugh LaFollette and Niall Shanks in *Brute Science*. LaFollette and Shanks argue that even if we hold that animals have considerably less moral worth than human beings do, it is doubtful that animal experimentation can be justified on the basis of its consequences. In making their argument, they point to three "moral asymmetries".

The first asymmetry has to do with acts versus omissions. It is widely (though not universally) held that it is worse to do evil than to fail to prevent evil. For example, it is worse to drown someone deliberately than to fail to rescue from drowning someone that you could have saved. In harming animals in their experiments, scientists deliberately bring about evil consequences, whereas refraining from doing these experiments would at worst mean failing to prevent some amount of human suffering. This suggests that, even if animals are presumed to be worth less than humans, the benefits to humans from experimentation must be substantially greater than the costs to animals if the experiments are to be morally acceptable.

The second asymmetry involves definite harms versus possible benefits. The harm inflicted on animals in experiments is definite. By contrast, at the time of doing the experiments it is merely possible, not definite, that beneficial consequences will result. This means it is difficult or impossible to quantify accurately the benefits to be derived from experiments.

The third asymmetry involves the creatures who suffer versus the creatures who benefit. The animals experimented on seldom benefit from whatever knowledge is gained. If there is any benefit, it is others — generally humans — who benefit. If we reject harming human beings solely for the benefit of other humans, it is not clear how we can justify harming non-humans solely for our benefit, even if we judge them to have less moral worth than we do.

But the problems involved in justifying animal experimentation in terms of beneficial consequences do not stop there, say LaFollette and Shanks. Animal models can sometimes be misleading. (See also Barnard and Kaufman 1997; Greek and Greek 2000.) We must factor into our calculations both the known and the possible costs of misleading experiments. LaFollette and Shanks claim, for example, that preoccupation with a misleading animal model delayed for many years the development of effective measures for preventing polio. Finally, and perhaps most importantly, we miscalculate if we place on the plus side of our scales all the benefits that research on animals has produced and will produce. The real question, after all, is what are the benefits that only animal research could produce. In other words, what is the increase, if any, in benefits relative to alternative programmes (those without animals)? There is no clear answer to this question. LaFollette and Shanks conclude that, while none of this shows that animal experimentation is worthless, it does show that the benefits are less than we are commonly led to believe and that an accounting of those benefits would be hard to give. Since animal experimentation involves significant moral costs, the onus is on those who wish to perpetuate the system to demonstrate clearly that its benefits exceed its costs. This they have failed to do.

The idea that animal experimentation is justified by its benefits for human beings is further undermined if we accept that we are confronted with the following dilemma. The closer a particular species of animal is to humans physiologically and/or psychologically, the more useful it is as an object of research where the idea is to use the animal to

An obvious paradox arises—the more a species is like us in its physiology, the more useful a model it is for human biomedical problems. But, precisely *because* a species resembles us biologically, the more likely it is that it experiences similar mental states. In short, the more justified the use of a species on scientific grounds, the less justified is its use on moral grounds.
—Harold Herzog, "Human Morality and Animal Research", p. 340

model human responses. Hence apes and monkeys are particularly useful as experimental models. For example, in their maternal-deprivation experiments Harry Harlow and his collaborators emphasized the psychological similarities between baby monkeys and baby humans, there being little difference between the two in terms of emotional and intellectual needs; they also pointed out that monkey mothers display the same sort of maternal affection as do human mothers. The dilemma for the responsible researcher is that the more closely an animal resembles humans, and thus the more useful it is in experiments where it would be unethical to use a human being, the more ethically questionable the use of that animal becomes. Ideally, what is wanted is an animal that resembles human beings very closely but whose use poses none of the ethical problems that using a human would pose. It is difficult to see how the researcher can have it both ways (LaFollette and Shanks 1996; Rachels 1990).

### Does the Rights View Rule Out Vivisection?

One way of avoiding this problem is simply to deny that any dilemma exists. Cohen, for instance, is prepared to admit that animals resemble human beings in many ways, physically and psychologically—including having emotions and perhaps an ability to reason—but finds all of that to be irrelevant. From his standpoint, it is only having the capacity to conduct oneself according to moral principles (or at least being a member of a species in which that capacity is normal) that entitles one to protection against being exploited for the benefit of others. Animals, not being moral agents, are not entitled to the protection afforded by moral rights and so are fair game for all manner of scientific research.

What follows from the contrary view that animals do, after all, have rights? At first glance it appears that a rights view must be inimical to vivisection. But just as the defence of vivisection in terms of its alleged beneficial consequences has been questioned, there are those who have denied that a rights view necessarily rules out all experimentation that harms animals. Certainly, the most prominent rights philosopher, Tom Regan (2004a), calls for the abolition of all scientific practices that harm animals, whether carried out for purposes of education, or to test the toxicity of new products and drugs, or for purposes of original or applied research. However, some writers (Lehman 1988; Varner 1994a) suggest that Regan is drawing the wrong conclusion from his own principles, or at least that an abolitionist conclusion does not necessarily follow from his basic rights view.

The argument here for permitting some vivisection runs broadly as follows. Yes, if animals have rights, many ways we currently treat them are wrong. If they have rights, it is almost always wrong to eat meat. In terms of nutritional requirements, everyone can at least survive on a vegetarian diet and, arguably, most people would actually be healthier if they stopped eating meat. Sport hunting is unnecessary, even if it does give some hunters a feeling of being connected with nature. Similarly, we do not need to confine animals in zoos, or make them perform in circuses, or use them in rodeos. But scientific research is a different case. If we do not discover cures for the diseases and injuries that afflict us, we shall die prematurely or live lives filled with suffering that could have been prevented. So when it comes to the issue of preventable suffering and death, it's "us or them". In short, we are in a lifeboat situation and since human beings would be harmed more by suffering and premature death than animals would be, this justifies sacrificing animals for our well-being.

For his part, Regan maintains that we cannot apply the worse-off principle to biomedical experimentation because of a special consideration: namely, that risks of being harmed are not morally transferable to those (animals, in this instance) who do not voluntarily choose to take them. Regan does not agree that animal experimentation is an example of a lifeboat case. Lifeboat cases, as he sees them, are exceptional cases and the application of the worse-off principle in exceptional cases cannot fairly be generalized to unexceptional cases, since doing so would allow the institutionalized subordination of some individuals (indeed, many individuals, including human ones) to other individuals. Routinely to subordinate some individuals to others would be to treat the former without the respect they deserve.

Susan Finsen (1988b), Alan Clune (1996), and Julian Franklin (2001) agree with Regan that the worse-off principle cannot be invoked to justify routine animal experimentation. Unlike the dog in Regan's lifeboat example, healthy animals are not in imminent peril — they are not in the lifeboat to begin with. They do not face harm until we decide to use them for research. Like Regan, Finsen and Clune say that the rights view does not insist on an end to all experimentation but demands that science apply the same basic ethical restrictions to the use of animals as to

In short, the continuing practice of killing nonhuman animals for medical purposes ... cannot be painted as a party of innocents trapped in a lifeboat. The only lifeboat situation that would be parallel to this one would be one in which a healthy young individual, minding her own business, is forced onto a lifeboat at gunpoint and made to serve as one's lunch, organ supplier, or vaccine tester. We could even breed her first so that we do not have to leave the lifeboat so often. We have a "deathboat" here, not a lifeboat!
—Evelyn B. Pluhar, *Beyond Prejudice*, p. 297

the use of human beings. Clune argues that tests on animals should aim to benefit them and should be allowed only in cases where some humans afflicted with the same medical condition give informed consent to undergo such testing themselves. Steve Sapontzis (1987) similarly maintains that animals employed in research should be afforded the same sort of moral protection afforded human research subjects and stresses the need for freely given consent, if necessary by a guardian acting on the animals' behalf.

## Feminists Emphasize the Legitimate Role of Feeling

In recent decades the vaunted objectivity of science has been called into question, first by scholars influenced by Marxism and then by feminists. These critics have maintained that the notion of "objectivity" often masks ideological biases. Feminists have emphasized that the demand for objectivity typically involves a distancing of the scientist from what is being studied; in particular, any emotional response on the part of the researcher is equated with bad science. Thus biologist Lynda Birke (1994) maintains that the dispassionate, technical form of language employed in describing experimental animals and the procedures performed on them distances scientists and readers of scientific reports from any sense that the creatures used are living, sentient individuals. Even when they are put to death they are usually not "killed"; rather, they are "sacrificed" or "culled". Animals are seen not as *subjects* of research toward whom an emotional response of some sort is appropriate but as standardized and interchangeable objects or "models".

According to Brian Luke (2007), use of the word "sacrifice" is entirely appropriate. He argues that vivisection is a modern-day form of the sacrificial rituals found in many religious traditions. It is a ritual in which a specially designated class of men (priests or researchers) display their alleged power to sustain human life and maintain the well-being of society by regularly killing animals. Sacrifice constructs men as fathers who can rival women in the reproduction of human life. Vivisection also perpetuates the attitude evident in the scientific revolution of the seventeenth century, when Francis Bacon and others explicitly characterized the natural world as female and extolled science (including vivisection) as the masculine means to dominate and exploit her.

As has been noted, feminist philosophers tend to be sceptical of the application of abstract principles to moral problems, and this includes the issue of animal experimentation. Although she has an antipathy to animal experimentation, Deborah Slicer (1991) rejects what she sees as the attempt by Singer, Regan, and others to arrive at some pat formula for solving problems. Instead, she says, we must recognize that every case has its own particular features that must be attended to. In particular, emotional bonds with family members, friends, and other human beings should count for something in our moral decision-making, even though these bonds should not count as automatic trump cards against the suffering of animals.

## Genetic Engineering of Animals

In February of 1997 came the announcement that scientists in Scotland had made a major breakthrough in genetic engineering. The product of their endeavours, born the previous July and named Dolly, was the genetic copy, or clone, of a sheep that had been born years before and that had probably already been slaughtered by the time Dolly arrived. Dolly did not come into being as a result of the union of a sperm and an egg but was created from genetic material taken from the udder of the sheep that, as the result of the procedure of cloning, became her lost twin.

Cloning is a dramatic instance of genetic engineering. It involves replacing the nucleus of an egg cell with the nucleus from a non-egg cell, usually from another individual. The egg, now with new genetic material, is then implanted in the womb of a surrogate mother so that it develops to produce an individual genetically identical to the individual who donated the nucleus. Dolly was not the first clone. Other animals, including sheep, had been produced by cloning. What was new about Dolly was that the genetic material used came not from the undifferentiated cell of an early embryo but from the differentiated (specialized) cell of an adult sheep. The advantage of using the genetic material of an adult is that identical copies can be made of an animal whose traits are already known.

The announcement of the arrival of Dolly immediately fuelled speculation about the possibility of cloning human beings. Ian Wilmut, leader of the research team, dismissed the idea as unethical and—somewhat naïvely—as pointless and unlikely to be implemented. At the same time, neither he nor most of those who reported for the mass media saw any ethical problems attendant on the cloning of animals. It is true that, in itself, cloning animals is not likely to raise as many moral issues as the cloning of humans. However, the cloning of non-human creatures becomes more questionable when we consider that it is linked in practice to another aspect of genetic engineering: the creation of transgenic animals. Transgenic animals are ones whose genetic constitution has been deliberately modified by the insertion of foreign genetic material. Dolly was created as part of a commercial project to produce drugs in sheep's milk in order to treat human diseases like haemophilia and cystic fibrosis. The idea was to grow cells from sheep in the laboratory and then add genes that would direct the cells to produce the desired drugs. The altered cells would then be used to make sheep clones that would become "living drug factories". Cloning could also be used to produce copies of animals with genetically engineered defects to serve as models for the study of human diseases (Kolata 1998; Wilmut 1998).

The use of transgenic animals for the study of human disease is already well established. In 2008 the UK government reported that, of the 3.2 million experiments on animals in Britain the previous year, more than a third involved transgenic animals, typically mice or fish. For example, transgenic mice have been used as models for the study of cystic fibrosis and diabetes (LaFollette and Shanks 1996). Transgenic pigs are considered good prospective candidates for use in xenotransplantation — the transplantation of organs from one species to another. In 1984 surgeons in California transplanted a baboon's heart into an infant girl who had been born with a fatal heart defect. The girl lived only twenty days after the operation. Rejection of foreign organs by the immune system is a major impediment on the road to routine xenotransplantation. Pigs that have been engineered with human genes may provide a source of organs that the human immune system will not reject.

Much less has been written by philosophers about the moral implications of the genetic engineering of animals than about the morality of vivisection. This is largely due to the fact that genetic engineering is a more recent phenomenon. Also, perhaps, it is due to the fact that the full possibilities and moral implications of genetic engineering are not yet clear. What is clear is that the issues raised by genetic engineering will become increasingly pressing in years to come.

Jeremy Rifkin has been a leading critic of genetic engineering. As

Rifkin (1983, 1998) sees it, the new technology is part and parcel of a way of looking at the world that devalues living individuals. The natural world is no longer seen as a realm whose member organisms have intrinsic value. Nature has been "desacralized", drained of all meaning except as a storehouse of material to be manipulated and exploited. This change has not happened overnight. From the seventeenth century until recently, physics has described the world in mechanical terms. Many commentators have seen in Darwin's theory of evolution parallels with the social and economic values of the industrial age. Rifkin argues that Darwin succeeded in establishing the idea of organisms as mechanical assemblages of inanimate parts. Now, he says, in line with the modern sciences of cybernetics and genetics, including an understanding of the role played by DNA in programming the development of organisms, the idea that life is mere machinery is being replaced by the idea that it is mere information. In the modern desacralized world, carrots, foxes, and human beings are not essentially carrots, foxes, and human beings; they are essentially bundles of genetic information that can be used for industrial purposes. There is no respect for the integrity of the individual organism. By reducing individuals in theory and in practice to the level of their genes, science is opening the door to a possible future in which human destinies have been programmed from before birth and in which, as a result, human beings have ceased to be part of the planet's community of freely living creatures.

Rifkin's concern is echoed by Michael W. Fox (not to be confused with Michael Allen Fox). While seeing potential benefits in genetic technology, Fox (1992) deplores the attitude that reduces animals to genetic material that can be exploited for industrial purposes. He claims that the creation of transgenic animals has already caused considerable suffering, much of it from unanticipated health problems. As long as the primary purpose of genetic engineering is not to benefit animals but to fit them more efficiently into the industrial system, their suffering is likely to increase; and as society becomes more dependent on the products of such animals, this suffering will be excused as being "necessary".

The idea that through genetic engineering we are repudiating any sense of the sacredness of the natural world is given explicitly theological expression by Andrew Linzey (1994, 2000). The genetic engineering of animals, in his opinion, is the ultimate manifestation of the view that they are mere things for human use. Through technology we are now manipulating the very nature of animals so that they are treated totally as human property—an attitude given legal form through the patenting of animals. (An example is the "oncomouse", a mouse engineered to develop cancer. See Orlans et al. 1998.) But just as making other human beings our slaves is wrong, so is this absolute subjugation of animals, says Linzey. In theological terms, our claim of absolute ownership of animals is idolatrous, since only God owns the creatures of this world and we have no right to misappropriate what belongs to God.

Many of the fears expressed by critics of genetic engineering are addressed at length by Bernard Rollin in *The Frankenstein Syndrome*. The title of the book refers to the widespread concern about creating new forms of life. The original story of Doctor Frankenstein, by Mary Shelley, portrays a scientist who, with the best of motives, creates from human parts a creature that proceeds to wreak destruction on its creator and others. The story has struck a powerful chord in the modern imagination, symbolizing as it does the potentially harmful consequences of scientific progress and suggesting that there are aspects of nature that we meddle with at great peril.

Although he is one of the leading animal-rights philosophers, Rollin sees nothing intrinsically wrong with the genetic engineering of animals. This is not to say that genetic engineering cannot be used in unacceptable ways, but that it is not wrong in itself. Rollin rejects Rifkin's notion that genetic engineering necessarily involves a reductionist way of looking at organisms. Rollin thinks that part of the objection here may be the idea that viewing living things as merely collections of chemicals or information is not conducive to what is essential to a good society, namely respect for individual dignity and uniqueness. However, says Rollin, we cannot make genetic engineering go away. As with other scientific and technological advances, the way to deal with it is through education and rational discussion.

Genetic engineering may be believed to be intrinsically wrong for a number of reasons, says Rollin. It may be thought that there is a clear division between nature and culture and that it is wrong to breach the gap by introducing artifice into nature. Rollin points out that not only are human beings part of nature themselves, but throughout history they have altered nature in innumerable ways, including the domestication and breeding of animals. Some environmentalists and environmental philosophers may reject meddling with the characteristics of species because they see nature as intrinsically valuable. But Rollin argues that species do not have the moral status that sentient individuals do and that the focus of our concern should be the welfare of individuals. (More will be said in the next chapter about the moral status of individuals in relation to species and ecosystems.) Some people may object on theological grounds to the mixing of human and animal traits — but we already insert animal parts, such as skin and heart valves from pigs, into humans for medical reasons. Suppose that an animal were found to contain a gene that could prevent cancer and that had no undesirable side effects. Why should this gene not be transferred to human beings? Why should human genes — say, genes that help an organism resist disease — not be transferred to animals in cases where the animals would benefit?

Rejecting the idea that there is something intrinsically wrong about the genetic engineering of animals, Rollin affirms that particular applications of this technology must be morally evaluated according to their consequences. In particular, Rollin proposes what he calls *the principle of conservation of welfare*. This says that any animal that is genetically engineered to serve human purposes or for environmental benefit should be no worse off in terms of suffering, and preferably should be better off, after the new traits are introduced than the parent stock was. In other words, to be morally acceptable, an application of genetic engineering must be either neutral or beneficial in terms of its consequences for the animals affected.

In Chapter 3 it was mentioned that Rollin holds that every animal should have its *telos* (intrinsic nature) respected. One might assume that this would lead him to reject genetic engineering as a violation of an animal's *telos*. This is not the case, however. Rollin's point is that, given an animal's particular nature, one should not violate the interests that constitute that nature. He is not maintaining that it is necessarily wrong to change an animal's nature. What is wrong is to change it in a way that violates the principle of conservation of welfare. Suppose that we can produce a chicken that has no nesting urge and prefers to lay eggs in a battery cage. Rollin sees nothing wrong with this, since the new chicken is better able to satisfy its nature than its predecessor was.

What I did assert was that given an animal's telos, and the interests that are constitutive thereof, one should not violate those interests. I never argued that the telos itself could not be changed. If the animals could be made happier by changing their natures, I see no moral problem in doing so (unless, of course, the changes harm or endanger other animals, humans, or the environment). Telos is not sacred; what is sacred are the interests that follow from it.
—Bernard E. Rollin, *The Frankenstein Syndrome*, pp. 171-72

141

Would we accept the genetic engineering of human beings to make them fit their environment better? In his famous novel, *Brave New World*, first published in 1932, Aldous Huxley pictures a time when, by alteration of embryos and later with drugs and indoctrination, people are tailor-made to fit their respective environments and to be happy, productive members of society. The catch is that happiness has been bought by giving up freedom — or at least by giving up the sort of freedom that arguably makes us who we are and that gives our lives meaning even in the face of much unhappiness. Huxley clearly thinks that this engineered happiness is happiness that has been bought at too high a price. Does the same criticism apply to Rollin's endorsement of the genetically engineered chicken?

Rollin is aware of the *Brave New World* objection. There is an important difference, he says, between engineering chickens to be content with their cages and engineering humans to be content with the human equivalent of cages. The difference is that autonomy and reason are goods that human beings refuse to relinquish but that are not valued by animals. Furthermore, says Rollin, we already have a long tradition of modifying the *telos* of domesticated animals through artificial selection in order to serve human needs and, if we consider it essential to continue confining hens in battery cages, it is reasonable to consider changing their nature to fit them to their environment.

These justifications can in turn be challenged. Birke (1994) says that the rapid growth of molecular biology, in particular genetics and DNA technology, has encouraged us to see animals as "puppets of their genes". On the contrary, she argues, animals not only have genetic dispositions but, like humans, are also active agents who make themselves from the time they are born by interacting with their physical and social environments. As we have seen, the idea that animals are active agents in the world is fundamental to the rights view. Although animals are not able to reason about their actions in the way that humans can, many of them exhibit what Regan calls preference autonomy: they have preferences and the ability to initiate actions with a view to satisfying them. If, then, it is wrong to change human nature in order to alter the way that humans typically choose to live their lives, why is it not wrong to change the nature of a particular kind of animal — a chicken, for example — in order to alter the way it typically chooses to live its life?

You and I might be horrified at living the life of an inhabitant of the society depicted in *Brave New World*, but members of that society clearly are not horrified: they like their lives and would be horrified at the thought of living our sort, with its attendant miseries. If the principle of conservation of welfare can condone creating chickens that like their cages, why can it not condone creating human beings who are ecstatic about a society like that in *Brave New World*? As for the fact that we humans have a long tradition of modifying the *telos* of animals to suit our purposes, this in itself does not constitute an argument for continuing to do so. It may indeed be best to change the nature of chickens if we are going to insist on keeping them in tiny cages, but should we insist on keeping them in tiny cages?

Henk Verhoog (1992) says that the idea of engineering animals to adapt them to cages that would normally cause suffering goes against the moral intuition of many people. Verhoog suggests that Rollin's endorsement of the idea is inconsistent with Rollin's own exposition of the significance of animal *telos* in *Animal Rights and Human Morality*. By genetically engineering an animal, are we not imposing our own purpose on the animal, rather than allowing it to realize the *telos* intrinsic to it? And by judging what is best for an animal by reference to its experiences of pleasure or suffering, are we not implying a too limited concept of what constitutes the animal's real nature? (Recall from Chapter 3 Rollin's assertion that a sentient creature need not be aware of all the intrinsic functions and aims that constitute its *telos*.)

Verhoog maintains that the nature of a wild animal involves much more than experiences of pleasure and suffering. It includes both its social relations to members of the same species and its relations with the ecological bio-community. The animal's well-being depends on its ability to function in its natural environment according to its historically evolved nature. We should reject the temptation to think of domesticated animals as quite different, to think of them simply as artifacts whose further modification by genetic engineering poses no moral problems. The quality of life of domesticated animals includes the quality of their relations with us. To the extent that genetic engineering violates the species-specific interests of animals and leads to their being reduced in our eyes to exploitable material, says Verhoog, it is to be rejected in all but cases of life-and-death necessity.

Although he ascribes rights to animals, Rollin is also a pragmatist. He is aware of the enormous pressure exerted by industrial society for the maximization of productivity at the expense of animal welfare and he is prepared to consider measures that improve the lives of animals even though falling short of liberating them. He suggests too that we might consider rendering food animals "decerebrate", either surgically or through genetic engineering—in other words, rendering them incapable of conscious experience, so that they exist in a merely vegetative state and hence without any suffering. This procedure might also be considered for transgenic animals designed to model human diseases, animals that would suffer greatly if conscious. No violation of the principle of conservation of welfare would result, since animals incapable of subjective experience could not be said to have a welfare in any significant sense of the term.

## Conclusion

Although human beings exploit animals for many different purposes, the use of animals in scientific research, especially in research where they are deliberately subjected to harm, has long provoked intense controversy outside philosophical circles. Anti-vivisectionists tend to see the practice as particularly odious from a moral standpoint. On the other hand, most scientists defend vivisection as necessary for the progress of science and medicine and point to the advances in knowledge that have resulted from animal experimentation.

Those philosophers and activists who take a broadly utilitarian approach to the issue are likely to accept some vivisection while at the same time pressing for the utmost possible implementation of the "three Rs"—replacement, reduction, and refinement. On the other hand, those with a rights view are likely to say that all research that harms animals should be abandoned, even if that means forgoing the benefits that would have accrued. Even here, however, there are dissenters. There are those who argue that a rights view can condone some vivisection because total abolition would make some humans worse off than the animals harmed in research.

Genetic engineering has opened a moral can of worms. The creation of transgenic animals and their use for the production of drugs, as models for the study of disease, and for other purposes raises issues around animal suffering and death. In addition there is the issue of whether we do wrong when we alter the fundamental nature, or *telos*, of an animal in order to use that creature for our purposes. Developments in the field during the twenty-first century are bound to confront us with questions that touch upon our very nature as human beings and force us to re-evaluate our notions of the place we occupy in the planet's web of life.

In 2003 Dolly the sheep, who suffered from arthritis and possibly from premature aging, was put to death after developing a severe lung infection.

# CHAPTER SIX

# CAN LIBERATIONISTS BE ENVIRONMENTALISTS?

Well, then, in our exercise of our power and in our guardianship of the rights of animals, must we not protect the weak among them against the strong? Must we not put to death blackbirds and thrushes because they feed on worms, or (if capital punishment offends our humanitarianism) starve them slowly by permanent captivity and vegetarian diet? What becomes of the "return to nature" if we must prevent the cat's nocturnal wanderings, lest she should wickedly slay a mouse?

*D.G. Ritchie*[1]

Even liberationists are unlikely to say that worms have rights. Nevertheless, in his response of 1894 to animal-rights advocate Henry Salt, Ritchie puts his finger on an issue that has enlivened — or plagued — the debate about the moral status of animals in recent times: is promoting animal liberation compatible with promoting a flourishing natural environment?

Most people probably assume that the animal-liberation movement is part of the wider environmental movement. After all, animals are an element of the physical and social world that surrounds us and, in particular, wild animals are a prominent and important element of our natural environment. Undoubtedly there is much truth to the idea of an

---

[1] David G. Ritchie, *Natural Rights* (London: George Allen and Unwin, 1894), p. 109.

intimate connection between the two movements. The animal-liberation movement emerged as a significant public presence at roughly the same time as the environmental movement and has been part of the growing concern with the way we treat the non-human world.

At the philosophical level, however, things are not so straightforward. Some environmental philosophers have maintained that the individualistic orientation of liberationist philosophies is fundamentally at odds with the holistic orientation of any ethic whose focus is the well-being of ecosystems. More than that, liberationists are charged with being ignorant of the processes of nature and of being sentimentalists who are unwilling to face up to realities of life and death (Herscovici 1985; Lynge 1992; Rolston 1988). J. Baird Callicott (1989), a prominent environmental philosopher, has argued that there are "intractable practical differences" between environmental ethics and the animal-liberation movement. He charges liberationists with having a "life-loathing philosophy", one that if pursued in practice would have "ruinous consequences" for the environment. From the other side, Tom Regan (2004a) calls the kind of position espoused by Callicott "environmental fascism". These salvoes have fuelled a sometimes acrimonious debate.

## A Bad Marriage?

The environmentalist case against animal liberation can be introduced with a look at an essay by Mark Sagoff, the title of which puts the matter succinctly: "Animal Liberation and Environmental Ethics: Bad Marriage, Quick Divorce". Sagoff considers the utilitarian and rights versions of animal liberation and finds both of them incapable of being reconciled with any environmental ethic that gives pride of place to promoting the flourishing of species and ecosystems.

Sagoff makes the point that all animal species produce in excess—in many cases, greatly in excess—of the number who survive long enough to reproduce themselves. Few animals in the wild die of old age; most die from predation, starvation, disease, parasitism, cold, and so forth. The sum of misery experienced by animals in the wild is enormous. Someone who takes the utilitarian position of Peter Singer seriously, says Sagoff, must logically be committed to intervening in wild nature to lessen the misery. There are many things that might be done. We might initiate a programme to reduce the numbers of wild animals born, perhaps by laying out food laced with contraceptives. We might convert wilderness areas, especially national parks, into humanely managed farms. People could be urged to adopt starving deer as pets. Earthworms could be saved by the construction of birdhouses where birds could feed on imitation worms made of textured soybean protein. We might build shelters and heated dens for wild animals so that they will not freeze to death in winter.

Sagoff, it need hardly be said, does not take these proposals seriously. He makes them as a *reductio ad absurdum*, that is, as a means of refuting his opponent's position by showing that it entails absurd consequences. At least, the above proposals will strike environmentalists as absurd. Sagoff's point is that someone like Singer, who is committed to the utilitarian version of animal liberation, does have to take such proposals seriously and hence cannot be an environmentalist.

Does the animal-rights position fare any better? According to Sagoff, it does not. Only individuals — not collectivities like species and ecosystems — can have moral rights. But in promoting the flourishing of species and ecosystems we must recognize that individual animals are normally expendable. An environmental ethic of this kind, then, cannot be grounded in, or derived from, the idea that individual animals have rights.

Similarly, Bryan Norton (1982) believes that neither a utilitarian nor a rights position can form the basis of an ethic that protects ecosystems from degradation. Minimizing the suffering of wild animals does not necessarily mean refraining from destroying their original habitats; in principle, Norton points out, the animals might be removed to live elsewhere, or even sterilized years in advance of the destruction. Alternatively, we might be tempted to ascribe rights to non-human entities so that environmental destruction is ruled out as a violation of these rights; but to ensure environmental protection we would have to expand the class of rights holders to such a degree that it would become impossible to satisfy all the resulting obligations. Norton's conclusion is that a holistic environmental ethic cannot be generated on the basis of the interests of individuals.

## Leopold's Land Ethic

In opposing environmental ethics to animal liberation, Sagoff takes as his standard the "land ethic" of Aldo Leopold (1887-1949), whose ideas have had a formative influence on environmental philosophy. Callicott, in particular, owes much to Leopold and has been the leading exponent and defender of Leopold's philosophy. Leopold argues that we must cease to regard the natural environment as simply an economic resource, as something that we conquer and control. Instead, we must realize that we, like the other elements of the biosphere—soils, waters, plants, and animals (or, collectively, the land)—are plain members and citizens of what he calls the "biotic community". Our ethical horizons, which have been restricted to the human family, must be enlarged to encompass the ecosystems of which we are a part. Leopold (1966, p. 240) formulates the core idea of his environmental ethic in the following maxim: "A thing is right when it tends to preserve the integrity, stability, and beauty of the biotic community. It is wrong when it tends otherwise."

Leopold's ethic is holistic. It evaluates actions in terms of their effects on the well-being of entire ecosystems rather than on the well-being of the individual components of those systems. The flourishing of individual plants and animals is not what is important. What is important is the flourishing of the wholes of which these plants and animals are parts, in other words, the flourishing of species and ecosystems.

Leopold's maxim has an intuitive appeal about it. It captures the sense that many people have that we must stop putting our narrow personal interests first and start appreciating and caring for the greater whole in which the lives of all of us, human and non-human, are rooted. But do we really want to accept Leopold's rule of conduct at face value? Do we really want to treat other individuals, including other human individuals, strictly according to the effect that this treatment will have on the ecosystem? The way people live these days often has deleterious effects on the natural environment. Suppose, all things considered, that the integrity, stability, and beauty of the biotic community would best be served by turning our wasteful, environmentally ignorant next-door neighbours into compost for our organic vegetable garden—or perhaps by stranding them out in the woods where they could be hunted down and devoured by wolves. Once we begin to imagine the whole range of scenarios that a truly holistic environmental ethic might welcome, we are likely to want to qualify our endorsement of such an ethic—even if we like gardens and wolves better than we like our next-door neighbours.

It is the untempered land ethic's emphasis on the health of the biotic community at the possible expense of any given component member that leads Regan to describe it as environmental fascism. He insists that such an ethic is irreconcilable with his own position: "Environmental fascism and the rights view are like oil and water: they don't mix" (Regan 2004a, p. 362). Fascist ideology insists that the individual has value only as a member of the biologically-based community. In one essay Callicott (1989) maintains that for the land ethic even human beings have value only as members of the biotic community. Maurice Wade (1990) questions whether an environmental ethic of this type can really avoid fascist implications. He wonders whether hunting human beings for sport — especially those people for whom we feel little sympathy — might not be a good way of promoting the well-being of the biotic community. (Leopold, it might be noted, was an enthusiastic hunter, though not of humans.)

Now, one does not have to accuse Leopold himself of being a fascist to see that a strict reading of his words might engender the sort of concern voiced by Regan and Wade. For his part, Regan is not saying that his rights view is incompatible with environmental ethics, only that it is incompatible with any environmental ethic that effectively deprives subjects-of-a-life of basic rights by evaluating human treatment of these subjects simply in terms of the integrity, stability, and beauty of the biotic community. The question remains, though, whether indeed the rights view, or any version of animal liberation, can be reconciled with the flourishing of the natural environment.

## Callicott's Search for an Ecocentric Ethic

Recognizing the problematic nature of an untempered holism, Callicott, in his own articulation of Leopold's land ethic, has moved to meet at least some of the objections of critics (e.g., E. Johnson 1981) by acknowledging the significant moral standing of individuals. In doing so, Callicott (1989, 1993) proposes a reconciliation of animal liberation and environmental ethics, albeit on terms explicitly favourable to the latter. Drawing on David Hume's notion that morality is rooted in natural sympathy for our fellows (a fact that, according to Charles Darwin, can be explained in terms of the evolutionary advantages of group solidarity), and on the point made by Mary Midgley (1983a) that human beings have long existed in mixed animal-human communities, Callicott argues that how we ought to treat one another, including animals, depends on the organization of communities. Our strongest duties, he says, are to members of our immediate families. We have certain obligations to them that we do not have even to our neighbours. In turn, we have obligations to our neighbours that we do not have to more remote fellow citizens. We have obligations to our fellow citizens that we do not have to human beings in general, and we have obligations to human beings in general that we do not have to animals in general. Some animals, however, have a special relationship with us: pet animals are surrogate family members and are owed special treatment on that account; barnyard animals have an unspoken social contract with us that permits us to use them for their labour and even to kill them for food, so long as we observe certain norms of good treatment.

Callicott (1989, 1993, 1994) is impressed by the traditional ways in which Native-American peoples have related to their environments, and he believes that we can all learn much from these ways in arriving at a viable environmental ethic. He sees the views of Aboriginal peoples as the key to reconciling the holism of Leopold's land ethic with the concept of treating individual animals respectfully. In traditional Aboriginal views, the whole world is imbued with spirit, and plants and animals are viewed with reverence. In particular, Callicott points to Ojibwa culture, in which animals are seen as participating in a voluntary economic exchange with human beings. As in Inuit culture (see Chapter 4), hunted animals are believed to be intelligent beings who allow themselves to be killed by hunters who have the proper attitude. Hunters must refrain from using animal bodies wastefully; they must bury their skeletal remains so that the animals who have sacrificed themselves can be reborn.

Callicott is thus led to propose two ethical limitations on our use of the natural environment. The first, following Leopold, is that our use of the environment should enhance the diversity, integrity, stability, and beauty of the biotic community. The second is that we should treat individual plants, animals, even rocks and rivers, with respect. Callicott means that in using these things we ought to do so thoughtfully and without being wasteful. Thus we show respect for an animal when we select it thoughtfully, kill it quickly, and use it without wasting it.

Callicott's attempt to enlist the Native-American world-view against

A secular environmental ethic that is as thoroughly informed by ecology as by evolution would have a holistic *as well as* an individualistic dimension. That is, *both* the biotic community as such *and* (not, I emphasize, instead of) its individual members, would be morally considerable.
—J. Baird Callicott, "The Search for an Environmental Ethic", p. 360

the animal-rights position is questionable (A. Taylor 2002). Despite the fact that traditional Aboriginal cultures condone the killing of animals for food and clothing, they typically recognize animals as active agents in the world, beings who must never be treated simply as means to our ends. If we are going to use an animal, we must do so only with the animal's consent. As mentioned previously, this concept of respect means that the Aboriginal attitude toward animals has something fundamental in common with the rights view, even if there remains an important difference of opinion over whether animals do in fact give consent to being killed. It must be remembered that, for traditional hunter-gatherer cultures, the use of animals to provide food and clothing was normally a necessity. The respect that Aboriginal people displayed toward animals not only reflected their spiritual attitude toward non-human nature but also served to limit their exploitation of animals to what was required for their own sustenance. It is difficult to invoke necessity in defence of hunting done by non-Natives who have other means of obtaining food and clothing.

Although Callicott endorses the hunting of animals for food and also defends the raising of animals for food using traditional barnyard practices, he rejects factory farming. This is because factory farming violates the traditional contract that he believes we have with domesticated animals, because factory farming has serious adverse effects on the environment (including rain-forest destruction and the extinction of species), and because it is an inefficient way of feeding the world's human population. Hence he advocates a primarily vegetarian diet for people, supplemented when desired by meat "respectfully" obtained from wild animals.

## Top Predators: Nature and Culture

In earlier chapters, we have seen a sustained attack against the traditional view that human beings have a unique moral worth and that, conversely, animals are to be excluded from the moral community because they are different from humans in significant ways. While not everyone is convinced by the critiques of the traditional view, in general the case for human domination of animals on the basis of "human exceptionalism" has become more difficult to defend. But the ecological reasoning of Callicott and others presents a very different case for asserting the dominant place of human beings in nature.

In the traditional view, the natural world and culture are distinct. As uniquely rational beings, humans have unique moral worth. We have few, if any, obligations to nature itself, though we should recognize its instrumental value. Animals are by nature radically *other*, and therefore legitimate objects of exploitation by us. By contrast, the new argument insists on an overlap between nature and culture. As natural beings we retain our prerogatives as top predators, even while culture supervenes to limit the morally acceptable ways we can treat each other. We respect and have obligations to nature in terms of preserving and enhancing ecosystemic values. It is now our intimate natural connectedness with non-humans that renders them legitimate objects of exploitation (Luke 2007; A. Taylor 2008a).

The new argument from nature offers a possible escape from the looming spectre of moral inclusiveness. It denies that the intrinsic qualities of those outside the human community can give them any claim to equal moral standing with us. In doing so, it circumvents the argument from marginal cases. What counts is not the capacity to suffer or even, in the last analysis, the capacity to reason, but rather the ecological niche of one's species. It is right that we hunt, kill, eat, exploit, and experiment upon members of other species for the simple reason that that's how nature works. The approach here is not to draw a line in the sand between human and non-human qualities, but to erase or blur the line in order all the better to let loose the beast in the human. At the same time, this letting loose is presented as virtuous — as facilitating the development of those positive traits of character that, paradoxically perhaps, make us truly human.

The new argument from nature differs from social Darwinism in that it is not about competition within human society or about progress; its focus is ecological process and balance. Its common refrain is that moral rights have no ecological meaning or applicability. Animals can have no moral claims against each other, and insofar as our interactions with animals (such as hunting and eating) are *natural*, no claims can be made against us. At the same time, proponents of the new argument are likely to lament industrial society's tendency to view the natural world as having value only instrumentally: as simply raw material for the production process.

Holmes Rolston III (1993) provides us with a fine example of the new argument. He makes an eloquent case for ascribing intrinsic value to more than just sentient life, on the grounds that every organism is a self-maintaining system; each has its own *telos* and pursues its own good as it responds to its environment. So the organism is an evaluative system, even if it is not yet a moral system. If we are to have an ethic that respects life, says Rolston, we must take into account how our behaviour affects these amoral evaluative systems. Even the species has its own *telos*, and an ecosystem *produces* value, though it has no value *for* itself. To believe that morality is purely a matter of interpersonal relations and has nothing to do with our place in the web of nature is to be blind to the way that value is embedded in natural processes.

But Rolston is no egalitarian when it comes to moral standing. Though good and value are embedded in nature, he says, only humans are moral beings. This, it turns out, makes all the difference. Humans, he says, live both in the realm of culture and in the realm of nature. Our interpersonal relations are cultural and hence bound by moral rules not applicable to the realm of nature: we are bound to assist each other in emergencies and to refrain from eating each other. At the same time, the standards for our dealings with non-humans are quite different and arise from ecosystemic processes of predation and natural selection. We have evolved as omnivores and may rightly eat animals, since, in effect, the law of the jungle applies to our dealings with them—a law that would be inexcusable to apply to our interpersonal behaviour. "The boundary between animals and humans has not been rubbed out after all; only what was a boundary line has been smeared into a boundary zone" (Rolston 1993, p. 140). And a most convenient boundary zone it is from our point of view, one into which we may conduct frequent and well-armed raids in search of food and resources.

Laura Westra (1989) also has attempted to integrate environmental ethics with the idea of respect, but not rights, for animals. She deplores the emphasis that liberationists place on sentience as a criterion for moral standing and believes that the liberationist point of view fails to respect the realities that govern all life. In particular, she says, we must recognize that relations among members of different species are typically characterized by hostility and indifference. With this in mind, she suggests that the conflict between individualism and environmental holism can be resolved by adopting an attitude of what she calls "respectful hostility" toward animals. In other words, we should show respect for animals by limiting our hostility toward them to those actions required for our survival. What this implies, according to Westra, is that we may legitimately kill animals for food as well as for "unavoidable" medical research.

Westra's argument has the merit of invoking the criterion of necessity as a means of reconciling the taking of animal life with the view that non-human creatures should be respected. However, her defence of meat-eating is vulnerable to the criticism that killing animals for food is seldom, if ever, necessary for most people today and that, without the justification provided by necessity or by the consent of those we kill, it is difficult to see how we can show respect for individuals when we kill them. As for medical experimentation, this practice is unique to humans and not easily defended in terms of ecological imperatives.

**Utilitarianism and Environmental Ethics**
Environmental philosophers often attack liberationists for being too restrictive in their moral concern. Why stop at sentient creatures, they ask. An environmental ethic needs to recognize that all elements of the natural world, not only those who are conscious, have intrinsic value. To attribute some elevated moral status to creatures on the basis of sentience is to be blind to what is required to sustain the wholes of which these creatures are parts. What Callicott finds particularly disturbing about animal-liberation philosophies is the implication, as he sees it, that we ought to intervene in wild nature to protect prey animals from predators. Such intervention, he maintains, would devastate biotic communities. Like Sagoff, and for similar reasons, Callicott rejects both the utilitarian and the rights versions of animal liberation on this score.

The claim that environmentalists must reject the utilitarian version of animal liberation seems particularly strong, at least on the surface. A utilitarian, it appears, must be committed to human intervention in nature in order to reduce suffering, at least up to the point at which the benefits of further intervention are outweighed by costs to human welfare. In addition to the sorts of proposals mooted by Sagoff (like contraceptive-laced food, heated dens, soybean worms for birds), there is at least the possibility that a utilitarian cost/benefit analysis would favour exterminating (as humanely as possible) many predator species. Think of the suffering that might be averted if wolves were exterminated and healthy, well-fed populations of deer and caribou had their numbers kept in check by contraceptives. Surely a utilitarian who is committed to animal liberation cannot be an environmentalist in any standard sense of that term.

A liberationist of utilitarian persuasion might respond that human intervention in the lives of wild animals is likely to cause more harm than good. In the first place, as environmentalists fear, large-scale intervention could easily do severe damage to ecosystems, resulting in a lower quality of life for human beings as well as for those animals still remaining at large in the wild. This consideration must immediately bring into question any plan to reduce suffering by intervening in nature on a large scale. Occasional and limited intervention might be beneficial, but the costs of diverting resources from human social needs and the long-run dangers attendant on meddling with ecosystems will probably deter utilitarians from anything more. Apart from the uncertain consequences of intervention, attempting to calculate the aggregate costs and benefits to different species is likely to prove extremely difficult, if not impossible (Gunn 1983).

Second, can we really be confident that wild animals would be happier if they spent their lives in carefully-controlled artificial conditions? According to John Stuart Mill (1957, p. 14), happiness has a qualitative aspect and consequently "It is better to be a human being dissatisfied than a pig satisfied; better to be Socrates dissatisfied than a fool satisfied." Arguably, then, it is better to be a wild boar dissatisfied than to be its domesticated cousin satisfied, better to be an animal exercising its full natural powers in the struggle for survival than to be the same sort of animal, fat and pampered in captivity. Admittedly, animals do not have the human capacity rationally to reflect on and appreciate the value of freedom. Hence there would seem to be no incentive for an animal to prefer a state of wild nature, with its many hardships, to a comfortable captivity. Nevertheless, every wild animal has its *telos*, the intrinsic capacities and drives that evolution has fitted it with for living in a particular kind of natural environment. A utilitarian might argue that removing a wild animal from its natural environment, or radically altering that environment, is unlikely to increase its true well-being. The kinds of satisfactions enjoyed by an animal in its natural environment

Judging by our past record, any attempt to change ecological systems on a large scale is going to do far more harm than good. For that reason, if for no other, it is true to say that, except in a few very limited cases, we cannot and should not try to police all of nature. We do enough if we eliminate our own unnecessary killing and cruelty toward other animals.
—Peter Singer, *Animal Liberation*, p. 226

may be more profound than the satisfactions of captivity, whether or not that creature can reflect on the existence it is leading. So it would seem that, contrary to first appearance, a case might be made on utilitarian grounds for the compatibility of animal liberation and environmental ethics. Whether such a case would be persuasive is another matter.

## Rights and Environmental Ethics

The rights version of animal liberation would appear to be a more promising candidate for wedding to environmental ethics than the utilitarian version. The rights view is founded on the notion of respect for the capacity of animals to conduct their own lives, free from human interference. Regan (2004a) explicitly denies that his rights view requires us to intervene in wild nature to protect some animals from other animals. On the contrary, he says, recognizing the rights of wild animals means "letting them be", giving them the opportunity to live their own lives, free from interference either in the direct form of sport hunting and trapping or in the indirect form of commercial development that destroys habitat.

Despite Regan's unequivocal statement on the subject, Callicott insists that the ascription of rights to wild animals — in particular, the right to life — must commit us to the ecologically ruinous attempt to save prey animals from predators. Callicott interprets the notion of a right to life as including a right to be saved from being killed, even by non-moral sources. In support of this interpretation, he points out that we try to save people from attacks by the criminally insane, not just from attacks by those who can be held morally responsible for their behaviour. So even though predator animals are not morally responsible for harming their prey, is it not our duty — if we take the putative rights of animals seriously — to prevent this harm? In fact, suggests Callicott, a consistent application of either Regan's or Singer's sort of view might mean undertaking to exterminate predators.

Callicott and Regan have different interpretations of what it means to have a right to life. The right to life, like the right to liberty and the right not to be made to suffer unnecessarily, is commonly (though not always) understood simply as a claim of non-interference against moral agents. The right to life, that is, is simply the right not to be killed by moral agents against one's wishes. This may include a right to be ren-

The total amount of suffering animals cause one another in the wild is not the concern of morally enlightened wildlife management. Being neither the accountants nor managers of felicity in nature, wildlife managers should be principally concerned with *letting animals be*, keeping human predators out of their affairs, allowing these "other nations" to carve out their own destiny.
— Tom Regan, *The Case for Animal Rights*, p. 357

158

dered assistance if one is in danger of being killed by a moral agent. So conceived, the right to life does not imply that others have a duty to prevent you from being killed by non-moral sources such as heart attacks, falling trees, or hungry cougars. There are, it is true, philosophers (e.g., McCloskey 1979) who maintain that the right to life entails a right to be defended by others against being killed even by non-moral sources, and who, like D.G. Ritchie, thus see an insurmountable problem inherent in ascribing a right to life to wild animals. But as long as we understand clearly what we mean by a right to life—that in this case we mean a right to life in the more restricted sense—the problem does not arise.

Or does it? Stephen Clark (1997) wonders whether Ritchie's *reductio ad absurdum* about saving mice from cats can be so easily dismissed. If we look upon suffering as an evil, he asks, why are we not under an obligation to prevent the evil just because it has not been caused by a moral agent? And just because it would often be difficult to prevent the suffering of wild animals, is that any good reason for not intervening when it is easy to prevent suffering? If the mouse has a right to life, it may indeed have a *prima facie* claim on us to be rescued from harm. However, Clark goes on to remind us, *prima facie* rights can conflict. The cat also has a right to life. That being so, we have a duty to let the cat live in the way that is natural to her kind. The rights of wild animals are rights to lead a natural existence, and leading a natural existence includes facing the usual dangers. This does not rule out our occasionally intervening, when we can, to rescue them from unusual dangers. The conclusion we are to draw from Clark's analysis is, after all, that Ritchie's *reductio* can be put to rest; ascribing rights to wild animals does not in normal circumstances obligate us to rescue them from non-human predators or other non-moral sources of harm.

Does the dispute between Regan and Callicott in the end simply come down to different understandings of what is meant by having a right to life? If so, it would seem that a great deal of ink has been spilled unnecessarily. There may be more involved, however. It appears that a rights view, insofar as it is understood to demand that we leave wild animals and their habitats alone, is the position that least of all condones human intervention in wild nature. Regan insists that what we need to manage is not wild animals but human wrongs. By contrast, the land ethic encourages us to manage ecosystems, including animals, with the object of promoting such values as diversity, integrity, stability, and beauty. Callicott is sympathetic both to hunting and to the idea of culling animals, when necessary, to preserve (for example) endangered plant species. The substantial objection made to the animal-rights position by Callicott and others of similar mind may be that it allows too little human intervention in nature, not that it requires too much.

While generally sympathetic to Regan's rights view, Julian Franklin (2005) believes there will often be unavoidable environmental conflict between legitimate human needs for space and the good life, and the needs of wild animals. Insofar as such conflicts can legitimately be understood as lifeboat situations, upholding the primacy of essential human interests is justified. None of this refutes the right of wild animals to be treated with respect, or justifies mindless exploitation of nature. Indeed, points out Franklin, protecting the natural environment is in our basic interest.

Although many philosophers reject extending rights to animals because they believe this is giving animals more than their due, it has also been argued that the widespread extension of rights to animals should be rejected because it reflects human arrogance and the desire to dominate and manipulate the non-human world. According to John Livingston (1984, 1994), the need for rights arises in human societies characterized by structural inequalities of power. In these conditions rights serve to protect the interests of individuals against the interests of the collective. Hence, the concept of rights has no meaning in wild nature: individual wild animals stand in no need of protection against the rest of wild nature. To extend rights to all of nature would be to bring the whole planet under human control. It would mean treating nature as something that needs fixing through human intervention. But nature needs no fixing.

To Livingston's thesis it may be objected that today all sentient life on the planet is effectively under our control. Whether we like it or not, all wild creatures already exist within the power relations of human society in the sense that they are vulnerable *en masse* to being harmed by our economic activity and our political decisions. If this is the case, then doesn't refraining from extending rights to wildlife simply leave these creatures without needed protection? In practice, does it not send a message to the general public that, because they lack rights, wild creatures have no moral claim against our exploiting them in any way we see fit? One possible response to this concern is, as we have seen, to try to elaborate some idea of how we might show respect for animals even while exploiting them. According to this way of thinking, there is nothing wrong with hunting and eating animals—indeed, it may be commendable to do so—so long as we are not wasteful and do not degrade the natural environment. This position will be rejected by liberationists, who are likely to insist that, at most, animals can legitimately be harmed or killed only when we have no other way of satisfying our vital needs. Whether or not they invoke the language of rights, liberationists are likely to say that, for the most part, we should leave wild animals alone to pursue their own destinies; if we do intervene in their affairs, it should be to enhance the environmental conditions that allow them to exercise their natural powers (A. Taylor 1996a).

Historically, the concept of individual moral rights arose in the context of the view that society is a contract among essentially isolated, self-seeking individuals. Ecocentric environmental philosophy emphasizes that individuals, whether human or not, are natural beings situated in intricate webs of relations with other beings, and that their flourishing requires appropriate ecological conditions. From this perspective the idea that our treatment of animals should be understood in terms of their having rights may well appear inadequate. Rod Preece and Lorna Chamberlain (1993) make the point that our growing awareness of being part of the larger ecological community has led us in two different directions. On the one hand, we see the need to apply collectivist criteria that give the well-being of the ecosystem priority over the interests of individuals. At the same time, insofar as we come to recognize ourselves as part of the animal world and hence come to feel a bond with non-human animals, we find it difficult to ignore the demands of individual justice. As a result, we find ourselves caught on the horns of a dilemma. Preece and Chamberlain find no neat abstract solution to the often conflicting claims of individuals and communities. Instead, they recommend that we recognize that all animal life, even non-sentient animal life, has value, value that is sometimes individual and sometimes communal. We must not harm any of it except to protect our "significant and natural interests". This does not mean, though, that all animal life is of equal value or that we have the same degree of moral responsibility toward all forms. Preece and Chamberlain maintain that there is an essential inequality among animal species in terms of morally relevant characteristics, which characteristics include quality of life, capacity for suffering, rationality, sociability, and awareness of self or community. In view of this, fair consideration for members of different species is likely to involve a variety of different treatments.

### Warren's Compromise

Is it possible to adhere to a rights view while retaining the land ethic's injunction to manage nature in the interests of flourishing biotic communities? A noteworthy attempt along these lines has been made by Mary Anne Warren. Liberationists, says Warren (1983), are correct to say that animals have significant moral rights, but they must recognize that these rights are not as extensive or as strong as the rights of human beings. What this means is that the rights of animals may be overridden in situations where it would not be acceptable to override the rights of human beings for similar reasons. On the other side, she says, it is correct to claim, as many environmental philosophers do, that non-sentient elements of the biosphere have intrinsic value. However, it must be recognized that the basis for attributing value to these non-sentient elements is not the same as the basis for attributing value to humans and animals.

Unless we recognize that suffering is an intrinsic evil, says Warren, we shall not be able to understand why we believe that treating human beings in certain ways is wrong. She concludes that all creatures who are sentient have certain basic rights. Having the capacity to experience pain gives creatures the right not to have pain intentionally and needlessly inflicted on them, while having the capacity to experience pleasure gives them the right not to be prevented from pursuing the pleasures and fulfilments natural to creatures of their kind. However, the human right to freedom is more extensive than the right to freedom of animals; this is because human beings require freedoms, such as freedom of speech and of political association, that do not apply to animals. Warren also maintains that animal lives are not as valuable as human lives are, since human lives are worth more to their possessors. Hence she finds that, though it makes sense to attribute a right to life to animals, that right is generally not as strong as the human right to life. The moral autonomy of most human beings, she suggests, is an additional reason for attributing stronger rights to humans. Animal rights to life and liberty, then, are weaker than the corresponding human rights.

Warren sees no fundamental conflict between the land ethic and the ascription of moral rights to sentient animals. If animal rights were identical to those of humans, there would indeed be a fundamental conflict, since it would then be unacceptable to eliminate animals for the good of ecosystems. But since animals have weaker rights than humans do, animal rights are more easily overridden for utilitarian or ecological reasons. Warren concludes that it is not wrong to kill animals when there is no other way of achieving a vital goal—for example, the preservation of a threatened species. True, sentient creatures have a moral standing that non-sentient things lack. The latter cannot be said to have interests, and therefore cannot have moral rights, certainly not in the sense that animals can. Yet mountains, trees, and so forth should be protected, not simply because of their direct value to humans, but also because they have value (what we can call intrinsic value) as elements of the biosphere. Biological communities, says Warren, are unified systems that at the same time contain many sentient individuals, each with its own needs and interests. Hence it is only by combining the environmentalist and the animal-rights perspectives that we can account for the full range of our obligations with respect to the non-human world.

Warren's position is a thoughtful compromise between the sort of full-fledged rights view advocated by Regan and the holism (tempered or not) of the land ethic. However, it is bound to encounter objections from both sides. Many advocates of the land ethic will be reluctant to ascribe any rights at all to animals because of a commitment to environmental holism. On the other hand, Warren's assertion that the rights of animals, being weaker than human rights, can be more easily overridden for utilitarian or ecological reasons will meet with resistance from those, like Regan, for whom the notion of moral rights implies a barrier against having the interests of the individual outweighed by the aggregate interests of the group. With regard to sport hunting, Warren (1997) says that this activity clearly falls short of the moral ideal that we never harm any sentient being except from necessity. But then she claims that because sport hunting is for many people a way to satisfy important needs and because animals are not the moral equals of human beings, it may be acceptable after all. Given this sort of analysis, liberationists are

The tension between what we owe to individual persons and other living things, and what we owe to our social and biological communities, is a ubiquitous part of our moral reality; to seek to resolve it by eliminating one of these principles in favour of the other is a mistake.
—Mary Anne Warren, *Moral Status*, p. 240

likely to be left wondering whether Warren's ascription of rights to animals has much practical significance.

## Taylor's Individualistic Environmental Ethic

Another alternative to environmental holism is the individualistic theory of environmental ethics developed by Paul Taylor in *Respect for Nature*. Key to Taylor's view is the idea that all living members of the planet's natural ecosystems have equal inherent worth. In the first place, he says, as members of the planet's community of life, wild organisms deserve our moral consideration. This means that the good of each ought to be accorded value and given weight in our deliberations. By the good of a non-human organism, whether animal or plant, Taylor means the full development of its biological powers, such that it is strong and healthy, able to cope with its environment. Further, the good of each animal and plant is something to be promoted as intrinsically valuable; wild living organisms are never to be regarded as simply means to the good of other beings. In this regard Taylor points to the fact that each living organism is what he calls a "teleological centre of life", that is, each is a unified system of goal-oriented activities, the aim of which is the preservation and well-being of the organism — and this is true whether or not the animal or plant in question is conscious. The good of a population or community of organisms is to be understood as referring to a state in which the average good of its individual organisms is at an optimal level.

The concept of the inherent worth of wild living things will remind one of Regan's concept of the inherent value of subjects-of-a-life, though Taylor casts his net much wider. (Taylor recognizes the similarity between the two concepts, which were developed independently.) Because animals and plants, unlike human persons, do not claim rights for themselves based on self-respect and the idea of equal treatment, Taylor would prefer not to employ the language of rights when describing our duties to animals and plants. Nonetheless, he does acknowledge that, given that their good makes a valid claim on moral agents, there is a sense it which it is meaningful to speak of their having moral rights. In light of all this, it would seem that animal liberation might be more easily wed to an environmental ethic of Taylor's type than to a holistic environmental ethic. However, there still remains the question of how we are to evaluate conflicts between human values and the good of non-human organisms.

To resolve competing moral claims Taylor proposes several priority principles, principles that are impartial with regard to species, not implying any greater inherent worth of human beings. These include a principle of self-defence (against harmful or dangerous organisms) and four principles applying to non-human organisms that are not harmful or dangerous to humans. Taylor's principles rule out overriding the basic interests of non-humans to serve any non-basic human interests that are incompatible with respect for nature. (Hence recreational hunting and fishing are ruled out, since the hunters and fishers treat the animals as mere means to their ends: they engage in their activities for pleasure and not because they must hunt or fish in order to have enough food to survive.) However, where non-basic human interests are not themselves incompatible with respect for nature, but where satisfying them will override the basic interests of non-humans (as in the case of destroying natural habitat to build an art museum or make room for a highway), then the acceptability of proceeding will depend on the degree to which the activity is judged necessary in order for society to maintain a high level of culture or for the true good of individuals to be realized. It will also depend on there being no way to accomplish these goals by means that involve fewer wrongs to wild living things. If we judge that the art museum is necessary for our cultural life, then we may build it so long as we do all we can to minimize harm to wild animals and plants.

Of course, we must eat to live. This means that in order to satisfy our basic interests we must override the basic interests of some non-human organisms. If we accord plants the same inherent worth as animals, it might seem that consuming animals for food is no worse than consuming plants for food. However, says Taylor, while the fact that some animals are sentient does not give them greater inherent worth than plants, it does mean that the good of an animal is not realized when it is made to suffer in ways that do not contribute to its well-being. Hence it is less wrong to kill plants for food than to kill animals that are made to suffer in being taken for food. Also—and this is the main reason to prefer a vegetarian diet in Taylor's opinion—far less cultivated land is required to sustain vegetarians than to sustain a meat-eating population, and the less human beings use of the surface of the planet, the more room there is for other species. (For a sympathetic critique of Taylor's theory, see Sterba 1995.)

## Managing the Biotic Community

The idea that, as much as possible, we should simply leave wild nature alone to take care of itself may sound appealing, but a little thought reveals the matter to be far from simple. To begin with, just what is wild nature? For millennia human beings have altered the landscape, sometimes in subtle, often in profound ways. In a significant sense the physical world that we inhabit is a human creation—a point made by Karl Marx in the nineteenth century. It is impossible to return to some ideal primordial state of nature, not only because of the effects of human activity over the ages but because, with or without human beings, ecosystems are in flux. There is no original, perfect state of nature. Furthermore, it is not clear that "nature knows best", if what is meant by this phrase is that, without further human intervention, nature would produce a state of affairs that would be in our best interests, or even in the best interests of sentient beings as a whole. If we cannot say with confidence that nature knows best, then why not step in to impose our values on the natural world?

In the context of the debate over animals, the conflict between animal liberation and the management of natural environments is illustrated by three disputes in the 1990s. The first case involved managing an ecosystem primarily to preserve a human resource. In the second case aesthetic values were a key motive for active intervention in an ecosystem. In both of these disputes liberationists found themselves allied with many environmentalists in opposition to those who felt it necessary to kill deer for ecological reasons. In the third case, fox-hunting was defended as a key element in a traditional way of life.

The Quabbin is a large reservoir and watershed in Massachusetts that provides drinking water for the city of Boston. It is valued by many people in the area for its natural beauty, including its wildlife. Hunting is forbidden and there are few natural predators. By the late 1980s the commission in charge of managing the Quabbin became convinced that the large and growing deer population in the reservation had to be reduced. As the result of a voracious appetite for tree saplings, the deer were making it difficult for the forest around the reservoir to regenerate itself, thus jeopardizing the stability and purity of the water supply. After considering and in some cases experimenting with various alternatives to shooting the deer (alternatives that included placing tubes around saplings, enclosing areas of forest with electrified fencing, using birth-control implants in deer, introducing new and larger predators to the area, and capturing deer in order to relocate them away from the reservation), the commission rejected all these options as impracticable for reasons of cost or logistics. In the case of relocation, the high mortality rate among captured and transported deer was also a factor. And large predators like wolves and cougars need more territory than the reservation provided. The commission decided to call upon local hunters to reduce the deer population.

In his study of the emotional public controversy that followed the commission's decision, Jan Dizard (1994) notes the alliance that developed between advocates of animal liberation and many environmentalists. Although the emphasis of liberationists on the rights of individual animals made for some tension with those environmentalists who took a holistic view of the Quabbin, both groups were united by their opposition to human intervention in wild nature. Dizard argues that both groups saw nature as characterized by harmony and balance, which human intervention would disrupt. For the liberationists, he says, the fundamental right of wild animals was the right to liberty, the right to be left alone. For their environmentalist allies, hunters were not custodians of nature, as hunters often claim, but one more interest group pressing for greater exploitation of nature.

The liberationists and environmentalists of the Quabbin Protective Alliance failed to reverse the commission's decision. During a nine-day period in December 1991, hunters with permits killed hundreds of deer in the Quabbin. Two years later a similar fate befell deer in Rondeau Provincial Park on the shore of Lake Erie in southwestern Ontario. The park is home to many tree species, such as tulip, sassafras, and black walnut, that are rare in Canada. This "Carolinian" forest is also the resting place of migrating monarch butterflies. A growing deer population had been eating the saplings of the shade-intolerant prized tree species in preference to maple and beech, thus threatening to alter radically the nature of the forest over time. Attempts to capture deer and move them elsewhere met with little success. When the Ontario Ministry of Natural Resources decided to kill many of the deer in order to protect the fragile forest ecosystem, the plan was opposed, for different reasons, by animal-rights activists, cottagers, Aboriginal people, and even hunters.

In the third case, some 100,000 demonstrators from the British countryside filled Hyde Park in London on July 10, 1997 to demand that the government resist a proposal to ban fox-hunting with hounds. Such hunting has long provoked intense opposition and groups of saboteurs have regularly attempted to disrupt hunts. The issue divides Britain roughly on urban/rural lines. Opponents of the hunt tend to see it as a cruel relic of pre-modern times. Those in favour say it is an effective and relatively painless way of keeping down the fox population, which poses a threat to farmers' lambs and chickens. For the demonstrators who came to London, however, more was at stake than just the hunt itself; for them hunting was intimately bound up with a whole way of rural life. In even larger demonstrations in March 1998 and September 2002, hundreds of thousands of country dwellers came to London to protest against what they perceived to be various threats to their traditional liberties and livelihoods. On each occasion the proposed fox-hunting ban (which has since become law) was a prime target. It was predicted by some that a ban on hunting with hounds would be followed by a campaign against angling.

Hunting and fishing are matters over which environmentalists are divided. The case of the Quabbin illustrates that some of those who see themselves as environmentalists join with liberationists in taking a general "hands off" attitude toward wild nature and deplore not only sport hunting but hunting designed to secure the integrity of ecosystems. However, Gary Varner (1998) believes that even liberationists should be able to endorse hunting when it is carried out for what he calls "therapeutic" purposes, that is, when hunting is done to promote the aggregate welfare of the targeted species or to secure the integrity of its ecosystem. Therapeutic hunting, he says, is a "precision tool" for maintaining animal populations within the carrying capacity of their habitats. Until scientists perfect non-lethal methods, such as genetically-engineered viruses that cause temporary infertility, liberationists with a hedonistic utilitarian outlook have no excuse for rejecting therapeutic hunting, since it results in a less painful death for surplus animals than they would otherwise experience.

Turning to Regan's rights view, Varner invokes the miniride principle to mandate therapeutic hunting. (Recall that, according to Regan's miniride principle, in cases where we must override the rights of some individuals and where the harm that individuals would suffer is comparable, we should override the rights of as few individuals as possible.) Given that normal members of the same species are harmed equally by death, and given that fewer animals will die if the population of animals is regulated by therapeutic hunting than otherwise, such hunting is morally mandatory if we are to respect animal rights. Varner recognizes that Regan might respond by saying that the miniride principle is not applicable in such a case because rights can be violated only by moral agents and hence no violation of rights is involved when animals die from natural attrition. Still, Varner doubts that we ought to stand by and let harm occur just because it is not caused by moral agents. Even though Regan refuses ever to condone hunting, Varner maintains that a full-fledged animal-rights position can support therapeutic hunting in cases where it is the only means of preventing a larger number of foreseeable deaths.

It is not surprising that liberationists should advocate a policy of non-intervention when the issue is whether to harm animals. But what about intervention designed to rescue animals from harm? Writing as a proponent of environmental holism and as one who believes in the necessity of managing ecosystems, Robert Loftin (1985) recognizes that liberationists and environmentalists may agree on many things, but he claims that they must be divided on the issue of administering medical treatment to injured wild animals. Liberationists, he says, must feel we have some obligation to provide assistance if we are able to. Loftin argues that while such treatment is not actually wrong, we have no obligation to help injured wild animals (unless perhaps they are members of endangered species) and we would be doing more good by devoting our time and resources to benefiting the whole ecosystem. It would seem, however, that liberationists are divided on whether we have an obligation to assist injured wild animals. Utilitarians, as Loftin himself recognizes, might calculate that the greater good would be better served by devoting our time and resources to the good of the ecosystem as a whole. Many rights advocates stress the duty of non-interference and may regard the rendering of assistance to the injured as optional in most circumstances where no rights would be violated by intervention.

What of removing animals entirely from their natural habitats? Taking animals from the wild and keeping them in zoos is wrong because it deprives them of the freedom to live a natural life, says Dale

Jamieson (2002); there should be a presumption in favour of liberty quite apart from considerations of longevity or happiness. By contrast, David DeGrazia (2002) argues that captivity (as distinct from confinement) does not *necessarily* significantly interfere with an animal's ability to live well. He suggests that in order to justify keeping an animal in a zoo—or keeping an animal as a companion (pet)—we must satisfy two conditions. First, the basic physical and psychological needs of the animal must be met; second, the animal must be provided with a life that is at least as good as she would be likely to have in the wild. Although most zoos today do not meet both these conditions with respect to their animals, it is not intrinsically impossible for at least some zoos to do so. Those that cannot or will not meet the basic-needs and comparable-life conditions ought to close.

## The Individual Embedded in the Environment

Those who are optimistic about the compatibility of animal liberation and environmental ethics are likely to point to the connection between habitat and the well-being of wild animals, as does Mary Midgley. Although Callicott draws on Midgley's idea of the mixed animal-human community in propounding his ecocentric environmental ethic, her position on animals is different from his. Midgley (1983a) recognizes what she calls "ecological" claims on us and distinguishes these from the "social" claims of sentient beings. The special importance of sentience, she says, is that, in cases where another being has experiences sufficiently like ours, it brings into play the Golden Rule: treat others as you would wish them to treat you. By thus invoking the Golden Rule, Midgley takes a liberationist stance on the moral treatment of animals. In short, she rejects the idea that our treatment of sentient creatures is to be guided exclusively by the well-being of the biotic community. At the same time, she contends—contrary to the charges made by Callicott, Sagoff, and others—that there is no inherent conflict between animal liberation and the flourishing of ecosystems. Because habitat is so important to animals, she says, ecological claims on us and the social claims of sentient beings converge much more often than they conflict. As Susan Finsen (1988a) argues, to value the autonomy and dignity of animals is to affirm the value of the ecosystems to which they have been adapted by evolution and on which their ways of life depend.

Sentience is important because of the very dramatic difference it makes in the kind of needs which creatures have, and the kind of harm which can be done to them. The duty which we can owe to a particular being capable of suffering and enjoyment must centre on those capacities. It therefore takes a different form from any duty we may have for example to a redwood, or to the species of redwoods. … Both sorts seem quite real, and, since habitat is so important to animals, they converge much more often than they conflict.
—Mary Midgley, *Animals and Why They Matter*, pp. 90-91

The idea that the crucial importance of habitat for animals may entail the convergence of animal liberation and environmental ethics is explored by Ted Benton, who develops an eco-socialist position in *Natural Relations: Ecology, Animal Rights, and Social Justice.* Like Midgley, Benton (1993, 1996) is a liberationist who is sceptical about the usefulness of ascribing rights to animals and who would prefer to talk in terms of human duties or responsibilities. Although not totally rejecting Regan's "liberal-individualist" rights view, he aims to move beyond it to a broader perspective. He criticizes the traditional liberal conception of rights for failing to understand the human individual in the context of his or her natural and social environments. Human beings, he says, are not only embodied, they are also ecologically and socially embedded. Their sense of self and their capacity to pursue what is good for themselves are indissolubly bound up with the ecological and social aspects of their being. To flourish, it is not enough that they be left alone by others; they require appropriate conditions of life. The rights of animals (or, alternatively put, our duties to animals) must similarly be understood in terms of the ecological and social conditions of their lives.

If we wish to speak in terms of the rights of animals, says Benton, then we can distinguish three sorts of rights they may have. First, there are negative, or non-interference, rights. To say that animals have non-interference rights is to say that we have a responsibility not to confine them or obstruct them from exercising their preference autonomy. Second, there are enablement rights. Our responsibility in this case is to preserve or to provide the conditions of life that enable the animals, by exercising their autonomy, to meet their needs or to secure their well-being. Third, there are security rights. To say that animals have security rights is to say that we have the responsibility to ensure that their needs are met or that their well-being is secured. Benton notes that non-interference rights are of little use to humans or animals if they are deprived of the means of exercising their autonomy in pursuit of well-being. Further, he insists, not only for human moral agents but arguably for some animals the exercise of autonomy is an important aspect of well-being. The liberation of animals will in many instances require more than just refraining from interfering with them. Hence he favours the ascription of enablement rights (assuming that we wish to use the language of rights) to such animals.

By associating the well-being of animals with the existence of those environmental conditions necessary for them to live according to the natural needs of their species, Benton makes the liberation of wild creatures dependent on the flourishing of ecosystems. At the same time, he recognizes that human needs for food and living space, and the widely perceived need to protect biotic diversity, including the need to preserve plant species, would complicate the implementation of a liberation ethic. He emphasizes that fulfilling our responsibilities toward animals will call for radical transformations in human social and economic arrangements, including our pattern of land use, and will require broad alliances between those working on behalf of animals and those who are committed to such changes on other grounds.

Brian Luke (1995) says that what animal liberation has in common with non-anthropocentric environmentalism (that is, environmentalism that respects nature for its own sake) is a rejection of the view that non-human nature exists essentially as an instrument for human purposes. This is a point also made by Lisa Mighetto (1991) in her study of the evolving view of wild animals in the US conservation movement since the nineteenth century. Not surprisingly, then, those who support animal liberation are often deeply concerned about human destruction of the natural environment. To the extent that the well-being of both humans and animals is imperilled by the technological reduction of the expanse and diversity of habitats, a shared interest emerges; far from animals being any longer our competitors in the struggle for survival, their welfare is now to a great degree in our hands and it makes sense for us to speak on their behalf (Schalow 2000).

Luke believes that concern for nature can be expressed in terms of a variety of sources of value (rationality, sentience, ecosystemic integrity, species beauty, and so on). In his opinion these sources of value are not reducible to a single common property and it is neither necessary nor desirable to rank them relative to each other. Luke offers no specific guidance, much less a formula, for ecological decision-making. He rejects the expectation of irreconcilable conflict between different sources of value and is confident that with an acceptance of pluralism we can work through ecological conflicts. Like Luke, Rick O'Neil (2000) is sympathetic to the feminist care perspective. He suggests that a viable environmental ethic must combine the justice perspective's approach to individual moral standing with the care perspective's recognition of the concern for others that flows from our relationships and emotional attachments—a concern that will be sensitive to the intrinsic value of nature. In cases of conflict, rights will normally take priority over considerations of care, but not always. There are no tidy rules here; as feminists emphasize, much depends on context and particularity. Environmental care should encourage us to seek ways to respect rights while protecting intrinsic value.

For his part, Anthony Weston (1992) reminds us that there is no such thing as "an animal" pure and simple: there are many kinds of creatures, human beings among them, and each has its own characteristic qualities. He mentions, as examples, the "exuberance" of gulls playing above water and the "alien grace" of a cat or spider or snake. Non-human creatures are not to be assessed morally as if they were incomplete or diminished versions of humans. Rather, we must recognize the multiplicity and diversity of values that are to be taken into account in our dealings with the natural world. Weston also insists that our mental well-being depends on the existence of a diversity of animal life and on having real relationships with some other animals. What this means, he says, is that there is a congruence between "selfish" concerns and concerns about the larger natural whole of which we are part.

Indeed, the "biophilia" thesis of zoologist Edward O. Wilson maintains that there is an inherent human affinity for the other forms of life on this planet, an affinity that is rooted in our evolutionary history (Kellert and Wilson 1993; E. Wilson 1984). This idea, that our sense of well-being and even our sense of who we are is bound up with the well-being of non-human life around us, can also be found in the "deep ecology" of Norwegian philosopher Arne Naess. According to Naess (1985), the process of maturing as a person means developing a wider sense of self, in which one comes to identify one's own interests with the interests of other beings, human and non-human, animate and even inanimate. He does not claim that this process of widening identification totally obliterates the distinction between oneself and others or eliminates all conflicts of interest. As a founder of the deep-ecology movement, which emphasizes the intrinsic value of non-human nature, he stresses that the flourishing of human and non-human life will require an end to the growth of human population and to society's drive for ceaseless economic growth.

They are pigs, rhinoceroses, rabbits, and hamsters (and humans) before they are animals. … We should thus proceed from the specific to the general, starting not with ideas of *animal* rights and *animal* wellbeing but with the wellbeing and rights of cobras, racoons, and zebras. Moreover, since the wellbeing and the rights of the bird and the cat, the rat and the weasel, the zebra and the lion cannot be squared, we should never expect full and final answers from any philosophical ethic, however prima facie persuasive, however philosophically brilliant.
—Rod Preece, *Brute Souls, Happy Beasts, and Evolution*, p. 378

## Conclusion

Several reasons can be identified to account for the reluctance of many environmentalists to embrace animal liberation. One is a belief that we would be obligated to rescue wild animals from harm, in violation of the predator-prey relation. A second reason is a desire on the part of many environmentalists for continued intervention in wild nature in the form of hunting and fishing. Third, there is the belief that maintaining ecosystems in a flourishing state sometimes requires us to reduce animal populations by killing some of their members.

The first reason — that we would be obligated to rescue wild animals from harm caused by predators or cold or disease, or by other natural factors — typically involves a misunderstanding of what is intended by the attribution of rights to animals. Regan and other liberationists deny that animals' having rights normally entails any duty on our part to rescue them from non-moral sources of harm. Even a utilitarian liberationist is unlikely to advocate acts that would significantly degrade ecosystems. The second and third reasons have more bite, however. Liberationists are normally strongly opposed to the killing of wild animals, except in self-defence. Not all environmentalists are in favour of hunting and fishing; still, many consider these activities to be compatible with a proper attitude toward the environment and see no reason to abandon them, even when they are not needed for subsistence or for management purposes. Managing ecosystems to promote such values as diversity, integrity, stability, and beauty frequently involves killing (culling) animals. While liberation activists typically oppose measures that harm individual animals, at least some philosophers argue that such harm can sometimes be justified even from an animal-rights perspective.

The thesis that liberationists cannot be environmentalists rests on a perceived incompatibility between promoting the good of ecosystems considered as wholes and promoting or ensuring the good of their individual members. The contrary thesis, that liberationists can indeed be environmentalists, rests to a large extent on the idea that the good of individual wild animals cannot be divorced from the existence of flourishing environments that allow them to exercise their natural powers and live their own lives, as free as possible from human interference.

# CHAPTER SEVEN

# TO CHANGE THE WORLD

If animals did have voices, and they could speak with the tongues of angels ... they would be unable to save themselves from us. What good would language do? Their mysterious otherness has not saved them, nor have their beautiful songs and coats and skins and shells and eyes. We discover the remarkable intelligence of the whale, the wolf, the elephant—it does not save them, nor does our awareness of the complexity of their lives. Their strength, their skills, their swiftness, the beauty of their flights. It matters not, it seems, whether they are large or small, proud or shy, docile or fierce, wild or domesticated, whether they nurse their young or brood patiently on eggs.

*Joy Williams*[1]

There has been a remarkable change among philosophers in recent decades concerning the moral status of animals. With some notable exceptions, philosophers now agree that sentient creatures are at least of direct moral concern, even if there is disagreement about just how much they are to count in our moral reckoning. Also there is, running explicitly or implicitly through many philosophers' arguments, the idea that overriding the interests of animals can be justified, if it is to be justified, only in terms of some conception of satisfying important human interests. It is not enough simply to say that we desire the benefits that accrue to us from exploiting animals.

This still leaves a great deal of room for dispute, as this book has

---

[1] Joy Williams, *Ill Nature* (New York: Lyons Press, 2001), p. 147.

shown. Not only are philosophers divided broadly into pro-liberation and anti-liberation camps, but within each camp there are divisions. Much of the controversy is about what the facts are. For example, are some animals self-conscious? Do some animals have a concept of the future? What constitutes harm to a creature that lacks a sense of self or of the future? Even given agreement about the facts, different ethical theories can yield different conclusions about our moral responsibilities. The topic of the moral status of animals is fascinating in part because it raises so many philosophical issues. More than that, however, it is important because it bears directly on so many human practices, from diet, clothing, and recreation to science and public policy.

**Crossing the Line**

Philosophers sympathetic to the project of fundamentally rethinking our traditional view of animals were concerned in the beginning to show that the case for animal liberation could be made on strictly rational grounds, untainted by appeals to sentiment. While recognizing emotion as an impetus for moral concern, writers like Peter Singer and Tom Regan have employed the rigour of analytic philosophy to turn the tables on those who charge that the project of re-evaluating the moral status of animals is "merely" emotional or that it illegitimately anthropomorphizes animals. They have not sought to invent striking new ethical theories, but have used variations of traditional theories like utilitarianism and Kantianism. In effect, they have said to their readers, "Here are basic moral principles and intuitions that you already accept, explicitly or implicitly. If you apply them consistently, you will see that many of the ways in which we typically treat animals cannot be justified." This approach—basically conservative in method but often radical in implications—has succeeded in making the animal issue a thriving arena of philosophical inquiry.

At the same time, questions have been raised about the adequacy of this approach. Apart from the feminist critique of ethical theories that neglect emotion, there is the question of whether any theories that were originally formulated to describe and prescribe relations among human beings are transferable without loss to non-humans. Given that members of other species have lives that we will never be able fully to understand—never be able fully to enter into imaginatively—do we not tear our ethical theories out of context when we apply them to non-humans? Are we not in danger of giving animals too much credit, or *too little* credit, by evaluating them as if they have human-like experiences and desires? We also have to ask whether the individualist orientation of most animal-liberation philosophy—the focus on the rights or welfare of animals as individuals—can adequately express the ecological dimensions of our relations with other creatures.

The issue of our proper relationship with non-human animals tends to evoke strong emotions. There is more at work here than dispassionate argument over the correct application of moral principles. At stake is our conception of what it is to be human: Who are we, what value do our lives have, and what is our place in the universe? For some, animal liberation is a misguided and even misanthropic cause that attacks progress and human dignity. For its advocates, animal liberation is simply the consistent application of the Golden Rule ("Treat others as you wish to be treated").

In a famous debate at Oxford in 1860, Bishop Samuel Wilberforce mockingly asked Thomas Huxley (who became known as "Darwin's bulldog") whether it was through his grandfather or his grandmother that he claimed descent from a monkey. The theory of evolution has long been controversial, less in terms of its scientific standing than because many have taken it to threaten the doctrine of human exceptionalism—the idea that human beings stand at the pinnacle of creation. More than simply a claim about the superior mental powers of Homo sapiens, human exceptionalism holds that humans possess a unique moral worth that makes it unacceptable to treat them as mere means to the ends of others, but does permit humans to use non-humans as mere means to human ends. The idea that humans have this exceptional moral status is hardly new, but the fact that it has now become an "ism" reflects the current struggle over where to draw the boundaries of the moral community.

The division here is not between religious believers and sceptics. As Rod Preece (2005) makes clear, those who have defended animals on the basis of their kinship with humans have often, at least in the past, been motivated less by the idea of biological evolution than by a religious, and specifically a Christian, belief in the unity of God's creation. This was especially true of the nineteenth-century debate in Britain over

The truth is that we never conquered the world, never understood it; we only think we have control. We do not even know why we respond a certain way to other organisms, and need them in diverse ways, so deeply. The prevailing myths concerning our predatory actions toward each other and the environment are obsolete, unreliable, and destructive. The more the mind is fathomed in its own right, as an organ of survival, the greater will be the reverence for life for purely rational reasons.
—Edward O. Wilson,
*Biophilia*, pp. 139-40

vivisection. Conversely, it is not only those who long to be saved by God who can feel threatened by the idea that humans and non-humans are in the same boat, morally speaking, but also those who see evolution as certifying human moral superiority ("We've clawed our way to the top of the heap"). The longing to be assured that humans occupy a special place in the universe runs deep, and is not limited to religious believers.

The desire to draw a neat line in the sand, between all humans on one side and all non-humans on the other, is as much about whom we are determined to exclude from the moral community as about whom we wish to include within it. Perversely, as we have seen historically in relations among humans, a sense of personal or group worth can be bound up with the act of excluding others: *we* are special and have intrinsic worth because we are not like *them*. It is instructive to note the frequency with which it is asserted in public discourse that ascribing rights to animals is unacceptable because it would reduce human beings to a brutish, dog-eat-dog level and effectively mean the end of human rights. For Kenan Malik (2000), who believes that animals are Cartesian "zombies" lacking consciousness, human exceptionalism is about transcending the dictates of nature; if we think of humans as merely natural beings, he says, we reduce them to animals and undermine moral progress.

Human exceptionalism, as the doctrine of the uncrossable line, is very much alive in the public arena. However, as scientists and philosophers have increasingly called into question the idea that there is some morally relevant attribute that distinguishes all humans from all other animals, defence of human supremacy has begun to shift away from trying to draw a neat line in the sand and toward arguments couched in terms of our place in the natural world, in terms of predation and ecological balance. It is not because we transcend nature, the new story goes, but because as a species we are intrinsically part of it, that our exploitation of other creatures is justified. At the same time, proponents of animal liberation make their own claims about our intimate connections to animals, arguing that we should expand the circle of our moral concern. The issue, one might say, is whether we are to view the other creatures of this world as kindred spirits or as prey.

### An Uphill Struggle
In a famous line, Marx said that while philosophers have only inter-

preted the world in various ways, the point is to change it. The animal issue is one field where philosophers have had a real influence on people struggling for social change. But the question that remains is whether the animal-liberation movement itself has any real prospect of accomplishing its goals.

In recent years a small, but significant and growing, proportion of the population of Western countries has adopted the general position of animal liberation. Political activism on behalf of animals has grown to the extent that a "March for the Animals" in June 1990 brought some 30,000 people to Washington, D.C. In Britain a campaign against the transportation of live food animals across the English Channel became a leading political issue in 1994 and 1995, with sizeable demonstrations at ports (Benton and Redfearn 1996; Ryder 1996). In the Netherlands, *Partij voor de Dieren* (Party for the Animals), dedicated to advancing the interests of animals, has won seats in the country's parliament. In Canada the slaughter of seals and the hunting of bears continue to provoke protest and controversy; in Australia and New Zealand duck-hunting has become a contentious issue. Campaigns against the testing of shampoos and other commercial products on animals have resulted in "cruelty-free" items becoming widely available in shops. In many advanced industrial societies the proportion of the population that is vegetarian, though still a relatively small minority, has shown a rise in recent decades, especially among young people.

People generally do not like to think too much about unpleasant truths that may be accompanied by moral demands to change the way they live their lives (N. Williams 2008). Despite the intense efforts of animal-advocacy organizations, there has been little, if any, reduction in the overall use of animals for food, clothing, sport, and scientific research. World-wide, the demand for meat is growing significantly. True, growing revulsion in Western nations for the more blatant abuses of animal agriculture may provide an entry point for attempts to dismantle the system of industrial meat production (Marcus 2005). On the other hand, a veritable industry has sprung up to promote "happy meat", "compassionate carnivores", and "humane slaughter". These phrases may be oxymorons, but they strikingly illustrate a modern phenomenon: growing unease about the industrial treatment of animals, combined with a refusal to abandon the use of animals for food and

We have tried so hard for so long to identify the magic feature that qualitatively distinguishes the human from the nonhuman animals so as to justify the treatment we accord them. While the old favourites have been dismissed by science in the many decades since Darwin first said "evolution" (they can't reason, they don't think, they can't communicate, they don't feel pain ...) perhaps we have found one after all: let us never underestimate the unique power of the human mind to rationalize — and even make ourselves feel good about — behaviour that is harmful to others.
—Lesli Bisgould, "Power and Irony", p. 259

clothing—what industrial animal agriculture has been designed to provide on a mass scale.

In addition to entrenched public attitudes, activists face powerful economic interests. When protesters in London distributed copies of a "factsheet" accusing the fast-food giant McDonald's of being responsible for everything from the destruction of rain-forests to the exploitation of workers, to the torture and murder of animals, the corporation sued two activists who refused to recant. The McLibel trial, as it became known, lasted three years (Vidal 1997). In what turned into a public-relations disaster for the plaintiff, McDonald's spent some £10-million in legal fees in opposing Helen Steel, a waitress, and Dave Morris, a former postman, who conducted their own defence. In June 1997 the court awarded damages to McDonald's for libel, though finding that the corporation exploited children in its advertising, paid low wages to workers, and was "culpably responsible" for cruel practices in the raising and killing of chickens, including some of them having their throats slit while still conscious. Immediately after the verdict was delivered, Steel and Morris, together with their supporters, were out on the street, distributing "What's Wrong with McDonald's?" leaflets again.

Despite the forces arrayed against them, individuals can make a difference. The story of Henry Spira of New York is a prime example of how a dedicated activist can bring about significant changes in the treatment of animals (Singer 1998). Largely thanks to Spira's imaginative use of a combination of dialogue and the pressure of public opinion, there have been major reductions in the use of the Draize and LD50 tests, and some relief in the conditions of animals raised for food. Like Spira, the great majority of activists are non-violent, engaging in peaceful protests or forming advocacy groups such as the Animal Legal Defense Fund, a national association of lawyers in the United States dedicated to protecting animal interests. Also in the United States, the advocacy organization People for the Ethical Treatment of Animals (PETA) has a prominent national profile. (Although it is often taken by outsiders to be the voice of animal liberation, many within the broader movement question PETA's methods and even its principles.)

The Internet has become an important medium for communicating and organizing. Academic animal-ethics philosophy is increasingly moving on-line, with essays being published electronically as well as in print, or sometimes only electronically (as with the journal *Between the Species*). Many organizations and individual activists have websites. These sites are far too numerous to list, but include, for example, those of the Animal Concerns Community, the Oxford Centre for Animal Ethics, and philosopher Gary Francione ("Animal Rights: The Abolitionist Approach"), as well as the "Animal Rights" section at Change.org, and Mary Martin's blog, "Animal Person".

While most activists are committed to strictly peaceful behaviour, a minority are willing to employ violence, almost always against property rather than persons. In defence of whales and dolphins, the Sea Shepherd Conservation Society has sunk whaling ships in harbour and has rammed drift-net fishing boats on the high seas. In 1986 two of the society's members attacked a whale-processing plant in Iceland one night, causing a couple of million dollars worth of damage. They then drove to the harbour at Reykjavik, where they sank two whaling vessels before catching an early morning flight out of the country. In line with the society's rule against harming persons, they had refrained from sinking a third whaling ship in the harbour because it had a sleeping watchman on board (P. Watson 1993a, 1993b).

The Animal Liberation Front (ALF), which was founded in Britain in the 1970s and later spread to other countries, has carried out numerous raids on research laboratories, fur retailers, and farm operations where animals are confined. The goals of the ALF have been to set free confined and exploited animals, to inflict economic damage on those who operate the targeted facilities, and to expose the practices involved. Stop Huntingdon Animal Cruelty (SHAC) is an international campaign against a leading research laboratory that uses and kills large numbers of animals in the course of testing products for pharmaceutical and chemical companies. SHAC is particularly controversial, with tactics ranging from letter-writing and peaceful demonstrations to occasional property-damage and attempts to intimidate individuals and companies involved with Huntingdon Life Sciences. A few of the more militant SHAC activists have been sentenced to prison terms. The liberation movement, in its many forms, has in turn provoked reaction from opponents, often in science or industry, who have undertaken to counter the claims of liberationists (Guither 1998).

The animal-liberation movement is not united with respect to methods or even with respect to particular goals. While there is agreement that animals ought never to be treated as mere resources, there is disagreement about the extent to which it is possible to use them without treating them unacceptably. Can animals, like dogs or horses, work for and with human beings in ways that respect their integrity and autonomy? Is veganism mandatory, or might milk and eggs be obtained from animals in ways that would not cause suffering or result in their premature deaths or the suffering or premature deaths of their siblings or offspring (Burgat 2004; Zamir 2004)? And ought partial measures, such as promoting bigger cages for chickens or meat from grass-fed cattle, be welcomed as steps in the right direction that may lead to further positive change, or should they be rejected because they serve to legitimize inherently oppressive practices?

The "liberation" of sentient non-humans, if it happens, will be a long, complex struggle, not some overnight revolution. Recognizing this, some sympathetic philosophers and scientists have proposed attempting a breakthrough at the point of our relations with the great apes — or, rather, with the other great apes, insofar as we humans may be considered to be great apes ourselves. In "A Declaration on Great Apes" they have called for formal recognition that the moral community ("the community of equals") comprises not only human beings but also chimpanzees (common and pygmy), gorillas, and orangutans. This declaration is the centre-piece of The Great Ape Project, which aims to build a coalition to demand that our closest kin in the animal world be accorded legally-enforceable rights to life, to individual liberty, and to freedom from torture (Cavalieri and Singer 1993). (It can be noted that bonobos, or pygmy chimpanzees, who are the species perhaps most closely related to human beings, are now threatened with extinction as the result of human action — hunting and the destruction of their native habitat in central Africa. The same fate faces gorillas in Africa and orangutans in Indonesia.) The Great Ape Project aims to convince human persons that our ape relatives are persons too and that they should be treated as such, without suggesting that they should be accorded the whole range of rights that humans possess (Sapontzis 1993).

Though thinking of animals as persons may seem odd, it should be noted that "person" originally meant a mask, and referred to a character in a play. In this sense, a person is someone who is recognized as having an important role in life's drama (Midgley 1996). A person is some*one*, not some*thing*, a *who*, not a *what*. Drawing on the original idea of persons as characters who have roles in relation to each other, Elisa Aaltola (2008) makes the case for understanding personhood as the capacity to experience interaction with other conscious beings. Insofar as animals have this capacity to relate to others, she says, they ought to be regarded as persons.

Several of the contributors to The Great Ape Project make it clear that they would like many more kinds of animals to be recognized formally as members of the moral community. To admit to the moral community only our nearest kin in the animal world, creatures who bear striking physical resemblances to us and who have demonstrated a significant degree of intellectual capacity (including, arguably, some linguistic capacity), and to leave other sentient beings outside, may appear anthropocentric. Certainly, it falls far short of the ultimate goal of the animal-liberation movement. Nevertheless, it is argued, formal admission of the non-human great apes to the moral community is an achievable first step that would not only give the great apes their due but could eventually open the door for other animals. In this respect, a leader of the project in Spain has called the campaign on behalf of great apes "the point of the spear".

## The Global Challenge

As a number of philosophers and observers have remarked, the animal-liberation movement is unlikely to succeed in its goals unless it joins forces with other movements challenging the assumptions of industrial society (Benton 1993; M.A. Fox 1999; Nibert 2002; Torres 2007). Although it is frequently said that we are moving into a post-industrial society, or are already in one, this is misleading. True, the rate of technological innovation is astonishing. Computers, communications satellites, genetic engineering, and a host of other developments make this in some ways a world far different from the world of only half a century ago. But the basic form of industrialism remains: a society organized in the interests of maximizing production and consumption.

With the collapse of the state-socialist model of industrialism, capitalism has succeeded in creating an increasingly integrated world economy. Unlike centrally planned economies, capitalist economies are intrinsically expansive systems, in which market competition not only provides a hothouse for technological innovation, but also forces enterprises to pursue growth, on pain of economic ruin. With all value measured in terms of the market, the natural world is stripped of any sense of being sacred or having intrinsic value (Heilbroner 1985). Today no part of the globe is immune from the tendency to view all animate and inanimate elements of the world as exploitable material in the drive for capital accumulation. This fact militates against overturning the traditional view of animals as essentially resources for human use.

For David Nibert (2002) speciesism is not simply a form of individual prejudice; it is an ideology—that is, a set of socially shared beliefs that functions to legitimate a particular social order. As such, it has its roots in institutional arrangements. In particular, says Nibert, speciesism today is rooted in and reinforces capitalist economic structures. The oppression of non-humans is entangled with the oppression of humans in a system whose benefits are inequitably distributed. The struggle for animal liberation, then, must be associated with the struggle for human rights and against corporate globalization.

There can be little doubt that today the world faces multiple, interlocking economic, ecological, and political crises. Climate change, the end of the age of cheap oil, air and water pollution, water shortages, food shortages, volatility in financial markets, international competition for resources, terrorism, failed states, religious and cultural rivalries and grievances, the threat of pandemics, growing populations, enormous disparities between rich and poor, extinction of species and loss of biodiversity—together these threaten the very existence of industrial civilization and demand transformative, systemic change in institutions and in world-view (G. Taylor 2008). Seen in this context, our relations with animals are not only a matter of personal morality but also part of the moral imperative of building a sustainable human civilization in a sustainable global environment.

In 2008 the International Union for the Conservation of Nature, an international network of scientists and conservation organizations, reported that at least 25 percent of the world's land-mammal species face extinction, primarily through habitat loss and hunting. Large numbers of sea-mammal and amphibian species are also at risk. In 2006 the Food and Agriculture Organization (FAO) of the United Nations reported that the livestock sector of agriculture is growing faster than any other sector and generates more greenhouse-gas emissions than transport. Livestock uses 30 percent of the planet's land surface, including pasture as well as arable land used for producing feed for livestock. Animal wastes, antibiotics, fertilizers, pesticides, and overgrazing are major factors in water pollution and in biodiversity loss in marine ecosystems, including the degradation of coral reefs. The livestock sector is a prime contributor to deforestation and soil erosion. In recent years, vast areas of the Amazon tropical rainforest, home to countless species of flora and fauna and an important element in the planet's climate system, have been burned to make room for cattle ranches, while burnings in Indonesia have resulted in much of southeast Asia at times being covered with a dense pall of smoke. And because most of the calories and potential protein from plants is lost in their conversion into meat, the modern meat industry, with its heavy reliance on crop production, actually reduces the amount of food available for human consumption.

Thomas Auxter (1979) argues that concern for the natural environment gives us good reason to ascribe to animals a right not to be eaten: human life and health do not require us to consume animals, while meat production significantly reduces wild-animal populations and destroys the capacity of the natural environment to support a multitude of life-forms. In her eco-feminist look at the issue of so-called mad-cow disease (a progressive neurological disorder that is believed to have been passed through meat to some humans, with fatal results), Carol Adams (1997) points to the various severe environmental costs of the "animal industrial complex". She reports, for example, that more than half of water pollution in the United States can be linked to wastes of one form or another from the livestock industry. For Jeremy Rifkin (1992), modern meat production and consumption is "cold evil", in which technological rationality — the pursuit of efficiency through such means as mechanization and market forces — has severed our intimate relationship with living nature, reducing it in our eyes to nothing but commercial resources and hence robbing other sentient creatures of their intrinsic worth. Rifkin, who details the devastating effects of beef production on the environment in his study of our global "cattle culture", believes that the elimination of beef would be followed by a veritable ecological renaissance.

More than a century ago, in his novel *News from Nowhere*, William

> Simply put, large-scale meat production absorbs vast quantities of raw materials and energy of all types in order to produce relatively meager returns to humans. Ecologically, nutritionally, and calorically, it is a losing proposition. Nor does it make sense from the standpoint of collective human welfare and the quest for global equality and social justice.
> —Michael Allen Fox, *Deep Vegetarianism*, p. 97

How amazing are the inhabitants of these animal worlds around us! Even when complex behavior is dictated by instinct alone—when it is innate or hard-wired through genetic inheritance—it is wondrous. But when we also admit that, in addition, many species of animals, certainly mammals and birds, have personalities, minds, and feelings, we are humbled indeed.
– Jane Goodall, *The Ten Trusts* [with Marc Bekoff], p. 48

Morris (2003) imagined a post-industrial society built on the ruins of capitalism. His utopia is likely to strike today's reader as charming but impractical, in part because it largely rejects advanced technology in favour of a kind of egalitarian vision of the Middle Ages. Yet in an important respect it remains relevant. As in all his art and writings, Morris proclaimed the thesis that would later be called biophilia: that human beings innately have a deep psychological need for connectedness with the natural world and that they can only truly flourish if the rest of nature flourishes.

Whether capitalism's need for incessant growth can be sufficiently channelled into ecologically sustainable modes (e.g., growth in green industries and in non-material, information technologies) to avoid catastrophe is not yet clear. Whatever the answer, throughout the world there is a growing awareness of the possible dire consequences, on sundry levels, of a failure to preserve the health of the biosphere, including the well-being of its animal species.

Animal liberation, of course, demands something more: recognition that numerous non-human creatures are members of the moral community. Many people have come to embrace the claim that the liberation of animals is the logical next step in the evolution of our moral sensibility. Many more have not. The movement for animal liberation will not go away—indeed, it is likely to grow—but neither will it win majority support any time soon. The idea that animals are not just resources to be exploited, that they are individuals with lives that matter, is still too radical for most people to accept.

# BIBLIOGRAPHY, INCLUDING WORKS CITED

The following bibliography includes works cited in the text, as well as others relevant to the topic of the moral status of animals. Most of the works listed can be classed as philosophy; the rest deal in one way or another with matters that bear on the philosophical debate. While extensive, this bibliography is not intended to be comprehensive. All works listed are in English, with one exception. Material that has appeared only in electronic form is not included, but many journal articles listed can be accessed on-line.

Aaltola, Elisa. 2002. "'Other Animal Ethics' and the Demand for Difference", *Environmental Values* 11: 193-209.

———. 2005. "Animal Ethics and Interest Conflicts", *Ethics & the Environment* 10, no. 1: 19-48.

———. 2008. "Personhood and Animals", *Environmental Ethics* 30: 175-93.

Aaltola, Elisa, and Markku Oksanen. 2002. "Species Conservation and Minority Rights: The Case of Springtime Bird Hunting in Åland", *Environmental Values* 11: 443-60.

Abbey, Ruth. 2007. "Rawlsian Resources for Animal Ethics", *Ethics & the Environment* 12, no. 1: 1-22.

Acampora, Ralph R. 2005. "Zoos and Eyes: Contesting Captivity and Seeking Successor Practices", *Society and Animals* 13: 69-88.

———. 2006. *Corporal Compassion: Animal Ethics and Philosophy of Body.* Pittsburgh: University of Pittsburgh Press.

Adams, Carol J. 1994. *Neither Man nor Beast: Feminism and the Defense of Animals.* New York: Continuum.

———.1997. "'Mad Cow' Disease and the Animal Industrial Complex: An Ecofeminist Analysis", *Organization & Environment* 10: 26-51.

———. 2000. *The Sexual Politics of Meat: A Feminist-Vegetarian Critical Theory*, 10th-anniversary ed. New York: Continuum.

———. 2004. *The Pornography of Meat*. New York: Continuum.

———. 2006. "'A Very Rare and Difficult Thing': Ecofeminism, Attention to Animal Suffering, and the Disappearance of the Subject", in Paul Waldau and Kimberley Patton, eds., *A Communion of Subjects: Animals in Religion, Science, and Ethics*. New York: Columbia University Press.

Adams, Carol J., and Josephine Donovan, eds. 1995. *Animals and Women: Feminist Theoretical Explorations*. Durham: Duke University Press.

Aitken, Gill. 2008. "Animal Suffering: An Evolutionary Approach", *Environmental Values* 17: 165-80.

Allen, Colin. 1996. "Star Witness", in Joel Feinberg, ed., *Reason and Responsibility: Readings in Some Basic Problems of Philosophy*, 9th ed. Belmont: Wadsworth.

———. 2004. "Animal Pain", *Noûs* 38: 617-43.

Allen, Colin, and Marc Bekoff. 2007. "Animal Minds, Cognitive Ethology, and Ethics", *The Journal of Ethics* 11: 299-317.

Almeida, Michael J., and Mark H. Bernstein. 2000. "Opportunistic Carnivorism", *Journal of Applied Philosophy* 17: 205-11.

Alward, Peter. 2000. "The Naïve Argument against Moral Vegetarianism", *Environmental Values* 9: 81-89.

Anderson, Elizabeth. 2004. "Animal Rights and the Values of Nonhuman Life", in Cass R. Sunstein and Martha C. Nussbaum, eds., *Animal Rights: Current Debates and New Directions*. New York: Oxford University Press.

Andrews, Kristin. 1996. "The First Step in the Case for Great Ape Equality: The Argument for Other Minds", *Etica & Animali* 8: 131-41.

Aquinas, Thomas. 1945. *Basic Writings of Saint Thomas Aquinas*, vol. 2. Ed. by Anton C. Pegis. New York: Random House. See "Summa Contra Gentiles", bk. 3, chap. 111-113, pp. 219-24.

Aristotle. 1927. *The Works of Aristotle*. London: Oxford University Press. See vol. 9, "Ethica Nicomachea", bk. 8; and vol. 10, "Politica", bk. 1.

Arluke, Arnold, and Clinton R. Sanders. 1996. *Regarding Animals*. Philadelphia: Temple University Press.

Armstrong, Susan J., and Richard G. Botzler, eds. 2008. *The Animal Ethics Reader*, 2nd ed. Abingdon: Routledge.

Austin, Jack. 1979. "Buddhist Attitudes towards Animal Life", in David

Paterson and Richard D. Ryder, eds., *Animals' Rights: A Symposium*. London: Centaur Press.

Auxter, Thomas. 1979. "The Right Not to Be Eaten", *Inquiry* 22: 221-30.

Bailey, Cathryn. 2005. "On the Backs of Animals: The Valorization of Reason in Contemporary Animal Ethics", *Ethics & the Environment* 10, no. 1: 1-17.

Baird, Robert M., and Stuart E. Rosenbaum, eds. 1991. *Animal Experimentation: The Moral Issues*. Buffalo: Prometheus.

Baker, Steve. 1993. *Picturing the Beast: Animals, Identity, and Representation*. Manchester: Manchester University Press.

———. 2000. *The Postmodern Animal*. London: Reaktion.

Baldwin, Elizabeth. 1993. "The Case for Animal Research in Psychology", *Journal of Social Issues* 49: 121-31.

Barad, Judith. 1995. *Aquinas on the Nature and Treatment of Animals*. San Francisco: International Scholars Publications.

Barad-Andrade, Judith. 1992. "The Dog in the Lifeboat Revisited", *Between the Species* 8: 114-17.

Barber, J. 1997. "Trapped", in Eldon Soifer, ed., *Ethical Issues: Perspectives for Canadians*, 2nd ed. Peterborough: Broadview Press.

Barnard, Neal D., and Stephen R. Kaufman. 1997. "Animal Research Is Wasteful and Misleading", *Scientific American* 276, no. 2: 80-82.

Bartkowski, Frances. 2008. *Kissing Cousins: A New Kinship Bestiary*. New York: Columbia University Press.

Beers, Diane L. 2006. *For the Prevention of Cruelty: The History and Legacy of Animal Rights Activism is the United States*. Athens, Ohio: Swallow Press.

Beisecker, David. 2002. "Some More Thoughts about Thought and Talk: Davidson and Fellows on Animal Belief", *Philosophy* 77: 115-24.

Bekoff, Marc. 2007. *The Emotional Lives of Animals: A Leading Scientist Explores Animal Joy, Sorrow, and Empathy, and Why They Matter*. Novato: New World Library.

Bekoff, Marc, ed. 1998. *Encyclopedia of Animal Rights and Animal Welfare*. With Carron A. Meaney. Westport: Greenwood Press.

Benatar, David. 2001. "Why the Naïve Argument against Moral Vegetarianism Really Is Naïve", *Environmental Values* 10: 103-12.

Benson, John. 1978. "Duty and the Beast", *Philosophy* 53: 529-49.

Bentham, Jeremy. 1970. *An Introduction to the Principles of Morals and Legislation*. London: Athlone Press. First published in 1789.

Benton, Ted. 1993. *Natural Relations: Ecology, Animal Rights, and Social Justice.* London: Verso.

———. 1996. "Animal Rights: An Eco-Socialist View", in Robert Garner, ed., *Animal Rights: The Changing Debate.* New York: New York University Press.

Benton, Ted, and Simon Redfearn. 1996. "The Politics of Animal Rights – Where Is the Left?", *New Left Review* no. 215: 43-58.

Bernstein, Mark H. 1998. *On Moral Considerability: An Essay on Who Morally Matters.* New York: Oxford University Press.

———. 2004a. "Neo-speciesism", *Journal of Social Philosophy* 35: 380-90.

———. 2004b. *Without a Tear: Our Tragic Relationship with Animals.* Urbana: University of Illinois Press.

Berry, Rynn. 2004. *Hitler: Neither Vegetarian Nor Animal Lover.* New York: Pythagorean.

Best, Steven, and Anthony J. Nocella, II, eds. 2004. *Terrorists or Freedom Fighters? Reflections on the Liberation of Animals.* New York: Lantern.

Birke, Lynda. 1994. *Feminism, Animals, and Science: The Naming of the Shrew.* Buckingham: Open University Press.

Birnbacher, Dieter. 1996. "The Great Apes – Why They Have a Right to Life", *Etica & Animali* 8: 142-54.

Bisgould, Lesli. 2008. "Power and Irony: One Tortured Cat and Many Twisted Angles to Our Moral Schizophrenia about Animals", in Jodey Castricano, ed., *Animal Subjects: An Ethical Reader in a Posthuman World.* Waterloo: Wilfrid Laurier University Press.

Bleich, J. David. 1986. "Judaism and Animal Experimentation", in Tom Regan, ed., *Animal Sacrifices: Religious Perspectives on the Use of Animals in Science.* Philadelphia: Temple University Press.

Blum, Deborah. 1994. *The Monkey Wars.* New York: Oxford University Press.

Blumberg, Mark S., and Edward A. Wasserman. 1995. "Animal Mind and the Argument from Design", *American Psychologist* 50: 133-44.

Boonin-Vail, David. 1993. "The Vegetarian Savage: Rousseau's Critique of Meat Eating", *Environmental Ethics* 15: 75-84.

———. 1994. "Contractarianism Gone Wild: Carruthers and the Moral Status of Animals", *Between the Species* 10: 39-48.

Bostock, Stephen St C. 1993. *Zoos and Animal Rights: The Ethics of Keeping Animals.* London: Routledge.

Botting, Jack H., and Adrian R. Morrison. 1997. "Animal Research Is Vital to Medicine", *Scientific American* 276, no. 2: 83-85.

Bowd, Alan D., and Kenneth J. Shapiro. 1993. "The Case against Laboratory Animal Research in Psychology", *Journal of Social Issues* 49: 133-42.

Broadie, Alexander, and Elizabeth M. Pybus. 1974. "Kant's Treatment of Animals", *Philosophy* 49: 375-83.

Brophy, Brigid. 1989. "The Rights of Animals", in Brigid Brophy, *Reads*. London: Cardinal. First published in *The Sunday Times* (London), October 10, 1965.

Brown, Les. 1988. *Cruelty to Animals: The Moral Debt*. Basingstoke: Macmillan Press.

Bruckner, Donald W. 2007. "Considerations on the Morality of Meat Consumption: Hunted-Game versus Farm-Raised Animals", *Journal of Social Philosophy* 38: 311-30.

Bryant, John. 1990. *Fettered Kingdoms*. Winchester: Fox Press.

Budiansky, Stephen. 1992. *The Covenant of the Wild: Why Animals Choose Domestication*. New York: William Morrow.

———. 1998. *If a Lion Could Talk: Animal Intelligence and the Evolution of Consciousness*. New York: Free Press.

Bulliet, Richard W. 2005. *Hunters, Herders, and Hamburgers: The Past and Future of Human-Animal Relationships*. New York: Columbia University Press.

Burch, Robert W. 1977. "Animals, Rights, and Claims", *Southwestern Journal of Philosophy* 8: 53-59.

Burgat, Florence. 2004. "Non-Violence towards Animals in the Thinking of Gandhi: The Problem of Animal Husbandry", *Journal of Agricultural and Environmental Ethics* 14: 223-48.

Burgess-Jackson, Keith. 1998. "Doing Right by Our Animal Companions", *The Journal of Ethics* 2: 159-85.

Calarco, Matthew. 2008. *Zoographies: The Question of the Animal from Heidegger to Derrida*. New York: Columbia University Press.

Calarco, Matthew, and Peter Atterton, eds. 2004. *Animal Philosophy: Essential Readings in Continental Thought*. London: Continuum.

Callicott, J. Baird. 1989. *In Defense of the Land Ethic: Essays in Environmental Philosophy*. Albany: State University of New York Press.

———. 1993. "The Search for an Environmental Ethic", in Tom Regan, ed., *Matters of Life and Death: New Introductory Essays in Moral Philosophy*, 3rd ed. New York: McGraw-Hill.

———. 1994. *Earth's Insights: A Survey of Ecological Ethics from the Mediterranean Basin to the Australian Outback*. Berkeley: University of California Press.

Canadian Broadcasting Corporation. 1991. *Uneasy Dominion*. Toronto: CBC Ideas Transcripts, ID 9140.

Caplan, Arthur L. 1983. "Beastly Conduct: Ethical Issues in Animal Experimentation", *Annals of the New York Academy of Sciences* 406: 159-69.

Caras, Roger A. 1996. *A Perfect Harmony: The Intertwining Lives of Animals and Humans throughout History*. New York: Simon and Schuster.

Carruthers, Peter. 1992. *The Animals Issue: Moral Theory in Practice*. Cambridge: Cambridge University Press.

Carson, Gerald. 1972. *Men, Beasts, and Gods: A History of Cruelty and Kindness to Animals*. New York: Charles Scribner's Sons.

Carter, Alan. 2005. "Animals, Pain, and Morality", *Journal of Applied Philosophy* 22: 17-22.

Cartmill, Matt. 1993. *A View to a Death in the Morning: Hunting and Nature through History*. Cambridge, Mass.: Harvard University Press.

Castricano, Jodey, ed. 2008. *Animal Subjects: An Ethical Reader in a Posthuman World*. Waterloo: Wilfrid Laurier University Press.

Cataldi, Suzanne Laba. 2002. "Animals and the Concept of Dignity: Critical Reflections on a Circus Performance", *Ethics & the Environment* 7, no. 2: 104-26.

Causey, Ann S. 1989. "On the Morality of Hunting", *Environmental Ethics* 11: 327-43.

Cavalieri, Paola. 2001. *The Animal Question: Why Nonhuman Animals Deserve Human Rights*. New York: Oxford University Press.

———. 2008. "A Missed Opportunity: Humanism, Anti-humanism, and the Animal Question", in Jodey Castricano, ed., *Animal Subjects: An Ethical Reader in a Posthuman World*. Waterloo: Wilfrid Laurier University Press.

Cavalieri, Paola, and Will Kymlicka. 1996. "Expanding the Social Contract", *Etica & Animali* 8: 5-33.

Cavalieri, Paola, and Peter Singer, eds. 1993. *The Great Ape Project: Equality beyond Humanity*. London: Fourth Estate.

Cave, George P. 1982a. "Animals, Heidegger, and the Right to Life", *Environmental Ethics* 4: 249-54.

———. 1982b. "On the Irreplaceability of Animal Life", *Ethics and Animals* 3: 106-116.

Cavell, Stanley, et al. 2008. *Philosophy and Animal Life*. New York: Columbia University Press.

Cavendish, Margaret. 1972. *Poems and Fancies, 1653*. Menston: Scolar Press.

Cebik, L.B. 1981. "Can Animals Have Rights? No and Yes", *The Philosophical Forum* 12: 251-68.

Chapple, Christopher Key. 1993. *Nonviolence to Animals, Earth, and Self in Asian Traditions*. Albany: State University of New York Press.

Chartier, Gary. 2006. "On the Threshold Argument against Consumer Meat Purchases", *Journal of Social Philosophy* 37: 233-49.

Cheney, Dorothy L., and Robert M. Seyfarth. 1990. *How Monkeys See the World: Inside the Mind of Another Species*. Chicago: University of Chicago Press.

Churchill, John. 1989. "If a Lion Could Talk...", *Philosophical Investigations* 12: 308-24.

Cigman, Ruth. 1981. "Death, Misfortune, and Species Inequality", *Philosophy and Public Affairs* 10: 47-64.

Clark, Stephen R.L. 1977. *The Moral Status of Animals*. Oxford: Clarendon Press.

———. 1982. *The Nature of the Beast: Are Animals Moral?* Oxford: Oxford University Press.

———. 1997. *Animals and Their Moral Standing*. London: Routledge.

Clune, Alan C. 1996. "Biomedical Testing on Nonhuman Animals: An Attempt at a *Rapprochement* between Utilitarianism and Theories of Inherent Value", *The Monist* 79: 230-46.

Coady, C.A.J. 1992. "Defending Human Chauvinism", in Claudia Mills (ed.), *Values and Public Policy*. Fort Worth: Harcourt Brace Jovanovich.

Cockburn, David. 1994. "Human Beings and Giant Squids", *Philosophy* 69: 135-50.

Coetzee, J.M., et al. 1999. *The Lives of Animals*. Princeton: Princeton University Press.

Cohen, Andrew I. 2007. "Contractarianism, Other-regarding Attitudes, and the Moral Standing of Nonhuman Animals", *Journal of Applied Philosophy* 24: 188-201.

Cohen, Carl. 1986. "The Case for the Use of Animals in Biomedical Research", *The New England Journal of Medicine* 315: 865-70.

———. 1997. "Do Animals Have Rights?", *Ethics and Behavior* 7: 103-11.

Cohen, Carl, and Tom Regan. 2001. *The Animal Rights Debate*. Lanham: Rowman and Littlefield.

Cohn, Priscilla. 1999. "Exploding the Hunting Myths", in Priscilla Cohn, ed., *Ethics and Wildlife*. Lewiston: Edwin Mellen Press.

Comstock, Gary. 1992. "The Moral Irrelevance of Autonomy", *Between the Species* 8: 15-27.

Conn, P. Michael, and James V. Parker. 2008. *The Animal Research War*. New York: Palgrave Macmillan.

Cottingham, John. 1978. "'A Brute to the Brutes?': Descartes' Treatment of Animals", *Philosophy* 53: 551-59.

Cowen, Tyler. 2003. "Policing Nature", *Environmental Ethics* 25: 169-82.

Crisp, Roger. 1997. "Utilitarianism and Vegetarianism", in Eldon Soifer, ed., *Ethical Issues: Perspectives for Canadians*, 2nd ed. Peterborough: Broadview Press.

Crist, Eileen. 1999. *Images of Animals: Anthropomorphism and Animal Mind*. Philadelphia: Temple University Press.

Crossley, Ceri. 2005. *Consumable Metaphors: Attitudes towards Animals and Vegetarianism in Nineteenth-Century France*. Bern: Peter Lang.

Curnutt, Jordan. 1997. "A New Argument for Vegetarianism", *Journal of Social Philosophy* 28, no. 3: 153-72.

Cushing, Simon. 2003. "Against 'Humanism': Speciesism, Personhood, and Preference", *Journal of Social Philosophy* 34: 556-71.

Darwin, Charles. 1859. *On the Origin of Species by Means of Natural Selection*. London: John Murray.

———. 1872. *The Expression of the Emotions in Man and Animals*. London: John Murray.

———. 1890. *The Descent of Man, and Selection in Relation to Sex*, 2nd ed. London: John Murray.

Daston, Lorraine, and Gregg Mitman, eds. 2005. *Thinking with Animals: New Perspectives on Anthropomorphism*. New York: Columbia University Press.

Davis, Steven L. 2003. "The Least Harm Principle May Require that Humans Consume a Diet Containing Large Herbivores, Not a Vegan Diet", *Journal of Agricultural and Environmental Ethics* 16: 387-94.

Davis, William H. 1976. "Man-Eating Aliens", *The Journal of Value Inquiry* 10: 178-85.

Davy, Barbara Jane. 2007. "An Other Face of Ethics in Levinas", *Ethics & the Environment* 12, no. 1: 39-65.

Dawkins, Marian Stamp. 1980. *Animal Suffering: The Science of Animal Welfare*. London: Chapman and Hall.

———. 1993. *Through Our Eyes Only? The Search for Animal Consciousness*. Oxford: W.H. Freeman.

Dawkins, Richard. 1993. "Gaps in the Mind", in Paola Cavalieri and Peter Singer, eds., *The Great Ape Project: Equality beyond Humanity*. London: Fourth Estate.

Dawn, Karen. 2008. *Thanking the Monkey: Rethinking the Way We Treat Animals*. New York: HarperCollins.

Deckha, Maneesha. 2006. "The Salience of Species Difference for Feminist Theory", *Hastings Women's Law Journal* 17, no. 1: 1-38.

DeGrazia, David. 1996. *Taking Animals Seriously: Mental Life and Moral Status.* Cambridge: Cambridge University Press.

———. 2002. *Animal Rights: A Very Short Introduction.* New York: Oxford University Press.

———. 2008. "Moral Status As a Matter of Degree?", *The Southern Journal of Philosophy* 46: 181-98.

DeGrazia, David, and Andrew Rowan. 1991. "Pain, Suffering, and Anxiety in Animals and Humans", *Theoretical Medicine* 12: 193-211.

De Leeuw, A. Dionys. 1996. "Contemplating the Interests of Fish: The Angler's Challenge", *Environmental Ethics* 18: 373-90.

Denis, Lara. 2000. "Kant's Conception of Duties regarding Animals: Reconstruction and Reconsideration", *History of Philosophy Quarterly* 17: 405-23.

Derrida, Jacques. 1991. "'Eating Well', or the Calculation of the Subject: An Interview with Jacques Derrida", in Eduardo Cadava, Peter Connor, and Jean-Luc Nancy, eds., *Who Comes after the Subject?* New York: Routledge.

———. 2002. "The Animal That Therefore I Am (More to Follow)", *Critical Inquiry* 28: 369-418. Abridged in Matthew Calarco and Peter Atterton, eds., *Animal Philosophy: Essential Readings in Continental Thought.* London: Continuum, 2004.

Descartes, René. 1985. "Discourse on the Method of Rightly Conducting One's Reason and Seeking the Truth in the Sciences", in *The Philosophical Writings of Descartes*, vol. 1. Cambridge: Cambridge University Press. First published in 1637. See especially pp. 139-41.

———. 1991. *The Philosophical Writings of Descartes*, vol. 3: *The Correspondence.* Cambridge: Cambridge University Press. See especially pp. 99-100, 302-04, 365-66.

Devine, Philip E. 1978. "The Moral Basis of Vegetarianism", *Philosophy* 53: 481-505.

De Vries, Rob. 2006. "Genetic Engineering and the Integrity of Animals", *Journal of Agricultural and Environmental Ethics* 19: 469-93.

———. 2008. "Intrinsic Value and the Genetic Engineering of Animals", *Environmental Values* 17: 375-92.

De Waal, Frans. 1996. *Good Natured: The Origins of Right and Wrong in Humans and Other Animals.* Cambridge, Mass.: Harvard University Press.

———. 2006. *Primates and Philosophers: How Morality Evolved.* Princeton: Princeton University Press.

Diamond, Cora. 1978. "Eating Meat and Eating People", *Philosophy* 53: 465-79.

Diamond, Jared. 1993. "The Third Chimpanzee", in Paola Cavalieri and Peter Singer, eds., *The Great Ape Project: Equality beyond Humanity*. London: Fourth Estate.

Dieterle, J.M. 2008. "Unnecessary Suffering", *Environmental Ethics* 30: 51-67.

Dixon, Ben. 2007. "Darwinism and Human Dignity", *Environmental Values* 16: 23-42.

Dixon, Beth A. 1996. "The Feminist Connection between Women and Animals", *Environmental Ethics* 18: 181-94.

———. 2008. *Animals, Emotion, and Mortality: Marking the Boundary*. Amherst: Prometheus.

Dizard, Jan E. 1994. *Going Wild: Hunting, Animal Rights, and the Contested Meaning of Nature*. Amherst: University of Massachusetts Press.

Dol, Marcel, et al., eds. 1997. *Animal Consciousness and Animal Ethics: Perspectives from the Netherlands*. Assen: Van Gorcum.

———. 1999. *Recognizing the Intrinsic Value of Animals: Beyond Animal Welfare*. Assen: Van Gorcum.

Dolins, Francine L., ed. 1999. *Attitudes to Animals: Views in Animal Welfare*. Cambridge: Cambridge University Press.

Dombrowski, Daniel A. 1984. *The Philosophy of Vegetarianism*. Amherst: University of Massachusetts Press.

———. 1988. *Hartshorne and the Metaphysics of Animal Rights*. Albany: State University of New York Press.

———. 1997. *Babies and Beasts: The Argument from Marginal Cases*. Urbana: University of Illinois Press.

———. 2006. "Is the Argument from Marginal Cases Obtuse?", *Journal of Applied Ethics* 23: 223-32.

Donnelley, Strachan. 1989. "Speculative Philosophy, the Troubled Middle, and the Ethics of Animal Experimentation", *Hastings Center Report* 19, no. 2: 15-21.

Donnelley, Strachan, Charles R. McCarthy, and Rivers Singleton, Jr. 1994. "The Brave New World of Animal Biotechnology", *Hastings Center Report* 24, no. 1, special supplement: S1-S30.

Donner, Wendy. 1997. "Animal Rights and Native Hunters: A Critical Analysis of Wenzel's Defence", in Alex Wellington, Allan Greenbaum, and Wesley Cragg, eds., *Canadian Issues in Environmental Ethics*. Peterborough: Broadview Press.

Donovan, Josephine. 1990. "Animal Rights and Feminist Theory", *Signs* 15: 350-75.

———. 1991. "Reply to Noddings", *Signs* 16: 423-25.

———. 1996. "Attention to Suffering: A Feminist Caring Ethic for the Treatment of Animals", *Journal of Social Philosophy* 27, no. 1: 81-102.

———. 2006. "Feminism and the Treatment of Animals: From Care to Dialogue", *Signs* 31: 305-29.

Donovan, Josephine, and Carol J. Adams, eds. 1996. *Beyond Animal Rights: A Feminist Caring Ethic for the Treatment of Animals*. New York: Continuum.

———. 2007. *The Feminist Care Tradition in Animal Ethics: A Reader*. New York: Columbia University Press.

Dunayer, Joan. 2001. *Animal Equality: Language and Liberation*. Derwood: Ryce.

———. 2004. *Speciesism*. Derwood: Ryce.

Eaton, David. 2002. "Incorporating the Other: Val Plumwood's Integration of Ethical Frameworks", *Ethics & the Environment* 7, no. 2: 153-80.

Edwards, Rem B. 1993. "Tom Regan's Seafaring Dog and (Un)Equal Inherent Worth", *Between the Species* 9: 231-35.

Egonsson, Dan. 1997. "Kant's Vegetarianism", *The Journal of Value Inquiry* 31: 473-83.

Eisnitz, Gail A. 1997. *Slaughterhouse: The Shocking Story of Greed, Neglect, and Inhumane Treatment inside the U.S. Meat Industry*. Amherst: Prometheus.

Elliott, Robert. 1984. "Rawlsian Justice and Non-Human Animals", *Journal of Applied Philosophy* 1: 95-106.

———. 1987. "Moral Autonomy, Self-Determination, and Animal Rights", *The Monist* 70: 83-97.

———. 1996. "Solidarity, Property Rights, Redistribution, and the Great Apes", *Etica & Animali* 8: 34-43.

Engel, Mylan Jr. 2000. "The Immorality of Eating Meat", in Louis P. Pojman, ed., *The Moral Life: An Introductory Reader in Ethics and Literature*. New York: Oxford University Press.

Engels, Frederick. 1972. *Dialectics of Nature*. Moscow: Progress. See especially "The Part Played by Labour in the Transition from Ape to Man", pp. 170-83.

Engster, Daniel. 2006. "Care Ethics and Animal Welfare", *Journal of Social Philosophy* 37: 521-36.

Everett, Jennifer. 2001. "Environmental Ethics, Animal Welfarism, and the Problem of Predation", *Ethics & the Environment* 6, no. 1: 42-67.

Fadali, Moneim A. 1996. *Animal Experimentation: A Harvest of Shame*. Los Angeles: Hidden Springs Press.

Feeney, Dennis M. 1987. "Human Rights and Animal Welfare", *American Psychologist* 42: 593-99.

Feinberg, Joel. 1974. "The Rights of Animals and Unborn Generations", in
W.T. Blackstone, ed., *Philosophy and Environmental Crisis*. Athens, GA:
University of Georgia Press.

———. 1978. "Human Duties and Animal Rights", in Richard Knowles Morris
and Michael W. Fox, eds., *On the Fifth Day: Animal Rights and Human
Ethics*. Washington: Acropolis.

Fellenz, Marc R. 2007. *The Moral Menagerie: Philosophy and Animal Rights*.
Urbana: University of Illinois Press.

Fellows, Roger. 2000. "Animal Belief", *Philosophy* 75: 587-98.

Ferguson, Moira. 1998. *Animal Advocacy and Englishwomen, 1780-1900:
Patriots, Nation, and Empire*. Ann Arbor: University of Michigan Press.

Ferré, Frederick. 1986. "Moderation, Morals, and Meat", *Inquiry* 29: 391-406.

Fiddes, Nick. 1991. *Meat: A Natural Symbol*. London: Routledge.

Finsen, Lawrence, and Susan Finsen. 1994. *The Animal Rights Movement in
America: From Compassion to Respect*. New York: Twayne.

Finsen, Susan. 1988a. "Making Ends Meet: Reconciling Ecoholism and Animal
Rights Individualism", *Between the Species* 4: 11-20.

———. 1988b. "Sinking the Research Lifeboat", *The Journal of Medicine and
Philosophy* 13: 197-212.

Fjellström, Roger. 2002a. "Equality Does Not Entail Equality across Species",
*Environmental Ethics* 24: 339-52.

———. 2002b. "Specifying Speciesism", *Environmental Values* 11: 63-74.

———. 2003. "Is Singer's Ethics Speciesist?", *Environmental Values* 12: 91-106.

Fouts, Roger. 1997. *Next of Kin: What Chimpanzees Have Taught Me about
Who We Are*. With Stephen Tukel Mills. New York: William Morrow.

Fox, Michael Allen. 1986. *The Case for Animal Experimentation: An Evolutionary and Ethical Perspective*. Berkeley: University of California Press.

———. 1987. "Animal Experimentation: A Philosopher's Changing Views",
*Between the Species* 3: 55-60, 75, 80, 82.

———. 1995. "Nonhuman, All Too Human", *Queen's Quarterly* 102: 182-96.

———. 1996. "Planet for the Apes", *Etica & Animali* 8: 44-49.

———. 1999. *Deep Vegetarianism*. Philadelphia: Temple University Press.

Fox, Michael W. 1980. *Returning to Eden: Animal Rights and Human
Responsibility*. New York: Viking Press.

———. 1990. *Inhumane Society: The American Way of Exploiting Animals*. New
York: St. Martin's Press.

———. 1992. *Superpigs and Wondercorn: The Brave New World of Biotechnology and Where It All May Lead*. New York: Lyons and Burford.

Francione, Gary L. 1995. *Animals, Property, and the Law*. Philadelphia: Temple University Press.

———. 1996. *Rain without Thunder: The Ideology of the Animal Rights Movement*. Philadelphia: Temple University Press.

———. 2000. *Introduction to Animal Rights: Your Child or the Dog?* Philadelphia: Temple University Press.

———. 2008. *Animals As Persons: Essays on the Abolition of Animal Exploitation*. New York: Columbia University Press.

Francis, Leslie Pickering, and Richard Norman. 1978. "Some Animals Are More Equal Than Others", *Philosophy* 53: 507-27.

Frank, Joshua. 2002. "A Constraint-Utility Alternative to Animal Rights", *Environmental Values* 11: 49-62.

Franklin, Julian H. 2001. "Regan on the Lifeboat Problem: A Defense", *Environmental Ethics* 23: 189-201.

———. 2005. *Animal Rights and Moral Philosophy*. New York: Columbia University Press.

French, Richard D. 1975. *Antivivisection and Medical Science in Victorian Society*. Princeton: Princeton University Press.

Frey, R.G. 1980. *Interests and Rights: The Case against Animals*. Oxford: Clarendon Press.

———. 1983. *Rights, Killing, and Suffering: Moral Vegetarianism and Applied Ethics*. Oxford: Basil Blackwell.

———. 1987. "Autonomy and the Value of Animal Life", *The Monist* 70: 50-63.

Fudge, Erica. 2006. *Brutal Reasoning: Animals, Rationality, and Humanity in Early Modern England*. Ithaca: Cornell University Press.

Fuller, B.A.G. 1949. "The Messes Animals Make in Metaphysics", *The Journal of Philosophy* 46: 829-38.

Gaffney, James. 1986. "The Relevance of Animal Experimentation to Roman Catholic Ethical Methodology", in Tom Regan, ed., *Animal Sacrifices: Religious Perspectives on the Use of Animals in Science*. Philadelphia: Temple University Press.

Gaita, Raimond. 2002. *The Philosopher's Dog*. Melbourne: Text.

Galdikas, Biruté M.F., and Gary L. Shapiro. 1996. "Orangutan Ethics", *Etica & Animali* 8: 50-67.

Galvin, Shelly L., and Harold A. Herzog. 1992. "The Ethical Judgment of Animal Research", *Ethics and Behavior* 2: 263-86.

Garner, Robert. 2004. *Animals, Politics, and Morality*, 2nd ed. Manchester: Manchester University Press.

———. 2005a. *Animal Ethics*. Cambridge: Polity Press.

———. 2005b. *The Political Theory of Animal Rights*. Manchester: Manchester University Press.

Garner, Robert, ed. 1996. *Animal Rights: The Changing Debate*. New York: New York University Press.

Garrett, Jeremy R. 2007. "Utilitarianism, Vegetarianism, and Human Health: A Response to the Causal Impotence Objection", *Journal of Applied Ethics* 24: 223-37.

Gavrell Ortiz, Sara Elizabeth. 2004. "Beyond Welfare: Animal Integrity, Animal Dignity, and Genetic Engineering", *Ethics & the Environment* 9, no. 1: 94-120.

George, Kathryn Paxton. 2000. *Animal, Vegetable, or Woman? A Feminist Critique of Ethical Vegetarianism*. Albany: State University of New York Press.

Gluck, John P., Tony DiPasquale, and F. Barbara Orlans, eds. 2002. *Applied Ethics in Animal Research: Philosophy, Regulation, and Laboratory Applications*. West Lafayette: Purdue University Press.

Godfrey-Smith, William. 1980. "The Rights of Non-Humans and Intrinsic Values", in D.S. Mannison, M.A. McRobbie, and R. Routley, eds., *Environmental Philosophy*. Canberra: Department of Philosophy, Research School of Social Sciences, Australian National University.

Godlovitch, Roslind. 1971. "Animals and Morals", *Philosophy* 46: 23-33.

Godlovitch, Stanley, Roslind Godlovitch, and John Harris, eds. 1971. *Animals, Men, and Morals: An Enquiry into the Maltreatment of Non-Humans*. London: Victor Gollancz.

Goldman, Michael. 2001. "A Transcendental Defense of Speciesism", *The Journal of Value Inquiry* 35: 59-69.

Gómez, Juan Carlos. 1998. "Are Apes Persons? The Case for Primate Intersubjectivity", *Etica & Animali* 9: 51-63.

Gompertz, Lewis. 1997. *Moral Inquiries on the Situation of Man and of Brutes*. Lewiston: Edwin Mellen Press. First published in 1824.

Goodall, Jane. 1990. *Through a Window: My Thirty Years with the Chimpanzees of Gombe*. Boston: Houghton Mifflin.

———. 2005. *Harvest for Hope: A Guide to Mindful Eating*. With Gary McAvoy and Gail Hudson. New York: Warner.

Goodall, Jane, and Marc Bekoff. 2002. *The Ten Trusts: What We Must Do to Care for the Animals We Love*. San Francisco: HarperSanFrancisco.

Goodpaster, Kenneth E. 1978. "On Being Morally Considerable", *The Journal of Philosophy* 75: 308-325.

Graham, David, and Nathan Nobis. 2006. "Putting Humans First?", *Journal of Ayn Rand Studies* 8: 85-104.

Graft, Donald. 1997. "Against Strong Speciesism", *Journal of Applied Philosophy* 14: 107-18.

Grant, Douglas. 1957. *Margaret the First: A Biography of Margaret Cavendish, Duchess of Newcastle, 1623-1673*. London: Rupert Hart-Davis. See chap. 10, "The Pursuit of Nature".

Greek, C. Ray, and Jean Swingle Greek. 2000. *Sacred Cows and Golden Geese: The Human Cost of Experiments on Animals*. New York: Continuum.

Gregory, James. 2007. *Of Victorians and Vegetarians: The Vegetarian Movement in Nineteenth-century Britain*. London: Tauris Academic Studies.

Griffin, Donald R. 1981. *The Question of Animal Awareness: Evolutionary Continuity of Mental Experience*, rev. ed. New York: Rockefeller University Press.

———. 1984. *Animal Thinking*. Cambridge, Mass.: Harvard University Press.

———. 1992. *Animal Minds*. Chicago: University of Chicago Press.

Groves, Julian McAllister. 1997. *Hearts and Minds: The Controversy over Laboratory Animals*. Philadelphia: Temple University Press.

Gruen, Lori. 1991. "Animals", in Peter Singer, ed., *A Companion to Ethics*. Oxford: Basil Blackwell.

———. 1993. "Dismantling Oppression: An Analysis of the Connection between Women and Animals", in Greta Gaard, ed., *Ecofeminism: Women, Animals, Nature*. Philadelphia: Temple University Press.

Gruen, Lori, Peter Singer, and David Hine. 1987. *Animal Liberation: A Graphic Guide*. London: Camden Press.

Guither, Harold D. 1998. *Animal Rights: History and Scope of a Radical Social Movement*. Carbondale: Southern Illinois University Press.

Gunn, Alastair S. 1983. "Traditional Ethics and the Moral Status of Animals", *Environmental Ethics* 5: 133-53.

———. 2001. "Environmental Ethics and Trophy Hunting", *Ethics & the Environment* 6, no. 1: 68-95.

Gunnarsson, Logi. 2008. "The Great Apes and the Severely Disabled: Moral Status and Thick Evaluative Concepts", *Ethical Theory and Moral Practice* 11: 305-26.

Hadley, John. 2004. "Using and Abusing Others: A Reply to Machan," *Journal of Value Inquiry* 38: 411-14.

———. 2005. "Nonhuman Animal Property: Reconciling Environmentalism and Animal Rights", *Journal of Social Philosophy* 36: 305-15.

———. 2006. "The Duty to Aid Nonhuman Animals in Dire Need", *Journal of Applied Philosophy* 23: 445-51.

Hale, Benjamin. 2006. "The Moral Considerability of Invasive Transgenic Animals", *Journal of Agricultural and Environmental Ethics* 19: 337-66.

Hare, R.M. 1999. "Why I Am Only a Demi-vegetarian", in Dale Jamieson, ed., *Singer and His Critics*. Oxford: Blackwell.

Hargrove, Eugene C., ed. 1992. *The Animal Rights/Environmental Ethics Debate: The Environmental Perspective*. Albany: State University of New York Press.

Harrison, Peter. 1989. "Theodicy and Animal Pain", *Philosophy* 64: 79-92.

———. 1991. "Do Animals Feel Pain?", *Philosophy* 66: 25-40.

———. 1992. "Descartes on Animals", *The Philosophical Quarterly* 42: 219-27.

———. 1993. "The Neo-Cartesian Revival: A Response", *Between the Species* 9: 71-76.

Harrison, Ruth. 1964. *Animal Machines: The New Factory Farming Industry*. London: Vincent Stuart.

Hauskeller, Michael. 2005. "Telos: The Revival of an Aristotelian Concept in Present Day Ethics", *Inquiry* 48: 62-75.

Hawkins, Ronnie Zoe. 2002. "Seeing Ourselves As Primates", *Ethics & the Environment* 7, no. 2: 60-103.

Haworth, Lawrence. 1977-78. "Rights, Wrongs, and Animals", *Ethics* 88: 95-105.

Hearne, Vicki. 1994. *Animal Happiness*. New York: HarperCollins.

Heilbroner, Robert L. 1985. *The Nature and Logic of Capitalism*. New York: Norton.

Herscovici, Alan. 1985. *Second Nature: The Animal-Rights Controversy*. Toronto: CBC Enterprises.

Herzing, Denise L., and Thomas I. White. 1998. "Dolphins and the Question of Personhood", *Etica & Animali* 9: 64-84.

Herzog, Harold A. 1993a. "Human Morality and Animal Research: Confessions and Quandaries", *The American Scholar* 62: 337-49.

———. 1993b. "'The Movement Is My Life': The Psychology of Animal Rights Activism", *Journal of Social Issues* 49: 103-19.

Hill, John Lawrence. 1996. *The Case for Vegetarianism: Philosophy for a Small Planet*. Lanham: Rowman and Littlefield.

Hobbes, Thomas. 1983. *De Cive, The English Version*. Oxford: Clarendon Press. First published (in Latin) in 1642. See especially pp. 56, 120-21.

Hoff, Christina. 1980. "Immoral and Moral Uses of Animals", *The New England Journal of Medicine* 302: 115-18.

———. 1983. "Kant's Invidious Humanism", *Environmental Ethics* 5: 63-70.

Holland, Alan J. 1984. "On Behalf of Moderate Speciesism", *Journal of Applied Philosophy* 1: 281-91.

Houston, Pam, ed. 1995. *Women on Hunting.* Hopewell: Ecco Press.

Hudson, Hud. 1993. "Collective Responsibility and Moral Vegetarianism", *Journal of Social Philosophy* 24, no. 2: 89-104.

Hume, David. 1975. *Enquiries Concerning Human Understanding and Concerning the Principles of Morals.* Oxford: Clarendon Press. Reprinted from the edition of 1777. See especially "Of the Reason of Animals", pp. 104-08, and "Of Justice", pp. 190-91.

Huntley, William B. 1972. "David Hume and Charles Darwin", *Journal of the History of Ideas* 33: 457-70.

Hursthouse, Rosalind. 2000. *Ethics, Humans, and Other Animals: An Introduction with Readings.* London: Routledge.

Husak, Douglas N. 1980. "On the Rights of Non-Persons", *Canadian Journal of Philosophy* 10: 607-22.

Huxley, Aldous. 1932. *Brave New World.* London: Chatto and Windus.

Irvin, Sherri. 2004. "Capacities, Context, and the Moral Status of Animals", *Journal of Applied Philosophy* 21: 61-76.

Jacobsen, Knut A. 1994. "The Institutionalization of the Ethics of 'Non-Injury' toward All 'Beings' in Ancient India", *Environmental Ethics* 16: 287-301.

Jamieson, Dale. 1981. "Rational Egoism and Animal Rights", *Environmental Ethics* 3: 167-71.

———. 1983. "Killing Persons and Other Beings", in Harlan B. Miller and William H. Williams, eds., *Ethics and Animals.* Clifton: Humana Press.

———. 1990. "Rights, Justice, and Duties to Provide Assistance: A Critique of Regan's Theory of Rights", *Ethics* 100: 349-62.

———. 2002. *Morality's Progress: Essays on Humans, Other Animals, and the Rest of Nature.* Oxford: Clarendon Press.

———. 2008. "The Rights of Animals and the Demands of Nature", *Environmental Values* 17: 181-99.

Jasper, James M., and Dorothy Nelkin. 1992. *The Animal Rights Crusade: The Growth of a Moral Protest.* New York: Free Press.

Jeangène Vilmer, Jean-Baptiste. 2008. *Éthique Animale.* Paris: Presses Universitaires de France.

Jenni, Kathie. 1994. "Dilemmas in Social Philosophy: Abortion and Animal Rights", *Social Theory and Practice* 20: 59-83.

Jensen, Jon. 2001. "The Virtues of Hunting", *Philosophy in the Contemporary World* 8, no. 2: 113-24.

Jerolmack, Colin. 2003. "Tracing the Profile of Animal Rights Supporters: A Preliminary Investigation", *Society and Animals* 11: 245-63.

Johnson, Edward. 1981. "Animal Liberation versus the Land Ethic", *Environmental Ethics* 3: 265-73.

———. 1983. "Life, Death, and Animals", in Harlan B. Miller and William H. Williams, eds., *Ethics and Animals*. Clifton: Humana Press.

Johnson, Lawrence E. 1983. "Can Animals Be Moral Agents?", *Ethics and Animals* 4: 50-61.

———. 1991. *A Morally Deep World: An Essay on Moral Significance and Environmental Ethics*. Cambridge: Cambridge University Press.

Kalof, Linda. 2007. *Looking at Animals in Human History*. London: Reaktion.

Kalof, Linda, and Amy Fitzgerald, eds. 2007. *The Animals Reader: The Essential Classic and Contemporary Writings*. Oxford: Berg.

Kalof, Linda, Amy Fitzgerald, and Lori Baralt. 2004. "Animals, Women, and Weapons: Blurred Sexual Boundaries in the Discourse of Sport Hunting", *Society and Animals* 12: 237-51.

Kant, Immanuel. 1997. *Lectures on Ethics*. Cambridge: Cambridge University Press. See especially "Of Duties to Animals and Spirits", pp. 212-13.

Katz, Eric. 1990. "Defending the Use of Animals by Business: Animal Liberation and Environmental Ethics", in W. Michael Hoffman, Robert Frederick, and Edward S. Petry, Jr., eds., *Business, Ethics, and the Environment: The Public Policy Debate*. Westport: Quorum.

Kaufman, Frederik. 1998. "Speciesism and the Argument from Misfortune", *Journal of Applied Philosophy* 15: 155-63.

Kawall, Jason. 2000. "Is (Merely) Stalking Sentient Animals Morally Wrong?", *Journal of Applied Philosophy* 17: 195-204.

Kellert, Stephen R., and Edward O. Wilson, eds. 1993. *The Biophilia Hypothesis*. Washington: Island Press.

Kemmerer, Lisa. 2006. *In Search of Consistency: Ethics and Animals*. Leiden: Brill.

Kerasote, Ted. 1993. *Bloodties: Nature, Culture, and the Hunt*. New York: Random House.

Kete, Kathleen. 1994. *The Beast in the Boudoir: Petkeeping in Nineteenth-Century Paris*. Berkeley: University of California Press.

Kheel, Marti. 1985. "The Liberation of Nature: A Circular Affair",
    *Environmental Ethics* 7: 135-49.

———. 1995. "License to Kill: An Ecofeminist Critique of Hunters' Discourse",
    in Carol J. Adams and Josephine Donovan, eds., *Animals and Women:
    Feminist Theoretical Explorations*. Durham: Duke University Press.

Kistler, John M. 2000. *Animal Rights: A Subject Guide, Bibliography, and
    Internet Companion*. Westport: Greenwood Press.

Kline, A. David. 1995. "We Should Allow Dissection of Animals", *Journal of
    Agricultural and Environmental Ethics* 8: 190-97.

Kolata, Gina. 1998. *Clone: The Road to Dolly, and the Path Ahead*. New York:
    William Morrow.

Korsgaard, Christine M. 2005. "Fellow Creatures: Kantian Ethics and Our
    Duties to Animals", in Grethe B. Peterson, ed., *The Tanner Lectures on
    Human Values*, vol. 25. Salt Lake City: University of Utah Press.

LaFollette, Hugh, and Niall Shanks. 1996. *Brute Science: Dilemmas of Animal
    Experimentation*. London: Routledge.

Lal, Basant K. 1986. "Hindu Perspectives on the Use of Animals in Science", in
    Tom Regan, ed., *Animal Sacrifices: Religious Perspectives on the Use of
    Animals in Science*. Philadelphia: Temple University Press.

Lamb, David. 1982. "Animal Rights and Liberation Movements",
    *Environmental Ethics* 4: 215-33.

Lamey, Andy. 2007. "Food Fight! Davis versus Regan on the Ethics of Eating
    Beef", *Journal of Social Philosophy* 38: 331-48.

Langer, Monika. 1999. "The Role and Status of Animals in Nietzsche's
    Philosophy", in H. Peter Steeves, ed., *Animal Others: On Ethics, Ontology,
    and Animal Life*. Albany: State University of New York Press.

Langley, Gill, ed. 1989. *Animal Experimentation: The Consensus Changes*. New
    York: Chapman and Hall.

Lansbury, Coral. 1985. *The Old Brown Dog: Women, Workers, and Vivisection
    in Edwardian England*. Madison: University of Wisconsin Press.

Lansdell, Herbert. 1988. "Laboratory Animals Need Only Humane Treatment:
    Animal 'Rights' May Debase Human Rights", *International Journal of
    Neuroscience* 42: 169-78.

Lawlor, Leonard. 2007. *This Is Not Sufficient: An Essay on Animality and
    Human Nature in Derrida*. New York: Columbia University Press.

Leahy, Michael P.T. 1991. *Against Liberation: Putting Animals in Perspective*.
    London: Routledge.

Lehman, Hugh. 1988. "On the Moral Acceptability of Killing Animals", *Journal of Agricultural Ethics* 1: 155-62.

Lekan, Todd. 2004. "Integrating Justice and Care in Animal Ethics", *Journal of Applied Philosophy* 21: 183-95.

Leopold, Aldo. 1966. *A Sand County Almanac, with Other Essays on Conservation from Round River*. New York: Oxford University Press.

Levy, Neil. 2003. "What (if Anything) Is Wrong with Bestiality?", *Journal of Social Philosophy* 34: 444-56.

———. 2004. "Cohen and Kinds: A Response to Nathan Nobis", *Journal of Applied Philosophy* 21: 213-17.

Lewis, C.S. 1940. *The Problem of Pain*. London: Centenary Press. See chap. 9, "Animal Pain".

Linden, Eugene. 1999. *The Parrot's Lament, and Other True Tales of Animal Intrigue, Intelligence, and Ingenuity*. New York: Dutton.

Linzey, Andrew. 1976. *Animal Rights: A Christian Assessment of Man's Treatment of Animals*. London: SCM Press.

———. 1987. *Christianity and the Rights of Animals*. New York: Crossroad.

———. 1994. *Animal Theology*. London: SCM Press.

———. 2000. *Animal Gospel*. Louisville: Westminster John Knox Press.

Linzey, Andrew, and Paul Barry Clarke, eds. 2004. *Animal Rights: A Historical Anthology*. New York: Columbia University Press.

List, Charles J. 1997. "Is Hunting a Right Thing?", *Environmental Ethics* 19: 405-16.

———. 2004. "On the Moral Distinctiveness of Sport Hunting", *Environmental Ethics* 26: 155-69.

Livingston, John A. 1984. "Rightness or Rights?", *Osgoode Hall Law Journal* 22: 309-21.

———. 1994. *Rogue Primate: An Exploration of Human Domestication*. Toronto: Key Porter.

Lloyd, Genevieve. 1980. "Spinoza's Environmental Ethics", *Inquiry* 23: 293-11.

Locke, John. 1960. *Two Treatises of Government*. Cambridge: Cambridge University Press. First published in 1689.

———. 1979. *An Essay Concerning Human Understanding*. Oxford: Clarendon Press. First published in 1690. See especially bk. 2, chap. 9, "Of Perception", chap. 10, "Of Retention", chap. 11, "Of Discerning, and Other Operations of the Mind".

Lockwood, Michael. 1979. "Singer on Killing and the Preference for Life", *Inquiry* 22: 157-70.

Loftin, Robert W. 1984. "The Morality of Hunting", *Environmental Ethics* 6: 241-250.

———. 1985. "The Medical Treatment of Wild Animals", *Environmental Ethics* 7: 231-39.

Lombardi, Louis G. 1983. "Inherent Worth, Respect, and Rights", *Environmental Ethics* 5: 257-70.

Lowry, Jon W. 1975. "Natural Rights: Men and Animals", *Southwestern Journal of Philosophy* 6: 109-22.

Luke, Brian. 1995. "Solidarity across Diversity: A Pluralistic Rapprochement of Environmentalism and Animal Liberation", *Social Theory and Practice* 21: 177-206.

———. 1997. "A Critical Analysis of Hunters' Ethics", *Environmental Ethics* 19: 25-44.

———. 2007. *Brutal: Manhood and the Exploitation of Animals*. Urbana: University of Illinois Press.

Lund, Vonne, and I. Anna S. Olsson. 2006. "Animal Agriculture: Symbiosis, Culture, or Ethical Conflict?", *Journal of Agricultural and Environmental Ethics* 19: 47-56.

Lynch, Joseph J. 1994. "Is Animal Pain Conscious?", *Between the Species* 10: 1-7.

Lynge, Finn. 1992. *Arctic Wars, Animal Rights, Endangered Peoples*. Hanover: University Press of New England.

Machan, Tibor R. 1991. "Do Animals Have Rights?", *Public Affairs Quarterly* 5: 163-73.

———. 2004. *Putting Humans First, Why We Are Nature's Favorite*. Lanham: Rowman and Littlefield.

MacIntosh, J.J. 1996. "Animals, Morality, and Robert Boyle", *Dialogue* 35: 435-72.

MacIver, A.M. 1948. "Ethics and the Beetle", *Analysis* 8: 65-70.

Mack, Arien, ed. 1999. *Humans and Other Animals*. Columbus: Ohio State University Press.

Malik, Kenan. 2000. *Man, Beast, and Zombie: What Science Can and Cannot Tell Us about Human Nature*. London: Weidenfeld & Nicolson.

Marcus, Erik. 2005. *Meat Market: Animals, Ethics, and Money*. Boston: Brio Press.

Marquardt, Kathleen. 1993. *AnimalScam: The Beastly Abuse of Human Rights*. With Herbert M. Levine and Mark LaRochelle. Washington: Regnery Gateway.

Marx, Karl. 1974. *Economic and Philosophic Manuscripts of 1844*. Moscow: Progress. See especially pp. 67-69.

———. 1976. *Capital*, vol. 1. Harmondsworth: Penguin. First published (in German) in 1867. See especially pp. 283-84.

Mason, Jim. 1993. *An Unnatural Order: Uncovering the Roots of Our Domination of Nature and Each Other*. New York: Simon and Schuster.

Mason, Jim, and Peter Singer. 1980. *Animal Factories*. New York: Crown.

Masri, B.A. 1986. "Animal Experimentation: The Muslim Viewpoint", in Tom Regan, ed., *Animal Sacrifices: Religious Perspectives on the Use of Animals in Science*. Philadelphia: Temple University Press.

Masson, Jeffrey Moussaieff. 2003. *The Pig Who Sang to the Moon: The Emotional World of Farm Animals*. New York: Ballantine.

Masson, Jeffrey Moussaieff, and Susan McCarthy. 1995. *When Elephants Weep: The Emotional Lives of Animals*. New York: Delacorte Press.

Matheny, Gaverick. 2002. "Expected Utility, Contributory Causation, and Vegetarianism", *Journal of Applied Philosophy* 19: 293-97.

———. 2003. "Least Harm: A Defense of Vegetarianism from Steven Davis's Omnivorous Proposal", *Journal of Agricultural and Environmental Ethics* 16: 505-11.

Matheny, Gaverick, and Kai M.A. Chan. 2005. "Human Diets and Animal Welfare: The Illogic of the Larder", *Journal of Agricultural and Environmental Ethics* 18: 579-94.

Matthews, Gareth B. 1978. "Animals and the Unity of Psychology", *Philosophy* 53: 437-54.

McCloskey, H.J. 1979. "Moral Rights and Animals", *Inquiry* 22: 23-54.

———. 1987. "The Moral Case for Experimentation on Animals", *The Monist* 70: 64-82.

McGinn, Colin. 1979. "Evolution, Animals, and the Basis of Morality", *Inquiry* 22: 81-99.

———. 1999. "Animal Minds, Animal Morality", in Arien Mack, ed., *Humans and Other Animals*. Columbus: Ohio State University Press.

McGrew, W.C. 1992. *Chimpanzee Material Culture: Implications for Human Evolution*. Cambridge: Cambridge University Press.

McGrew, William C., Linda F. Marchant, and Toshisada Nishida, eds. 1996. *Great Ape Societies*. Cambridge: Cambridge University Press.

McKenna, Erin. 1994. "Feminism and Vegetarianism: A Critique of Peter Singer", *Philosophy in the Contemporary World* 1, no. 3: 28-35.

———. 1996. "Women, Power, and Meat: Comparing *The Sexual Contract* and *The Sexual Politics of Meat*", *Journal of Social Philosophy* 27, no. 1: 47-64.

McLeod, Carmen M. 2007. "Dreadful/Delightful Killing: The Contested Nature of Duck Hunting", *Society and Animals* 15: 151-67.

McMahan, Jeff. 2002. *The Ethics of Killing: Problems at the Margins of Life*. New York: Oxford University Press.

———. 2005. "Our Fellow Creatures", *The Journal of Ethics* 9: 353-80.

———. 2008. "Eating Animals the Nice Way", *Dædalus* 137, no. 1: 66-76.

Melden, A.I. 1988. *Rights in Moral Lives: A Historical-Philosophical Essay*. Berkeley: University of California Press. See chap. 6, "Animal Rights?"

Melin, Anders. 2004. "Genetic Engineering and the Moral Status of Non-Human Species", *Journal of Agricultural and Environmental Ethics* 17: 479-95.

Midgley, Mary. 1973. "The Concept of Beastliness: Philosophy, Ethics, and Animal Behaviour", *Philosophy* 48: 111-35.

———. 1983a. *Animals and Why They Matter*. Harmondsworth: Penguin.

———. 1983b. "Duties Concerning Islands", in Robert Elliot and Arran Gare, eds., *Environmental Philosophy*. St. Lucia: University of Queensland Press.

———. 1995. *Beast and Man: The Roots of Human Nature*, rev. ed. London: Routledge.

———. 1996. *Utopias, Dolphins, and Computers: Problems of Philosophical Plumbing*. London: Routledge.

Mighetto, Lisa. 1991. *Wild Animals and American Environmental Ethics*. Tucson: University of Arizona Press.

Mill, John Stuart. 1957. *Utilitarianism*. New York: Liberal Arts Press. First published in 1861.

Miller, Harlan B., and William H. Williams, eds. 1983. *Ethics and Animals*. Clifton: Humana Press.

Miller, Peter. 1983. "Do Animals Have Interests Worthy of Our Moral Interest?", *Environmental Ethics* 5: 319-33.

Mitchell, John G. 1980. *The Hunt*. New York: Alfred A. Knopf.

Montgomery, Charlotte. 2000. *Blood Relations: Animals, Humans, and Politics*. Toronto: Between the Lines.

Moore, Eric. 2002. "The Case for Unequal Animal Rights", *Environmental Ethics* 24: 295-312.

Moriarty, Paul Veatch, and Mark Woods. 1997. "Hunting ≠ Predation", *Environmental Ethics* 19: 391-404.

Morris, Richard Knowles, and Michael W. Fox, eds. 1978. *On the Fifth Day: Animal Rights and Human Ethics*. Washington: Acropolis.

Morris, William. 2003. *News from Nowhere, or, An Epoch of Rest, Being Some*

*Chapters from a Utopian Romance*. Peterborough: Broadview Press. First published in 1890.

Morton, Timothy. 1994. *Shelley and the Revolution in Taste: The Body and the Natural World*. Cambridge: Cambridge University Press.

Mukerjee, Madhusree. 1997. "Trends in Animal Research", *Scientific American* 276, no. 2: 86-93.

Musschenga, Albert W. 2002. "Naturalness: Beyond Animal Welfare", *Journal of Agricultural and Environmental Ethics* 15: 171-86.

Naess, Arne. 1985. "Identification As a Source of Deep Ecological Attitudes", in Michael Tobias, ed., *Deep Ecology*. San Diego: Avant.

Nagel, Thomas. 1974. "What Is It Like to Be a Bat?", *Philosophical Review* 83: 435-50.

Namkoong, Gene, and Tom Regan. 1988. "The Question Is Not, 'Can They Talk?'", *The Journal of Medicine and Philosophy* 13: 213-21.

Narveson, Jan. 1977. "Animal Rights", *Canadian Journal of Philosophy* 7: 161-78.

———. 1983. "Animal Rights Revisited", in Harlan B. Miller and William H. Williams, eds., *Ethics and Animals*. Clifton: Humana Press.

———. 1987. "On a Case for Animal Rights", *The Monist* 70: 31-49.

———. 1999. *Moral Matters*, 2nd ed. Peterborough: Broadview Press. See chap. 6, "Morals and Animals".

Newman, Lex. 2001. "Unmasking Descartes's Case for the Bête Machine Doctrine", *Canadian Journal of Philosophy* 31: 389-425.

Newmyer, Stephen T. 2006. *Animals, Rights, and Reason in Plutarch and Modern Ethics*. New York: Routledge.

Nibert, David. 2002. *Animal Rights/Human Rights: Entanglements of Oppression and Liberation*. Lanham: Rowman and Littlefield.

Nicholson, Edward Byron. 1879. *The Rights of an Animal: A New Essay in Ethics*. London: C. Kegan Paul.

Nicoll, Charles S., and Sharon M. Russell. 1990. "Analysis of Animal Rights Literature Reveals the Underlying Motives of the Movement: Ammunition for Counter Offensive by Scientists", *Endocrinology* 127: 985-89.

Nielson, Kai. 1978. "Persons, Morals, and the Animal Kingdom", *Man and World* 11: 231-56.

Nobis, Nathan. 2002. "Vegetarianism and Virtue: Does Consequentialism Demand Too Little?", *Social Theory and Practice* 28: 135-56.

———. 2004. "Carl Cohen's 'Kind' Argument *For* Animal Rights and *Against* Human Rights", *Journal of Applied Philosophy* 21: 43-59.

Noddings, Nel. 1984. *Caring: A Feminine Approach to Ethics and Moral Education*. Berkeley: University of California Press.

———. 1991. "Comment on Donovan's 'Animal Rights and Feminist Theory'", *Signs* 16: 418-22.

Norcross, Alastair. 2004. "Puppies, Pigs, and People: Eating Meat and Marginal Cases", *Philosophical Perspectives* 18: 229-45.

Norton, Bryan G. 1982. "Environmental Ethics and Nonhuman Rights", *Environmental Ethics* 4: 17-36.

———. 1995. "Caring for Nature: A Broader Look at Animal Stewardship", in Bryan G. Norton, et al., eds., *Ethics on the Ark: Zoos, Animal Welfare, and Wildlife Conservation*. Washington: Smithsonian Institution Press.

Norton, Bryan G., et al., eds. 1995. *Ethics on the Ark: Zoos, Animal Welfare, and Wildlife Conservation*. Washington: Smithsonian Institution Press.

Noske, Barbara. 1997. *Beyond Boundaries: Humans and Animals*. Montreal: Black Rose.

Nozick, Robert. 1974. *Anarchy, State, and Utopia*. New York: Basic. See pp. 35-47.

Nussbaum, Martha C. 2001. "Animal Rights: The Need for a Theoretical Basis", *Harvard Law Review* 114: 1506-49.

———. 2004. "Beyond 'Compassion and Humanity': Justice for Nonhuman Animals", in Cass R. Sunstein and Martha C. Nussbaum, eds., *Animal Rights: Current Debates and New Directions*. New York: Oxford University Press.

———. 2006. *Frontiers of Justice: Disability, Nationality, Species Membership*. Cambridge, Mass.: Belknap Press of Harvard University Press.

———. 2007. "The Moral Status of Animals", in Linda Kalof and Amy Fitzgerald, eds., *The Animals Reader: The Essential Classic and Contemporary Writings*. Oxford: Berg.

Olsen, Len. 2003. "Contemplating the Intentions of Anglers: The Ethicist's Challenge", *Environmental Ethics* 25: 267-77.

O'Neil, Rick. 2000. "Animal Liberation versus Environmentalism: The Care Solution", *Environmental Ethics* 22: 183-90.

O'Neill, Onora. 1998. "Kant on Duties regarding Nonrational Nature", *The Aristotelian Society*, supplementary vol. 72: 211-28.

Orend, Brian. 2002. *Human Rights: Concept and Context*. Peterborough: Broadview Press.

Orlans, F. Barbara. 1993. *In the Name of Science: Issues in Responsible Animal Experimentation*. New York: Oxford University Press.

Orlans, F. Barbara, et al. 1998. *The Human Use of Animals: Case Studies in Ethical Choice*. New York: Oxford University Press.

Ortega y Gasset, José. 1972. *Meditations on Hunting*. New York: Charles Scribner's Sons.

Osborne, Catherine. 2007. *Dumb Beasts and Dead Philosophers: Humanity and the Humane in Ancient Philosophy and Literature*. Oxford: Clarendon Press.

Palmer, Clare. 2001. "'Taming the Wild Profusion of Existing Things'? A Study of Foucault, Power, and Human/Animal Relationships", *Environmental Ethics* 23: 339-58.

———. 2003. "Placing Animals in Urban Environmental Ethics", *Journal of Social Philosophy* 34: 64-78.

Palmer, Clare, ed. 2008. *Animal Rights*. Aldershot: Ashgate.

Pardes, Herbert, Anne West, and Harold Alan Pincus. 1991. "Physicians and the Animal-Rights Movement", *The New England Journal of Medicine* 324: 1640-43.

Paske, Gerald H. 1988. "Why Animals Have No Right to Life: A Response to Regan", *Australasian Journal of Philosophy* 66: 498-511.

Passmore, John. 1975. "The Treatment of Animals", *Journal of the History of Ideas* 36: 195-218.

Pateman, Carol. 1996. "The Sexual Contract and the Animals", *Journal of Social Philosophy* 27, no. 1: 65-80.

Paterson, David, and Richard D. Ryder, eds. 1979. *Animals' Rights: A Symposium*. London: Centaur Press.

Paterson, R.W.K. 1984. "Animal Pain, God, and Professor Geach", *Philosophy* 59: 116-20.

Patterson, Charles. 2002. *Eternal Treblinka: Our Treatment of Animals and the Holocaust*. New York: Lantern.

Patterson, Francine, and Eugene Linden. 1981. *The Education of Koko*. New York: Holt, Rinehart, and Winston.

Payne, Katy. 1998. *Silent Thunder: In the Presence of Elephants*. New York: Simon and Schuster.

Payne, Roger. 1995. *Among Whales*. New York: Scribner.

Peña, Lorenzo. 1996. "Anthropoid Rights and Paternalism", *Etica & Animali* 8: 154-77.

Perrett, Roy W. 1993. "Moral Vegetarianism and the Indian Tradition", in Ninian Smart and Shivesh Thakur, eds., *Ethical and Political Dilemmas of Modern India*. Basingstoke: Macmillan Press.

——. 1997. "The Analogical Argument for Animal Pain", *Journal of Applied Philosophy* 14: 49-58.

Peterson, Dale, and Jane Goodall. 1993. *Visions of Caliban: On Chimpanzees and People*. Boston: Houghton Mifflin.

Petrinovich, Lewis. 1999. *Darwinian Dominion: Animal Welfare and Human Interests*. Cambridge, Mass.: MIT Press.

Phelps, Norm. 2004. *The Great Compassion: Buddhism and Animal Rights*. New York: Lantern.

——. 2007. *The Longest Struggle: Animal Advocacy from Pythagoras to PETA*. New York: Lantern.

Pickover, Michelè. 2005. *Animal Rights in South Africa*. Cape Town: Double Storey.

Pierce, Christine. 1979. "Can Animals Be Liberated?", *Philosophical Studies* 36: 69-75.

Pinker, Steven. 1994. *The Language Instinct*. New York: William Morrow. See chap. 11.

Pleasants, Nigel. 2006. "Nonsense on Stilts? Wittgenstein, Ethics, and the Lives of Animals", *Inquiry* 49: 314-36.

Pluhar, Evelyn B. 1991. "The Joy of Killing", *Between the Species* 7: 121-28.

——. 1992. "Who Can Be Morally Obligated to Be a Vegetarian?", *Journal of Agricultural and Environmental Ethics* 5: 189-215.

——. 1993. "On Vegetarianism, Morality, and Science: A Counter Reply", *Journal of Agricultural and Environmental Ethics* 6: 185-213.

——. 1995. Beyond Prejudice: *The Moral Significance of Human and Nonhuman Animals*. Durham: Duke University Press.

——. 2006. "Legal and Moral Rights of Sentient Beings and the Full Personhood View", *Organization & Environment* 19: 275-79.

Plumwood, Val. 2000. "Integrating Ethical Frameworks for Animals, Humans, and Nature: A Critical Feminist Eco-Socialist Analysis", *Ethics & the Environment* 5, no. 2: 285-322.

Podberscek, Anthony L., Elizabeth S. Paul, and James A. Serpell, eds. 2000. *Companion Animals and Us: Exploring the Relationship between People and Pets*. Cambridge: Cambridge University Press.

Pojman, Louis P. 1995. "Animal Rights, Egalitarianism, and Nihilism", in John Howie and George Schedler, eds., *Ethical Issues in Contemporary Society*. Carbondale: Southern Illinois University Press.

Poole, Joyce H. 1998. "An Exploration of a Commonality between Ourselves and Elephants", *Etica & Animali* 9: 85-110.

Porphyry. 2000. *On Abstinence from Killing Animals.* Translated by Gillian Clark. Ithaca: Cornell University Press.

Povilitis, Anthony J. 1980. "On Assigning Rights to Animals and Nature", *Environmental Ethics* 2: 67-71.

Preece, Rod. 1999. *Animals and Nature: Cultural Myths, Cultural Realities.* Vancouver: UBC Press.

———. 2002. *Awe for the Tiger, Love for the Lamb: A Chronicle of Sensibility to Animals.* Vancouver: UBC Press.

———. 2005. *Brute Souls, Happy Beasts, and Evolution: The Historical Status of Animals.* Vancouver: UBC Press.

Preece, Rod, and Lorna Chamberlain. 1993. *Animal Welfare and Human Values.* Waterloo: Wilfrid Laurier University Press.

Preston, Christopher J. 2002. "Animality and Morality: Human Reason As an Animal Activity", *Environmental Values* 11: 427-42.

Pritchard, Michael S., and Wade L. Robison. 1981. "Justice and the Treatment of Animals: A Critique of Rawls", *Environmental Ethics* 3: 55-61.

Rabb, J. Douglas. 2002. "The Vegetarian Fox and Indigenous Philosophy: Speciesism, Racism, and Sexism", *Environmental Ethics* 24: 275-94.

Rachels, James. 1990. *Created from Animals: The Moral Implications of Darwinism.* Oxford: Oxford University Press.

———. 2004. "Drawing Lines", in Cass R. Sunstein and Martha C. Nussbaum, eds., *Animal Rights: Current Debates and New Directions.* New York: Oxford University Press.

Radner, Daisie, and Michael Radner. 1996. *Animal Consciousness.* Amherst: Prometheus.

Raterman, Ty. 2008. "An Environmentalist's Lament on Predation", *Environmental Ethics* 30: 417-34.

Rawls, John. 1971. *A Theory of Justice.* Cambridge, Mass.: Harvard University Press. See p. 512.

Regan, Tom. 1982. *All That Dwell Therein: Animal Rights and Environmental Ethics.* Berkeley: University of California Press.

———. 1985. "The Case for Animal Rights", in Peter Singer, ed., *In Defence of Animals.* Oxford: Basil Blackwell.

———. 1986a. "Honey Dribbles down Your Fur", in Philip P. Hanson, ed., *Environmental Ethics: Philosophical and Policy Perspectives.* Burnaby: Institute for the Humanities.

———. 2001. *Defending Animal Rights.* Urbana: University of Illinois Press.

———. 2003. *Animal Rights, Human Wrongs: An Introduction to Moral Philosophy*. Lanham: Rowman and Littlefield.

———. 2004a. *The Case for Animal Rights*, 2nd ed. Berkeley: University of California Press. First edition published in 1983.

———. 2004b. *Empty Cages: Facing the Challenge of Animal Rights*. Lanham: Rowman and Littlefield.

Regan, Tom, ed. 1986b. *Animal Sacrifices: Religious Perspectives on the Use of Animals in Science*. Philadelphia: Temple University Press.

Regan, Tom, and Peter Singer, eds. 1989. *Animal Rights and Human Obligations*, 2nd ed. Englewood Cliffs: Prentice Hall.

Reichmann, James B. 2000. *Evolution, Animal "Rights", and the Environment*. Washington: Catholic University of America Press.

Richards, Stewart. 1981. "Forethoughts for Carnivores", *Philosophy* 56: 73-87.

Rifkin, Jeremy. 1983. *Algeny*. New York: Viking Press.

———. 1992. *Beyond Beef: The Rise and Fall of the Cattle Culture*. New York: Dutton.

———. 1998. *The Biotech Century: Harnessing the Gene and Remaking the World*. New York: Jeremy P. Tarcher/Putnam.

Ritchie, David G. 1894. *Natural Rights*. London: George Allen and Unwin. See pp. 107-11.

Ritter, Erika. 2009. *The Dog by the Cradle, the Serpent Beneath: Some Paradoxes of Human-Animal Relationships*. Toronto: Key Porter.

Ritvo, Harriet. 1987. *The Animal Estate: The English and Other Creatures in the Victorian Age*. Cambridge, Mass.: Harvard University Press.

Robbins, John. 1987. *Diet for a New America*. Walpole: Stillpoint.

Roberts, Monty. 1997. *The Man Who Listens to Horses*. Toronto: Alfred A. Knopf.

Rodd, Rosemary. 1990. *Biology, Ethics, and Animals*. Oxford: Clarendon Press.

———. 1996. "Evolutionary Ethics and the Status of Non-Human Animals", *Journal of Applied Philosophy* 13: 63-72.

Rodman, John. 1979. "Animal Justice: The Counter-Revolution in Natural Right and Law", *Inquiry* 22: 3-22.

Rollin, Bernard E. 1989. *The Unheeded Cry: Animal Consciousness, Animal Pain, and Science*. Oxford: Oxford University Press.

———. 1995. *The Frankenstein Syndrome: Ethical and Social Issues in the Genetic Engineering of Animals*. Cambridge: Cambridge University Press.

———. 2006. *Animal Rights and Human Morality*, 3rd ed. Amherst: Prometheus.

———. 2007. "Animal Mind: Science, Philosophy, and Ethics", *The Journal of Ethics* 11: 253-74.

Rolston, Holmes, III. 1988. *Environmental Ethics: Duties to and Values in the Natural World*. Philadelphia: Temple University Press.

———. 1993. "Challenges in Environmental Ethics", in Michael E. Zimmerman et al., eds., *Environmental Philosophy: From Animal Rights to Radical Ecology*. Englewood Cliffs: Prentice Hall.

Rothschild, Miriam. 1986. *Animals and Man*. Oxford: Clarendon Press.

Rowan, Andrew N. 1984. *Of Mice, Models, and Men: A Critical Evaluation of Animal Research*. Albany: State University of New York Press.

Rowe, Martin, ed. 1999. *The Way of Compassion: Vegetarianism, Environmentalism, Animal Advocacy, and Social Justice*. New York: Stealth Technologies.

Rowlands, Mark. 1998. *Animal Rights: A Philosophical Defence*. Basingstoke and New York: Palgrave.

———. 2002. *Animals Like Us*. London: Verso.

Rudacille, Deborah. 2000. *The Scalpel and the Butterfly: The War between Animal Research and Animal Protection*. New York: Farrar, Straus and Giroux.

Rudnick, Abraham. 2007. "Other-Consciousness and the Use of Animals As Illustrated in Animal Experiments", *Journal of Applied Philosophy* 24: 202-08.

Rupke, Nicolaas A., ed. 1987. *Vivisection in Historical Perspective*. London: Croom Helm.

Ryder, Richard D. 1983. *Victims of Science: The Use of Animals in Research*, 2nd ed. London: National Anti-Vivisection Society.

———. 1996. "Putting Animals into Politics", in Robert Garner, ed., *Animal Rights: The Changing Debate*. New York: New York University Press.

———. 2000. *Animal Revolution: Changing Attitudes towards Speciesism*, rev. ed. Oxford: Berg.

———. 2001. *Painism: A Modern Morality*. London: Centaur Press.

Ryder, Richard D., ed. 1992. *Animal Welfare and the Environment*. London: Duckworth.

Sagoff, Mark. 1984. "Animal Liberation and Environmental Ethics: Bad Marriage, Quick Divorce", *Osgoode Hall Law Journal* 22: 297-307.

Salt, Henry S. 1980. *Animals' Rights Considered in Relation to Social Progress*. London: Centaur Press. First published in 1892.

Sapontzis, Steve F. 1987. *Morals, Reason, and Animals*. Philadelphia: Temple University Press.

———. 1988. "On Justifying the Exploitation of Animals in Research", *The Journal of Medicine and Philosophy* 13: 177-96.

———. 1993. "Aping Persons – Pro and Con", in Paola Cavalieri and Peter Singer, eds., *The Great Ape Project: Equality beyond Humanity*. London: Fourth Estate.

Sapontzis, Steve F., ed. 2004. *Food for Thought: The Debate over Eating Meat*. Amherst: Prometheus.

Sargent, Tony. 1996. *Animal Rights and Wrongs: A Biblical Perspective*. London: Hodder and Stoughton.

Savage-Rumbaugh, E. Sue. 1986. *Ape Language: From Conditioned Response to Symbol*. New York: Columbia University Press.

Savage-Rumbaugh, Sue, and Roger Lewin. 1994. *Kanzi: The Ape at the Brink of the Human Mind*. New York: John Wiley and Sons.

Savage-Rumbaugh, Sue, Stuart G. Shanker, and Talbot J. Taylor. 1998. *Apes, Language, and the Human Mind*. New York: Oxford University Press.

Sax, Boria. 2000. *Animals in the Third Reich: Pets, Scapegoats, and the Holocaust*. New York: Continuum.

Schalow, Frank. 2000. "Who Speaks for the Animals? Heidegger and the Question of Animal Welfare", *Environmental Ethics* 22: 259-71.

Schedler, George. 2005. "Does Ethical Meat Eating Maximize Utility?", *Social Theory and Practice* 31: 499-511.

Schicktanz, Silke. 2006. "Ethical Considerations of the Human-Animal Relationship under Conditions of Asymmetry and Ambivalence", *Journal of Agricultural and Environmental Ethics* 19: 7-16.

Schinkel, Anders. 2008. "Martha Nussbaum on Animal Rights", *Ethics & the Environment* 13, no. 1: 41-69.

Schmidt-Raghavan, Maithili. 1993. "Animal Liberation and Ahimsa", in Ninian Smart and Shivesh Thakur, eds., *Ethical and Political Dilemmas of Modern India*. Basingstoke: Macmillan Press.

Schmidtz, David. 1998. "Are All Species Equal?", *Journal of Applied Philosophy* 15: 57-67.

Schopenhauer, Arthur. 1965. *On the Basis of Morality*. Indianapolis: Bobbs-Merrill. First published (in German) in 1841.

Schwartz, Richard H. 2001. *Judaism and Vegetarianism*, 3rd ed. New York: Lantern.

Scruton, Roger. 2000. *Animal Rights and Wrongs*, 3rd ed. London: Metro.

Scully, Matthew. 2002. *Dominion: The Power of Man, the Suffering of Animals, and the Call to Mercy*. New York: St. Martin's Press.

Searle, John. 1994. "Animal Minds", *Midwest Studies in Philosophy* 19: 206-19.

Seidler, Michael J. 1977. "Hume and the Animals", *The Southern Journal of Philosophy* 15: 361-72.

Serpell, James. 1996. *In the Company of Animals: A Study of Human-Animal Relationships*, rev. ed. Cambridge: Cambridge University Press.

Shafer-Landau, Russ. 1994. "Vegetarianism, Causation, and Ethical Theory", *Public Affairs Quarterly* 8: 85-100.

Sheets-Johnstone, Maxine. 1996. "Taking Evolution Seriously: A Matter of Primate Intelligence", *Etica & Animali* 8: 115-30.

Shelley, Mary. 1992. *Frankenstein, or, The Modern Prometheus*. Harmondsworth: Penguin. First published in 1818.

Sherratt, Anna. 2007. "Vegetarians and Their Children", *Journal of Applied Philosophy* 24: 425-34.

Shevelow, Kathryn. 2008. *For the Love of Animals: The Rise of the Animal Protection Movement*. New York: Henry Holt.

Silverstein, Helena. 1996. *Unleashing Rights: Law, Meaning, and the Animal Rights Movement*. Ann Arbor: University of Michigan Press.

Simmons, Aaron. 2007. "A Critique of Mary Anne Warren's Weak Animal Rights View", *Environmental Ethics* 29: 267-78.

Singer, Peter. 1979. "Killing Humans and Killing Animals", *Inquiry* 22: 145-56.

———. 1980. "Utilitarianism and Vegetarianism", *Philosophy and Public Affairs* 9: 325-37.

———. 1981. *The Expanding Circle: Ethics and Sociobiology*. New York: Farrar, Straus and Giroux.

———. 1987. "Animal Liberation or Animal Rights?", *The Monist* 70: 3-14.

———. 1993a. "Animals and the Value of Life", in Tom Regan, ed., *Matters of Life and Death*, 3rd ed. New York: McGraw-Hill.

———. 1993b. *Practical Ethics*, 2nd ed. Cambridge: Cambridge University Press.

———. 1998. *Ethics into Action: Henry Spira and the Animal Rights Movement*. Lanham: Rowman and Littlefield.

———. 2002. *Animal Liberation*, 3rd ed. New York: Ecco/HarperCollins. First edition published in 1975.

Singer, Peter, ed. 1985. *In Defence of Animals*. Oxford: Basil Blackwell.

———. 2006. *In Defence of Animals: The Second Wave*. Oxford: Blackwell.

Singer, Peter, and Jim Mason. 2006. *The Way We Eat: Why Our Food Choices Matter*. Emmaus, PA: Rodale.

Skidmore, J. 2001. "Duties to Animals: The Failure of Kant's Moral Theory", *The Journal of Value Inquiry* 35: 541-59.

Slicer, Deborah. 1991. "Your Daughter or Your Dog? A Feminist Assessment of the Animal Research Issue", *Hypatia* 6: 108-24.

Smith, Ethan. 2007. *Building an Ark: 101 Solutions to Animal Suffering*. With Guy Dauncey. Gabriola Island: New Society.

Smith, Kimberly K. 2008. "Animals and the Social Contract: A Reply to Nussbaum", *Environmental Ethics* 30: 195-207.

Snow, Nancy. 1993. "Compassion for Animals", *Between the Species* 9: 61-66.

Sorabji, Richard. 1993. *Animal Minds and Human Morals: The Origins of the Western Debate*. Ithaca, NY: Cornell University Press.

Sowards, Stacey K. 2006. "Identification through Orangutans: Destabilizing the Nature/Culture Dualism", *Ethics & the Environment* 11, no. 2: 45-61.

Spencer, Colin. 1993. *The Heretic's Feast: A History of Vegetarianism*. London: Fourth Estate.

Spencer, Stuart, et al. 2006. "History and Ethics of Keeping Pets: Comparison with Farm Animals", *Journal of Agricultural and Environmental Ethics* 19: 17-25.

Sperling, Susan. 1988. *Animal Liberators: Research and Morality*. Berkeley: University of California Press.

Spiegel, Marjorie. 1996. *The Dreaded Comparison: Human and Animal Slavery*, rev. ed. New York: Mirror.

Sprigge, T.L.S. 1979. "Metaphysics, Physicalism, and Animal Rights", *Inquiry* 22: 101-43.

———. 1984. "Non-Human Rights: An Idealist Perspective", *Inquiry* 27: 439-61.

Squadrito, Kathy. 1992. "Descartes and Locke on Speciesism and the Value of Life", *Between the Species* 8: 143-49.

Stallwood, Kim. 1996. "Utopian Visions and Pragmatic Politics: Challenging the Foundations of Speciesism and Misothery", in Robert Garner, ed., *Animal Rights: The Changing Debate*. New York: New York University Press.

Steeves, H. Peter, ed. 1999. *Animal Others: On Ethics, Ontology, and Animal Life*. Albany: State University of New York Press.

Steinbock, Bonnie. 1978. "Speciesism and the Idea of Equality", *Philosophy* 53: 247-56.

Steiner, Gary. 2005. *Anthropocentrism and Its Discontents: The Moral Status of Animals in the History of Western Philosophy*. Pittsburgh: University of Pittsburgh Press.

———. 2008. *Animals and the Moral Community: Mental Life, Moral Status, and Kinship*. New York: Columbia University Press.

Stephens, William O. 1994. "Five Arguments for Vegetarianism", *Philosophy in the Contemporary World* 1, no. 4: 25-39.

———. 1998. "Masks, Androids, and Primates: The Evolution of the Concept 'Person'", *Etica & Animali* 9: 111-27.

Sterba, James P. 1995. "From Biocentric Individualism to Biocentric Pluralism", *Environmental Ethics* 17: 191-207.

Stich, Stephen P. 1979. "Do Animals Have Beliefs?", *Australasian Journal of Philosophy* 57: 15-28.

Sumner, L.W. 1988. "Animal Welfare and Animal Rights", *The Journal of Medicine and Philosophy* 13: 159-75.

Sunstein, Cass R., and Martha C. Nussbaum, eds. 2004. *Animal Rights: Current Debates and New Directions*. New York: Oxford University Press.

Swan, James A. 1995. *In Defense of Hunting*. New York: HarperCollins.

Swart, J.A.A. 2005. "Care for the Wild: An Integrative View on Wild and Domesticated Animals", *Environmental Values* 14: 251-63.

Sztybel, David. 1997. "Marxism and Animal Rights", *Ethics & the Environment* 2, no. 2: 169-85.

———. 2006a. "A Living Will Clause for Supporters of Animal Experimentation", *Journal of Applied Philosophy* 23: 173-89.

———. 2006b. "Can the Treatment of Animals Be Compared to the Holocaust?", *Ethics & the Environment* 11, no. 1: 97-132.

———. 2008. "Animals As Persons", in Jodey Castricano, ed., *Animal Subjects: An Ethical Reader in a Posthuman World*. Waterloo: Wilfrid Laurier University Press.

Talbert, Matthew. 2006. "Contractualism and Our Duties to Nonhuman Animals", *Environmental Ethics* 28: 201-15.

Tannenbaum, Jerrold. 1993. "Veterinary Medical Ethics: A Focus of Conflicting Interests", *Journal of Social Issues* 49: 143-56.

Tannenbaum, Jerrold, and Andrew N. Rowan. 1985. "Rethinking the Morality of Animal Research", *Hastings Center Report* 15, no. 5: 32-43.

Tantillo, James A. 2001. "Sport Hunting, *Eudaimonia*, and Tragic Wisdom", *Philosophy in the Contemporary World* 8, no. 2: 101-12.

Tardiff, Andrew. 1996. "Simplifying the Case for Vegetarianism", *Social Theory and Practice* 22: 299-314.

Taylor, Angus. 1996a. "Animal Rights and Human Needs", *Environmental Ethics* 18: 249-64.

———. 1996b. "Nasty, Brutish, and Short: The Illiberal Intuition That Animals Don't Count", *The Journal of Value Inquiry* 30: 265-77.

———. 2002. "Environmental Ethics and Respect for Animals", in Wayne Ouderkirk and Jim Hill, eds., *Land, Value, Community: Callicott and Environmental Philosophy*. Albany: State University of New York Press.

———. 2008a. "Electric Sheep and the New Argument from Nature", in Jodey Castricano, ed., *Animal Subjects: An Ethical Reader in a Posthuman World*. Waterloo: Wilfrid Laurier University Press.

———. 2008b. "Hunting for Consistency", *Philosophy Now* no. 67: 8-10.

Taylor, Chloë. 2008. "The Precarious Lives of Animals: Butler, Coetzee, and Animal Ethics", *Philosophy Today* 52: 60-72.

Taylor, Graeme. 2008. *Evolution's Edge: The Coming Collapse and Transformation of Our World*. Gabriola Island: New Society.

Taylor, Paul W. 1986. *Respect for Nature: A Theory of Environmental Ethics*. Princeton: Princeton University Press.

———. 1987. "Inherent Value and Moral Rights", *The Monist* 70: 15-30.

Taylor, Rodney L. 1986. "Of Animals and Man: The Confucian Perspective", in Tom Regan, ed., *Animal Sacrifices: Religious Perspectives on the Use of Animals in Science*. Philadelphia: Temple University Press.

Tester, Keith. 1991. *Animals and Society: The Humanity of Animal Rights*. London: Routledge.

Thomas, Keith. 1983. *Man and the Natural World: Changing Attitudes in England, 1500-1800*. London: Allen Lane.

Tobias, Michael. 1999. *Voices from the Underground: For the Love of Animals*. Pasadena: New Paradigm.

Tooley, Michael. 1998. "Speciesism and Basic Moral Principles", *Etica & Animali* 9: 5-36.

Torres, Bob. 2007. *Making a Killing: The Political Economy of Animal Rights*. Oakland: AK Press.

Townsend, Aubrey. 1979. "Radical Vegetarians", *Australasian Journal of Philosphy* 57: 85-93.

Turner, E.S. 1964. *All Heaven in a Rage*. London: Michael Joseph.

Turner, James. 1980. *Reckoning with the Beast: Animals, Pain, and Humanity in the Victorian Mind*. Baltimore: Johns Hopkins University Press.

VanDeVeer, Donald. 1979a. "Interspecific Justice", *Inquiry* 22: 55-79.

———. 1979b. "Of Beasts, Persons, and the Original Position", *The Monist* 62: 368-77.

———. 1980. "Animal Suffering", *Canadian Journal of Philosophy* 10: 463-71.

Varner, Gary E. 1994a. "The Prospects for Consensus and Convergence in the Animal Rights Debate", *Hastings Center Report* 24, no. 1: 24-28.

———. 1994b. "What's Wrong with Animal *By-products*?", *Journal of Agricultural and Environmental Ethics* 7: 7-17.

———. 1998. *In Nature's Interests? Interests, Animal Rights, and Environmental Ethics.* New York: Oxford University Press.

———. 1999. "Should You Clone Your Dog? An Animal Rights Perspective on Somacloning", *Animal Welfare* 8: 407-20.

———. 2001. "Sentientism", in Dale Jamieson, ed., *A Companion to Environmental Philosophy.* Oxford: Blackwell.

———. 2002. "Pets, Companion Animals, and Domesticated Partners", in David Benatar, ed., *Ethics for Everyday.* Boston: McGraw-Hill.

Verhoog, Henk. 1992. "The Concept of Intrinsic Value and Transgenic Animals", *Journal of Agricultural and Environmental Ethics* 5: 147-60.

Vidal, John. 1997. *McLibel: Burger Culture on Trial.* New York: New Press.

Violin, Mary Ann. 1990. "Pythagoras — The First Animal Rights Philosopher", *Between the Species* 6: 122-27.

Vitali, Theodore. 1990. "Sport Hunting: Moral or Immoral?", *Environmental Ethics* 12: 69-82.

Vyvyan, John. 1969. *In Pity and in Anger: A Study of the Use of Animals in Science.* London: Michael Joseph.

Wade, Maurice L. 1990. "Animal Liberation, Ecocentrism, and the Morality of Sport Hunting", *Journal of the Philosophy of Sport* 17: 15-27.

Waldau, Paul. 2002. *The Specter of Speciesism: Buddhist and Christian Views of Animals.* New York: Oxford University Press.

Waldau, Paul, and Kimberley Patton, eds. 2006. *A Communion of Subjects: Animals in Religion, Science, and Ethics.* New York: Columbia University Press.

Walker, Stephen. 1983. *Animal Thought.* London: Routledge and Kegan Paul.

Wallace, Alfred Russel. 1911. *The World of Life: A Manifestation of Creative Power, Directive Mind, and Ultimate Purpose.* London: G. Bell and Sons. See chap. 19, "Is Nature Cruel? The Purpose and Limitations of Pain".

Waller, David. 1997. "A Vegetarian Critique of Deep and Social Ecology", *Ethics & the Environment* 2, no. 2: 187-97.

Walters, Kerry S., and Lisa Portmess, eds. 1999. *Ethical Vegetarianism from Pythagoras to Peter Singer.* Albany: State University of New York Press.

Warren, Mary Anne. 1983. "The Rights of the Nonhuman World", in Robert

Elliot and Arran Gare, eds., *Environmental Philosophy*. St. Lucia: University of Queensland Press.

———. 1987. "Difficulties with the Strong Animal Rights Position", *Between the Species* 2: 163-73.

———. 1997. *Moral Status: Obligations to Persons and Other Living Things*. Oxford: Clarendon Press.

Watson, Paul. 1993a. "Raid on Reykjavik", in Peter C. List, ed., *Radical Environmentalism: Philosophy and Tactics*. Belmont: Wadsworth.

———. 1993b. "Tora! Tora! Tora!", in Peter C. List, ed., *Radical Environmentalism: Philosophy and Tactics*. Belmont: Wadsworth.

Watson, Richard A. 1979. "Self-Consciousness and the Rights of Nonhuman Animals and Nature", *Environmental Ethics* 1: 99-129.

Welchman, Jennifer. 2003. "Xenografting, Species Loyalty, and Human Solidarity", *Journal of Social Philosophy* 34: 244-55.

Wemmer, Christen, and Catherine A. Christen, eds. 2008. *Elephants and Ethics: Toward a Morality of Coexistence*. Baltimore: Johns Hopkins University Press.

Wennberg, Robert N. 2003. *God, Humans, and Animals: An Invitation to Enlarge Our Moral Universe*. Grand Rapids: William B. Eerdmans.

Wenz, Peter S. 1993. "Contracts, Animals, and Ecosystems", *Social Theory and Practice* 19: 315-44.

Wenzel, George. 1991. *Animal Rights, Human Rights: Ecology, Economy, and Ideology in the Canadian Arctic*. London: Belhaven Press.

Weston, Anthony. 1992. *Toward Better Problems: New Perspectives on Abortion, Animal Rights, the Environment, and Justice*. Philadelphia: Temple University Press. See chap. 4, "Other Animals".

Westra, Laura. 1989. "Ecology and Animals: Is There a Joint Ethic of Respect?", *Environmental Ethics* 11: 215-30.

White, Thomas I. 1990. "Ethics at Sea: The Dolphin-Tuna Controversy", in W. Michael Hoffman, Robert Frederick, and Edward S. Petry, Jr., eds., *Business, Ethics, and the Environment: The Public Policy Debate*. Westport: Quorum.

Wickins-Dražilová, Dita. 2006. "Zoo Animal Welfare", *Journal of Agricultural and Environmental Ethics* 19: 27-36.

Willard, L. Duane. 1982. "About Animals 'Having' Rights", *The Journal of Value Inquiry* 16: 177-87.

Williams, Joy. 1995. "The Killing Game", in Pam Houston, ed., *Women on Hunting*. Hopewell: Ecco Press.

———. 2001. "The Animal People", in Joy Williams, *Nature: Rants and*

*Reflections on Humanity and Other Animals.* New York: Lyons Press.

Williams, Meredith. 1980. "Rights, Interests, and Moral Equality",
*Environmental Ethics* 2: 149-61.

Williams, Nancy M. 2008. "Affected Ignorance and Animal Suffering: Why
Our Failure to Debate Factory Farming Puts Us at Moral Risk", *Journal of
Agricultural and Environmental Ethics* 21: 371-84.

Williams, R.M. 2003. "On the Tail-Docking of Pigs, Human Circumcision, and
Their Implications for Prevailing Opinion regarding Pain", *Journal of
Applied Ethics* 20: 89-93.

Wilmut, Ian. 1998. "Cloning for Medicine", *Scientific American* 279, no. 6: 58-63.

Wilson, Edward O. 1984. *Biophilia.* Cambridge, Mass.: Harvard University
Press.

Wilson, Scott. 2001. "Carruthers and the Argument from Marginal Cases",
*Journal of Applied Philosophy* 18: 135-47.

———. 2002. "Indirect Duties to Animals", *The Journal of Value Inquiry* 36: 15-25.

Wise, Steven M. 2000. *Rattling the Cage: Toward Legal Rights for Animals.*
Cambridge, Mass.: Perseus.

———. 2002. *Drawing the Line: Science and the Case for Animal Rights.*
Cambridge, Mass.: Perseus.

Wolfe, Cary. 2003a. *Animal Rites: American Culture, the Discourse of Species,
and Posthumanist Theory.* Chicago: University of Chicago Press.

Wolfe, Cary, ed. 2003b. *Zoontologies: The Question of the Animal.* Minneapolis:
University of Minnesota Press.

Wood, Allen W. 1998. "Kant on Duties regarding Nonrational Nature", *The
Aristotelian Society*, supplementary vol. 72: 189-210.

Wood, David. 2004. "Thinking with Cats", in Matthew Calarco and Peter
Atterton, eds., *Animal Philosophy: Essential Readings in Continental
Thought.* London: Continuum.

Wynne-Tyson, Jon, comp. 1989. *The Extended Circle: A Commonplace Book of
Animal Rights.* New York: Paragon House.

Yates, Roger. 2007. "Debating 'Animal Rights' On-Line: The Movement-
Countermovement Dialectic Revisited", in Piers Beirne and Nigel South,
eds., *Issues in Green Criminology: Confronting Harms against Environments,
Humanity, and Other Animals.* Cullompton, Devon: Willan.

Young, Richard Alan. 1999. *Is God a Vegetarian? Christianity, Vegetarianism,
and Animal Rights.* Chicago: Open Court.

Zamir, Tzachi. 2004. "Veganism", *Journal of Social Philosophy* 35: 367-79.

——. 2006. "Killing for Knowledge", *Journal of Applied Ethics* 23: 17-40.

——. 2007a. *Ethics and the Beast: A Speciesist Argument for Animal Liberation*. Princeton: Princeton University Press.

——. 2007b. "The Welfare-based Defense of Zoos", *Society and Animals* 15: 191-201.

# Index